SCHOOLING
AND
LANGUAGE
MINORITY
STUDENTS:
A THEORETICAL
FRAMEWORK

Developed by

California State Department of Education
Office of Bilingual Bicultural Education
Sacramento, California

Published by

Evaluation, Dissemination and Assessment Center
California State University, Los Angeles
Los Angeles, California

ISBN: 0-89755-011-0

Library of Congress Catalog Card Number: 81-71272

This publication was funded in whole or in part by a contract (G007902844) between the California State Department of Education and the United States Education Department. The opinions expressed herein do not, however, necessarily
reflect the positions or policy of the United States Education Department; no official endorsement by the United States Education Department should be
inferred.

Developed by
OFFICE OF BILINGUAL BICULTURAL EDUCATION
California State Department of Education
Sacramento, California

Published and Disseminated by
EVALUATION, DISSEMINATION AND ASSESSMENT CENTER
California State University, Los Angeles
Los Angeles, California

Printed in USA 1981   Thirteenth Printing 1988
Second Printing 1982   Fourteenth Printing 1989
Third Printing 1982   Fifteenth Printing 1990
Fourth Printing 1982   Sixteenth Printing 1990
Fifth Printing 1983   Seventeenth Printing 1991
Sixth Printing 1983
Seventh Printing 1984
Eighth Printing 1984
Ninth Printing 1985
Tenth Printing 1986
Eleventh Printing 1986
Twelfth Printing 1987

PREFACE

The growing interest in the problems of language minority students in the United States has been accompanied by the publication of an enormous number of books and articles. Often, however, advice regarding approaches, methods, strategies, and techniques for effectively educating language minority students is offered without any concern or explanation of empirical evidence. With the possible exception of legal concerns, the Office of Bilingual Bicultural Education in the California State Department of Education receives more inquiries regarding research evidence on the effectiveness of bilingual education than on any other issue. Educators want to know which types of programs actually work with non-English language background students.

The Office of Bilingual Bicultural Education has identified three major objectives for all instructional programs serving language minority students. Regardless of the approach taken, at the end of the treatment period, language minority students should exhibit: (1) high levels of English language proficiency, (2) appropriate levels of cognitive/academic development, and (3) adequate psychosocial and cultural adjustment. The articles included in this collection of papers explain the importance of these goals and describe the likelihood of various types of instructional approaches to achieve such outcomes. Instead of providing the reader with a series of unconnected suggestions and recommendations, the authors collectively advance a research-based theoretical framework for the design and implementation of instructional programs for language minority students.

This publication is a progress report, not a collection of proven answers. The theoretical framework implied in this volume is, however, based on the best information that science can provide at this time. The research herein reported does not lead to perfect programs with perfect outcomes, nor does it answer all the questions regarding language development, language acquisition, and cognitive/academic development in bilingual contexts. But, taken collectively, these articles form the beginning of a research-based theoretical framework for planning and improving bilingual education programs. We at the California State Department of Education view this as substantive progress. We iv

are encouraged by the potential practical applications of the research presented in this collection and shall continue with the refinement of this work. At the same time, we not only invite other researchers, teacher trainers, and school district personnel to put into practice the ideas and implications presented here but also to improve and expand their programs to meet all of the schooling needs of language minority students.

ACKNOWLEDGMENTS

Sincere appreciation is first expressed to the authors of the five papers appearing in this collection: James Cummins, Stephen Krashen, Dorothy Legarreta-Marcaida, Tracy Terrell, and Eleanor Thonis. The contributors have not only astutely synthesized their own research and the research of others but have also skillfully presented the information in a manner especially suitable to educators.

Special thanks are also due to the Project Team members in the Office of Bilingual Bicultural Education: Maria Ortiz, Dennis Parker, and Fred Tempes. These individuals were responsible for the design of the initial outline questions, review of the interim and final drafts, consultation with the authors, and preparation of the articles for the publisher. In turn, the work of the Project Team was ably promoted and supervised by several administrators at the California State Department of Education, including Ramiro Reyes, Guillermo Lopez, and Tomas Lopez. Charles Leyba, Director, and his staff at the Evaluation, Dissemination and Assessment Center, California State University, Los Angeles are to be commended for their professional preparation of this document. The Office of Bilingual Education and Minority Language Affairs of the United States Education Department provided the funds for this project.

Many more individuals and agencies, too many to list here, provided valuable assistance in the development of this collection; final responsibility for this volume, nevertheless, rests with the Office of Bilingual Bicultural Education, California State Department of Education.

David P. Dolson
Project Team Leader

Guillermo Lopez, Chief
Office of Bilingual Bicultural Education

BIOGRAPHICAL SKETCHES

JAMES CUMMINS is a Visiting Professor in the Modern Language Centre of the Ontario Institute for Studies on Education. He received his PhD from the University of Alberta in 1974. His research interests include minority group achievement, bilingualism, and reading disability. He is the recipient (with J. P. Das) of the International Reading Association 1979 Albert J. Harris Award for the best paper on detection and remediation of reading disability.

* * *

STEPHEN KRASHEN is Professor of Linguistics at the University of Southern California. He has published extensively on second language acquisition theory, second language teaching, and neurolinguistics. He is the author of **Second Language Acquisition and Second Language Learning** (Pergamon Press, 1981), co-author of **The Human Brain** (Prentice-Hall, 1977), and co-editor of **Research in Second Language Acquisition** (Newbury House, 1980).

* * *

DOROTHY LEGARRETA-MARCAIDA is Adjunct Professor of Basque Studies at the University of Nevada, Reno. Dr. Legarreta has published several articles on second language acquisition and primary language maintenance. Her earlier research was on Black dialect speakers. Her present book-in-progress is a study of ethnic identity and language maintenance among nearly 20,000 Basque children evacuated during the Spanish Civil War and sent to France, England, Belgium, the U.S.S.R., and Mexico.

* * *

TRACY DAVID TERRELL is the Chair of the Program in Linguistics and a member of the Department of Spanish and Portuguese at the University of California, Irvine. He has written many articles on Spanish phonology, especially on the phonology of Caribbean Spanish. His theoretical interest is sociolinguistics and, in particular, language change. His recent area of specialization is second language acquisition, especially language teaching. He is perhaps best known as the initiator of a "new" communicative approach to language instruction, "The

Natural Approach." He has published a text on applied linguistics with Maruxa Salgues de Cargill called **Linguistica aplicada** (J. Wiley and Sons) and another will appear shortly on Spanish phonetics with R. Barrutia, **Fonetica y fonologia españolas** (J. Wiley and Sons). He will also publish a book co-authored with S. Krashen entitled **The Natural Approach: Language Acquisition in the Classroom** (Pergamon Press).

*   *   *

ELEANOR WALL THONIS is the district psychologist for Wheatland Elementary School District; a part-time instructor, University of California, Berkeley; and the consultant for bilingual education in the Marysville Unified School District. She has served as the director of the area Reading Center and is the author of several publications on reading for language minority students.

INTRODUCTION

There are presently more than 375,000 students of limited English proficiency in California public schools. There are an additional 433,000 students of fluent English proficiency who have a home language other than English. This means that California's language minority student population in kindergarten through grade twelve approximates 810,000.

As a group, language minority students tend to do poorly in regular school programs. They do not acquire the language, academic, and sociocultural skills necessary to meet the challenges of vocational and higher education pursuits. Many language minority students achieve only low levels of primary language proficiency while acquiring less than native-like ability in English.

Making decisions about instructional offerings for language minority students has proven to be a complex and demanding task for school personnel and parents alike. Part of the difficulty can be attributed to the absence of a theoretical framework upon which programs for language minority students can be based. Without a framework, decision makers are often unable to focus consistently upon the psychosocial and educational factors that influence the school achievement of language minority students. While political and economic factors are also important, basing educational programs solely on such grounds tends to affect negatively the quality of the educational experience of language minority students. Only by clearly understanding what educational attainments are possible for language minority students can school personnel and parents judge the appropriateness of the educational practices currently utilized by local schools. Although political and economic compromises may be necessary, they are best made when decision makers understand as many of the pertinent dynamics as possible. This publication offers information related specifically to the educational consequences of program decisions on language minority students.

In the past, most knowledge about programs for language minority students was based entirely on authority (laws and experts), the personal experiences of educators, and the "common sense" reasoning of program designers and planners. Such information may be important but is in itself insufficient for making

x

critical educational decisions. Therefore, the Office of Bilingual Bicultural Education of the California State Department of Education has decided to turn to scientifically controlled studies to establish the validity of knowledge about instructional programs for language minority students. Empirical knowledge is certain to improve the ability of educators to predict individual student and program outcomes for specific types of students, given certain types of instructional treatments, and under different types of background conditions. Thus, the articles contained in this collection represent an initial step in the development of a research-based theoretical framework for the schooling of language minority students.

This collection of papers is divided into two major parts. The first section, consisting of papers by James Cummins and Stephen Krashen, addresses the theoretical underpinnings of primary language development, second language acquisition, and the relationship of both to normal school achievement. The second section contains a series of three papers, each expanding upon the theoretical works in the first section and providing the reader with numerous instructional methods and techniques, all consistent with each other and with the various hypotheses posited by Cummins and Krashen.

No pedagogical issue relating to the instruction of language minority students has been more vigorously debated than the role of minority languages in bilingual education programs. In his work, Cummins clarifies the role of the primary language by: (1) describing the nature of language proficiency and its connection to academic and cognitive development, (2) identifying different levels of bilingualism experienced by language minority students and predicting the corresponding effects of each level on academic achievement, and (3) suggesting a relationship between primary language development and eventual attainment in the second language through the notion of a common underlying dimension of language proficiency. Clearly, Cummins has developed several important hypotheses and constructs that help explain and reconcile the seemingly contradictory findings of many other researchers.

While Cummins' article focuses on primary language development and academic achievement, Krashen dedicates attention to the acquisition of a second language, specifically English. The author distinguishes between language **acquisition** and language **learning** environments. The former, it is suggested, leads to fluency, while the latter assists in the development of what Krashen calls the "Monitor." Krashen also suggests that the key to second language acquisition is exposure to "comprehensible input" in substantial amounts and under optimal conditions. In describing the conditions necessary for second language acquisition, Krashen analyzes the potential of various second language (grammar and communicative-based English-as-a-Second-Language) and bilingual education (immersion, transitional, and ideal) programs to meet the language and academic needs of minority students.

Based on the assumption that high levels of primary language proficiency promote adequate school achievement, Dorothy Legarreta-Marcaida explores the effective use of primary language in bilingual classrooms. The author addresses five key questions related to the design, management, and implementation of bilingual classes:

1. To what **extent** should the child's primary language be used overall in grades K-6?
2. In what **manner** should primary language instruction be delivered:
   a. Concurrent translation?
   b. Alternate immersion (direct method) usually through language dominant groupings?
3. What **variety** of the primary language should be used in the classroom?
4. How can we ensure the **prestige** of the primary language **vis à vis** the dominant language, English?
5. How can primary language use be **monitored:** a formative evaluation process?

The responses to these questions are based on the recent findings of empirical studies and the published material of experienced professionals.

Complementing Krashen's theoretical hypotheses, Tracy D. Terrell presents an acquisition model called the "Natural Approach." This model is one means of applying Krashen's theoretical constructs. Terrell not only describes the model in relationship to Krashen's work and the work of others but also addresses: (1) the principles of the Natural Approach, (2) natural language acquisition situations, (3) appropriate teacher behaviors, (4) sample teaching techniques and strategies, (5) the use of continua in the Natural Approach, and (6) student evaluation. Terrell's article is enhanced by the inclusion of many actual classroom examples related to suggested techniques and strategies.

The last paper, by Eleanor Thonis, deals with reading instruction in bilingual contexts. She expands upon Cummins' notion of a Common Underlying Proficiency (CUP) in the cognitive/academic language skills area as it relates to literacy acquisition among bilingual students. The potential for primary language reading skill transfer to English is discussed in detail. Additionally, the author suggests appropriate methods and techniques designed to promote primary language literacy in and out of the classroom. Thonis concludes her article with a description of the positive outcomes associated with biliteracy.

Finally, the compendium concludes with an Appendix and a Glossary. The appendix contains a sample copy of the 1981-82 version of the Bilingual Education Program Quality Review Instrument, Kindergarten Through Grade Six. The use of this instrument is one way the Office of Bilingual Bicultural Education promotes the principles and standards of implementation suggested by the theoretical framework implied in this compendium. Other promotional strategies include the development of Asian and minority group handbooks and periodic presentations at regional technical assistance workshops for local school district personnel as well as coordination meetings with resource agencies and county schools offices. The glossary of terms has been included to assist the reader by promoting consistency in the use of the key terms across articles. It is suggested that the reader become familiar with the entries in the glossary before attempting a thorough reading of any of the papers.

Most educators, government officials, parents, and community members would agree that the goal of educational programs designed for language minority students is to allow such students to develop the highest degree possible of language, academic, and social skills necessary to participate fully in all aspects of life. More specifically, as a result of an instructional treatment, language minority students should attain: (1) high levels of English language proficiency, (2) normal cognitive and academic achievement, (3) adequate psychosocial and cultural adjustment, and (4) sufficient levels of primary language development to promote normal school progress. Based on the empirical evidence presented in the five articles contained in this collection, properly designed and adequately implemented bilingual education programs are one means to achieve such goals.

As a result of the controversy regarding the legislation of state and federal requirements, some educators today erroneously believe that many parents and community members view bilingual education with disfavor. This is not necessarily the case. In a recent poll conducted for **Newsweek** by the Gallup Organization (March, 1981), 64 percent of the American public approved of classes conducted in a foreign language as well as in English for children who do not speak English. Another 14 percent did not know enough about the value of these classes to make a judgment. Contrary to the statements of a few political opportunists, uninformed newspaper columnists, and some special interest group representatives, the public is generally supportive of primary language instruction for language minority students, even though there may not be an awareness of the strong scientific case for such programs.

The task of educating language minority students is not simple. Nevertheless, creative and committed educators in cooperation with concerned parents and community members have designed and implemented educational programs that result in significantly improved school performance on the part of such students. In other words, under certain conditions, language-related problems are no longer as likely to interfere with the academic and vocational aspirations of language minority students and their families. To accomplish this, educators must rely upon empirical evidence rather than "folk remedies" as a guide to professional decisions for selecting and implementing instructional programs for language minority children. This publication is meant to be an important contribution toward this end.

David P. Dolson
Project Team Leader
Office of Bilingual Bicultural Education

CONTENTS

PART ONE: THEORETICAL FOUNDATIONS

PART TWO: STRATEGIES FOR IMPLEMENTATION

Part One
Theoretical Foundations

The Role of Primary Language Development in Promoting Educational Success for Language Minority Students*

James Cummins

IN ORDER TO ASSESS the role of language minority students' primary language (L1) development in the acquisition of English (L2) academic skills, it is necessary to consider two questions: (1) What is meant by "language proficiency"? and (2) What are the cross-lingual dimensions of language proficiency, i.e., how does the development of proficiency in L1 relate to the development of L2 proficiency? Confusion concerning the rationale for bilingual education, assessment of bilingual proficiency, and entry-exit criteria for bilingual programs stems from inadequate conceptualization of the nature of language proficiency and its cross-lingual dimensions.

To account for the research data on bilingual education, it is necessary to distinguish those aspects of language proficiency involved in the development of literacy skills from other aspects of language proficiency, and to note that these literacy-related aspects are interdependent across languages, i.e., manifestations of a common underlying proficiency.

This paper is organized into three sections. First, the nature of language proficiency and its relationship to academic and cognitive development is considered. In the second section, the origins of current misconceptions about bilingualism are examined, and a theoretical position regarding the nature of bilingual proficiency is formulated in light of the research data. The third section applies these theoretical positions regarding the nature of language proficiency and its cross-lingual dimensions to the current debate over the rationale for bilingual education, entry and exit criteria, and assessment of bilingual proficiency.

*Many people have contributed to the present paper through comments on previous versions of the theoretical framework which it elaborates. I would like to thank Michael Canale, Steve Chesarek, Lily Wong Fillmore, Fred Genesee, Steve Krashen, John Oller Jr., Muriel Saville-Troike, Bernard Spolsky, Merrill Swain, Rudolph Troike, and Benji Wald for their constructive criticisms. The suggestions of the editorial team for the present volume have also been extremely useful and for this I would like to thank David Dolson, Maria Ortiz, Dennis Parker, and Fred Tempes of the Office of Bilingual-Bicultural Education, California State Department of Education.

The Nature of Language Proficiency

How Misconceptions About English Proficiency Create Academic Deficits in Language Minority Students

The rationale for bilingual education in the United States (United States Commission on Civil Rights, 1975), as it is understood by most policy makers and practitioners, can be stated as follows:

> Lack of English proficiency is the major reason for language minority students' academic failure. Bilingual education is intended to ensure that students do not fall behind in subject matter content while they are learning English, as they would likely do in an all-English program. However, when students have become proficient in English, then they can be exited to an all-English program, since limited English proficiency will no longer impede their academic progress.

Despite its intuitive appeal, there are serious problems with this rationale. First, it ignores the sociocultural determinants of minority students' school failure which, it will be argued, are more fundamental than linguistic factors. Second, an inadequate understanding of what is meant by "English proficiency" is likely to result in the creation of academic deficits in language minority students.

Some concrete examples will help illustrate how this process operates. These examples are taken from a Canadian study in which the teacher referral forms and psychological assessments of over 400 language minority students were analyzed (Cummins, 1980c). Throughout the teachers' referral forms and psychologists' assessment reports are references to the fact that children's English communicative skills appear considerably better developed than their academic language skills. The following examples illustrate this point:

> PS (094). Referred for reading and arithmetic difficulties in second grade, teacher commented that "since PS attended grade one in Italy, I think his main problem is language, although he understands and speaks English quite well."
>
> GG (184). Although he had been in Canada for less than a year, in November of the grade one year, the teacher commented that "he speaks Italian fluently and English as well." However, she also referred him for psychological assessment because "he is having a great deal of difficulty with the grade one program" and she wondered if he had "specific learning disabilities or if he is just a very long way behind children in his age group."
>
> DM (105). Arrived from Portugal at age 10 and was placed in a second grade class; three years later in fifth grade, her

teacher commented that "her oral answering and comprehension is so much better than her written work that we feel a severe learning problem is involved, not just her non-English background."

These examples illustrate the influence of the environment in developing English communicative skills. In many instances in this study immigrant students were considered to have sufficient English proficiency to take a verbal IQ test within about one year of arrival in Canada. Similarly, in the United States, language minority students are often considered to have developed sufficient English proficiency to cope with the demands of an all-English classroom after a relatively short amount of time in a bilingual program (in some cases, as little as six months).

There is little doubt that many language minority students can develop a relatively high degree of English communicative skills within about two years of exposure to English-speaking peers, television, and schooling. However, in extrapolating from the considerable English proficiency that language minority students display in face-to-face communication to their overall proficiency in English, we risk creating academic deficits in these students.

Consider the following example:

PR (289). PR was referred in first grade by the school principal who noted that "PR is experiencing considerable difficulty with grade one work. An intellectual assessment would help her teacher to set realistic learning expectations for her and might provide some clues as to remedial assistance that might be offered."

No mention was made of the child's ESL background; this only emerged when the child was referred by the second grade teacher in the following year. Thus, the psychologist does not consider this as a possible factor in accounting for the discrepancy between a verbal IQ of 64 and a performance IQ of 108. The assessment report read as follows:

Although overall ability level appears to be within the low average range, note the significant difference between verbal and nonverbal scores....It would appear that PR's development has not progressed at a normal rate and consequently she is, and will continue to experience much difficulty in school. Teacher's expectations at this time should be set accordingly.

What is interesting in this example is that the child's English communicative skills are presumably sufficiently well developed that the psychologist (and possibly the teacher) is not alerted to the child's ESL background. This leads the psychologist to infer from her low verbal IQ score that "her development has not progressed at a normal rate" and to advise the teacher to set low academic expectations for the child since she "will continue to experience much difficulty in school." There is ample evidence from many contexts (Mercer, 1973) of how the attribution of deficient cognitive skills to language minority students can become self-fulfilling.

In many of the referral forms and psychological assessments analyzed in this study, the following line of reasoning was invoked:

> *Because language minority students are fluent in English, their poor academic performance and/or test scores cannot be attributed to lack of proficiency in English. Therefore, these students must either have deficient cognitive abilities or be poorly motivated ("lazy").*

The trend to exit students to all-English programs as quickly as possible in many United States bilingual programs inevitably gives rise to a similar line of reasoning. It is commonly observed that students classified as "English proficient" after a relatively short stay in a bilingual program and then exited to an all-English program often fall progressively further behind grade norms in the development of English academic skills. Because these students appear to be fluent in English, their poor academic performance can no longer be explained by their English language deficiency. Policymakers and educators are also reluctant to blame the school for minority students' poor performance because the school has accommodated the students by providing a bilingual program. Once again, the academic deficiency will be attributed to factors within the child.[1]

It is frequently assumed that language minority students have become "English proficient" when they have acquired relatively fluent and peer-appropriate face-to-face communicative skills. The examples cited above, as well as the research evidence reviewed in the remainder of this paper, strongly suggest that this misconception operates to impede the academic progress of language minority students. To understand the nature of this misconception, it is necessary to consider the question of what is meant by "English proficiency."

---

[1] This process is, in many respects, the opposite of the attribution of deficient cognitive or linguistic ability on the basis of surface structure dialectal differences (Shuy, 1977). In the present situation, the presence of adequate surface structure leads teachers to eliminate "lack of English proficiency" as an explanatory variable with the result that low academic performance is attributed to deficient cognitive abilities in language minority students.

What Is Meant By "English Proficiency"?

There is still little consensus among researchers as to the nature of "language proficiency" or "communicative competence."[2] For example, a model proposed by Hernandez-Chavez *et al*. (1978) comprised 64 separate proficiencies, each of which, hypothetically, is independently measurable. At the other extreme is Oller's (1978; 1979) claim that "...there exists a global language proficiency factor which accounts for the bulk of the reliable variance in a wide variety of language proficiency measures" (1978, p. 413). This factor is strongly related to cognitive abililty and academic achievement measures and is about equally well measured by certain types of listening, speaking, reading, and writing tasks.[3]

The communicative competence framework proposed by Canale (1981), on the basis of the earlier Canale and Swain (1980) theory, adopts an intermediate position in distinguishing four components. These are:

1. *Grammatical competence:* Mastery of the language code (e.g., lexical items and rules of word formation, sentence formation, literal meaning, pronunciation, and spelling).

2. *Sociolinguistic competence:* Mastery of appropriate language use in different sociolinguistic contexts, with emphasis on appropriateness of meanings and forms.

3. *Discourse competence:* Mastery of how to combine meanings and forms to achieve a unified text in different modes (e.g., telephone inquiry, argumentative essay, and recipe) by using (a) cohesion devices to relate utterance forms (e.g., pronouns and transition words), and (b) coherence rules to organize meanings (e.g., repetition progression, consistency, and relevance of ideas).

4. *Strategic competence:* Mastery of verbal and non-verbal strategies (a) to compensate for breakdowns in communication due to insufficient competence or performance limitations (e.g., strategies such as use of dictionaries, paraphrase, and gestures), and (b) to enhance communication effectiveness.

---

[2] Although language can be used for purposes not overtly communicative, e.g., problem-solving (Canale and Swain, 1980), these "analytic" (Bruner, 1975) language skills develop within a matrix of human interaction; thus, for purposes of this paper, the terms "language proficiency" and "communicative proficiency" are being used synonymously.

[3] It should be noted that Oller (1979) leaves open the possibility that there may be smaller specific components of language proficiency that are not encompassed by the global proficiency dimension.

There are two major problems in applying this or any other theoretical framework for communicative competence to minority students' acquisition of English proficiency. First, these theories tend to be static since the developmental aspects of communicative competence in L1 and L2 are left vague; second, in general, little consideration has been given to the role of specific acquisition contexts in determining the interrelationships and development of different aspects of communicative competence (however, see Canale, 1981). In particular, the nature of the communicative demands of schooling (e.g., processing language outside of one-to-one, face-to-face situations) has not been considered. The relevance of these problems can be seen by examining the development of English proficiency among native English-speaking children.

The Development of English Proficiency in School Contexts. The development of language proficiency can be considered in two very different ways. First is the acquisition of what Bruner (1975) has termed the "species minimum" involving the phonological, syntactic, and semantic skills that most native speakers have acquired by age six (there is little difference between the phonological competence of a six-year-old and a fourteen-year-old). Similarly, mastery of basic syntax approaches maturity by age six, although the development of more sophisticated rules and flexibility in grammatical control will continue into early adolescence (Chomsky, 1972). Also, semantic categories such as agent, instrument, and recipient of action are present at a very early age.

However, in contrast to the acquisition of this "species minimum" competence, other aspects of language proficiency continue to develop throughout the school years and beyond. Obvious examples are literacy-related language skills such as reading comprehension, writing ability, and vocabulary/concept knowledge. Within each of the four components of communicative competence distinguished by Canale (1981), native speakers achieve mastery levels in some subskills prior to others. For example, within grammatical competence virtually all native speakers master pronunciation before spelling. Similarly, some aspects of sociolinguistic, discourse, and strategic competence will be mastered at an early age and others much later, if at all.

However, within a second language context very different relationships may exist among the various subskills, depending upon the specific acquisition context, e.g., formal L2 classroom vs. real life exposure, or pre-school immigrant children vs. adolescent immigrant children whose L1 literacy skills are well developed. Also, the relationship of language proficiency to cognitive and academic variables will vary both between L1 and L2 contexts and also within L2 contexts, depending upon the conditions of acquisition. Thus, almost by definition, the "species minimum" will be attained by all native speakers regardless of academic or cognitive abilities; however, this will not necessarily be the case among L2 learners. For example, pronunciation skills may remain poorly developed among many older L2 learners. Also, cognitive and personality variables are likely to differentially influence the acquisition of different aspects of L2 proficiency in different contexts. As Fillmore (1979) suggests, personality variables (e. g., sociability) may be most influential in determining the acquisition rate of L2 face-to-face communication skills in a peer interaction situation; however, cognitive skills in a peer interaction situation; however, cognitive skills may be more involved in determining the acquisition rate of L2 literacy skills in a classroom context.

In short, current theories of communicative competence are not particularly helpful in elucidating issues related to the development of English proficiency by language minority students. This is because these theories (1) fail to incorporate a developmental perspective; (2) fail to consider the development of communicative competence explicitly in relation to specific contexts, in particular the school context; and (3) fail to examine the developmental relationships between L1 and L2. In other words, the usefulness of most current theories is limited because they either exist in a developmental and contextual vacuum or else have been proposed in a very different context from that of bilingual education in the United States.

The necessity for considering the question of what constitutes language proficiency in school contexts from a developmental perspective is highlighted by a recent study which shows that immigrant students arriving after age six take between six and seven years to approach grade norms in English academic skills (Cummins, 1981). Results of this study, conducted among 1,210 immigrant students in the Toronto Board of Education, are shown in Figure 1. The Picture Vocabulary Text (PVT) consisted of a group-administered vocabulary test, and results were broken down by Age on Arrival (AOA) and Length of Residence (LOR).

Clearly, it takes considerably longer for immigrant students to develop age-appropriate academic skills in English (five-seven years LOR) than it does to develop certain aspects of age-appropriate English communicative skills (approximately two years). The reason is not difficult to see. Literacy-related language skills (such as vocabulary range) continue to develop among native speakers throughout the school years, whereas some salient aspects of face-to-face communicative skills reach a plateau by about age six. Clearly, many other aspects of face-to-face com-

Figure 1

AGE ON ARRIVAL, LENGTH OF RESIDENCE, AND PVT
STANDARD SCORES

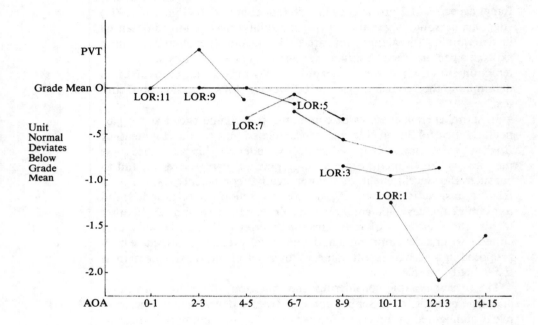

municative skills continue to develop throughout the school years; but the data considered above suggest that these are not particularly salient for teachers and psychologists.

In a previous section, it was pointed out that failure to distinguish these two dimensions of English proficiency can result in educational deficits for language minority students. At this point, it may be helpful to describe this distinction more completely and place it into a broader theoretical framework so that it can be used to examine the developmental relationships between L1 and L2 proficiency within bilingual education programs.

A Theoretical Framework[4]

To recapitulate, three minimal requirements for a theoretical framework of communicative proficiency relevant to bilingual education in the United States have been outlined: First, such a framework must incorporate a developmental perspective so that those aspects of communicative proficiency mastered early by native speakers and L2 learners can be distinguished from those varying across individuals as development progresses; second, the framework must permit differences between the linguistic demands of school and those of interpersonal contexts outside the school to be described; and third, the framework must allow for the developmental relationships between L1 and L2 proficiency to be described.

The framework developed in response to these requirements is presented in Figure 2. The framework proposes that in the context of United States bilingual education, communicative proficiency can be conceptualized along two continuums. A continuum related to the range of contextual support available for expressing or receiving meaning is described in terms of "context-embedded" versus "context-reduced" communication. The extremes of this continuum are distinguished by the fact that in context-embedded communication the participants can actively negotiate meaning (e.g., by providing feedback that the message has not been understood) and the language is supported by a wide range of meaningful paralinguistic (gestures, intonation, etc.) and situational cues; context-reduced communication, on the other hand, relies primarily (or at the extreme of the continuum, exclusively) on linguistic cues to meaning and may, in some cases, involve suspending knowledge of the "real" world in order to interpret (or manipulate) the logic of communication appropriately.[5]

In general, context-embedded communication derives from interpersonal involvement in a shared reality that reduces the need for explicit linguistic elaboration of the message. Context-reduced communication, on the other hand, derives from the fact that this shared reality cannot be assumed and thus linguistic messages must be elaborated precisely and explicitly so that the risk of misinterpretation is minimized. It is impor-

[4] This theoretical framework should be viewed within a social context. The language proficiencies described develop as a result of various types of communicative interactions in home and school. The nature of these interactions is, in turn, determined by broader societal factors, as described later in this paper.

[5] The term "context-reduced" is used rather than "disembedded" (Donaldson, 1978) or "decontextualized" because there is a large variety of contextual cues available to carry out tasks even at the context-reduced end of the continuum. The difference, however, is that these cues are exclusively *linguistic* in nature.

Figure 2

RANGE OF CONTEXTUAL SUPPORT AND DEGREE OF COGNITIVE INVOLVEMENT IN COMMUNICATIVE ACTIVITIES

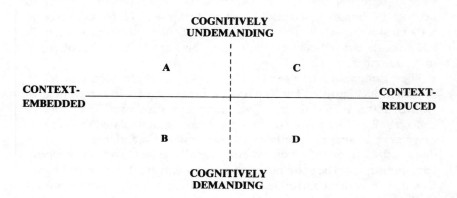

tant to emphasize that this is a continuum and not a dichotomy. Thus, examples of communicative behaviors going from left to right along the continuum might be: engaging in a discussion, writing a letter to a close friend, and writing (or reading) an academic article. Clearly, context-embedded communication is more typical of the everyday world outside the classroom, whereas many of the linguistic demands of the classroom reflect communication that is closer to the context-reduced end of the continuum. Recent research, reviewed by Tannen (1980), suggests that part of minority students' failure in mainstream classrooms may derive from application of context-embedded strategies in the school setting where context-reduced strategies (e.g., responding in terms of the logic of the text rather than in terms of prior knowledge) are expected and rewarded.

The vertical continuum is intended to address the developmental aspects of communicative competence in terms of the degree of active cognitive involvement in the task or activity. Cognitive involvement can be conceptualized in terms of the amount of information that must be processed simultaneously or in close succession by the individual in order to carry out the activity.

How does this continuum incorporate a developmental perspective? If we return to the four components of communicative competence (grammatical, sociolinguistic, discourse, and strategic) discussed by Canale (1981), it is clear that within each one some subskills are mastered more rapidly than others. In other words, some subskills (e.g., pronunciation and syntax within L1 grammatical competence) reach plateau levels at which there are no longer significant differences in mastery between individuals (at least in context-embedded situations). Other subskills continue to develop throughout the school years and beyond, depending upon the individual's communicative needs.

Thus, the upper parts of the vertical continuum consist of communicative tasks and activities in which the linguistic tools have become largely automatized (mastered) and thus require little active cognitive involvement for appropriate performance. At the lower end of the continuum are tasks and activities in which the communicative tools have not become automatized and thus require active cognitive involvement. Persuading other individuals that your point of view rather than theirs is correct, or writing an essay on a complex theme, are examples of such activities. In these situations, it is necessary to stretch one's linguistic resources (i.e., grammatical, sociolinguistic, discourse, and strategic competencies) to the limit in order to achieve one's communicative goals. Obviously, cognitive involvement can be just as intense in context-embedded as in context-reduced activities.

As mastery is developed, specific linguistic tasks and skills travel from the bottom towards the top of the vertical continuum. In other words, there tends to be a high level of cognitive involvement in task or activity performance until mastery has been achieved or, alternatively, until a plateau level at less than mastery levels has been reached (e.g., L2 pronunciation in many adult immigrants).[6] Thus, learning the phonology and syntax of L1, for example, requires considerable cognitive involvement for the two- and three-year-old child, and thus these tasks would be placed in quadrant B (context-embedded, cognitively demanding). However, as mastery of these skills develops, tasks involving them would move from quadrant B to quadrant A, since performance becomes

---

[6]Bereiter and Scardamalia (1980) point out that as children learn to write, the progressive automatization of lower level skills (e.g., handwriting, spelling of common words, punctuation, common syntactic forms, etc.) releases increasingly more mental capacity for higher level planning of large chunks of discourse. To illustrate what writing must be like for a young child, they suggest trying to do some original writing with the wrong hand. It is likely to be difficult to think much beyond the word being written.

increasingly automatized and cognitively undemanding. In a second
language context, the same type of developmental progression occurs. As
specific linguistic tasks and skills are mastered in L2, they move up the
vertical continuum.[7]

Literacy Development and Communicative Proficiency. Clearly,
within this theoretical framework, literacy is viewed as one aspect of
communicative proficiency. Although there are inherent characteristics
of literacy tasks that place them towards the context-reduced end of the
horizontal continuum, most theorists would agree that the more reading
and writing instruction can be embedded in a meaningful communicative
context (i.e., related to children's previous experience), the more successful it is likely to be. As the papers (this volume) by Krashen (1981)
and Terrell (1981) emphasize, the same principle holds for second
language instruction. The more context-embedded the initial L2 input,
the more comprehensible it will be and, paradoxically, the more successful in ultimately developing L2 skills in context-reduced situations.
Thus, a major pedagogical principle for both L1 and L2 teaching is that
language skills in context-reduced situations can be most successfully
developed on the basis of initial instruction which maximizes the degree
of context-embeddedness.

In terms of the vertical continuum, developmental relationships between cognitive ability and reading performance can be readily interpreted. Singer (1977) reviews data that show a change between grades 1

---

[7] An implication of this theoretical framework for theories of communicative competence
is that there is likely to be different relationships among language tasks in a first
language, compared to a second language context. This is because L2 learners are likely
to have lower levels of certain L2 skills as compared to native speakers. In other words,
tasks located close to the top of the vertical continuum for native speakers may be close
to the bottom for L2 learners. Also, acquisition contexts may vary between L2 learners
and native speakers. For example, skills acquired in context-embedded situations by
native speakers may have been learned in context-reduced situations (e.g., formal
classrooms) by L2 learners. This would also result in variable relationships among
language skills between native speakers and L2 learners. Thus, an important
characteristic of the theoretical framework is that although communicative tasks and activities can be mapped onto it in a general way (e.g., inherent text characteristics make
reading and writing less context-embedded than face-to-face communication), the exact
location of any particular task on the horizontal and vertical continuums will depend on
the individual's or group's proficiency level and acquisition context. Thus, for immigrant
students in the host country for two years, academic tasks in L2 are likely to be more
cognitively demanding and context-reduced than for native speakers.

Space does not permit the question of individual differences in learning styles among L2
learners to be discussed in detail. However, within the present framework, learning style
can be regarded as the way in which individual learners define the degree of cognitive involvement and context-embeddedness of particular tasks. Thus, at least three factors
must be taken into account in locating any particular task in relation to the two continuums: (1) the task's inherent characteristics, (2) the learner's general level of proficiency, and (3) the learner's individual learning style.

and 5 in the amount of common variance between IQ and reading achievement from 16 to 64 percent (correlations of .40 to .79). He interprets this in terms of the nature of the component skills stressed in reading instruction at different grade levels.[8]

> *As reading achievement shifts from predominant emphasis on word recognition to stress on word meaning and comprehension, the mental functions being assessed by intelligence and reading tests have more in common. (Singer, 1977, p. 48)*

As development progresses, word meaning and reasoning-in-reading (e.g., inferring and predicting text meaning) rather than word decoding skills account for the variance between good and poor readers. In terms of the present framework, word meaning and reasoning-in-reading skills remain in the lower end of the vertical continuum (i.e., variance between individuals in these skills remains large), whereas word recognition skills tend to climb towards the upper end of the continuum as development progresses. In other words, as fluency in reading is acquired, word recognition skills are first automatized and then totally short-circuited, since the proficient reader does not read individual words but engages in a process of sampling from the text to confirm predictions (Smith, 1978).

Relevance of the Theoretical Framework to the Achievement of Language Minority Students. A major aim of literacy instruction in schools is to develop students' abilities to manipulate and interpret context-reduced cognitively demanding texts (quadrant D). One reason why language minority students have often failed to develop high levels of academic skills is because their initial instruction has emphasized context-reduced communication, since instruction has been through English and unrelated to their prior out-of-school experiences. Attempts to teach English through context-reduced audiolingually-based ESL may very well have been counter-productive in some respects (Legarreta, 1979).

However, another contributing factor to minority students' academic failure, and one which is still operating even in the context of bilingual programs, is that many educators have a very confused notion of what it means to be proficient in English. If language minority students manifest proficiencies in some context-embedded aspects of English (quadrant A), they are often regarded as having sufficient English proficiency both to follow a regular English curriculum and to take psychological and educational tests in English. What is not realized by many educators is that

---

[8] Clearly, the relationships between IQ and early reading achievement may vary as a function of the instructional approach.

because of language minority students' ESL background, the regular English curriculum and psychological assessment procedures are considerably more context-reduced and cognitively demanding than they are for English-background students. As was pointed out earlier, research findings suggest that it takes much longer for language minority students to approach commonly accepted age/grade norms in context-reduced aspects of English proficiency (five to seven years on the average) than it does in context-embedded aspects (approximately two years on the average).[9] Hypothetical curves representing these data are presented in Figure 3.

Figure 3

LENGTH OF TIME REQUIRED TO ACHIEVE AGE-APPROPRIATE LEVELS OF CONTEXT-EMBEDDED AND CONTEXT-REDUCED COMMUNICATIVE PROFICIENCY

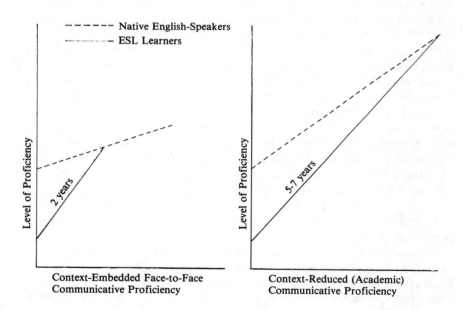

[9]Native-speakers also, of course, take much longer to develop proficiency in processing language in context-reduced situations.

In summary, I have tried to show how certain misconceptions regarding the notion of language proficiency are currently contributing to the academic failure of language minority students. To more adequately address the issue of the acquisition of English proficiency in bilingual programs, a theoretical framework has been developed in which two continuums are distinguished. One deals with the range of contextual supports for the communicative activity while the other is concerned with the degree of active cognitive involvement in the activity. Literate cultures typically require their members to become proficient in communicative activities which are context-reduced and cognitively demanding (e.g., reading and writing). There tends to be large individual differences both within and between socio-economic groups in the extent to which this dimension of communicative proficiency is developed.[10] In the remainder of this paper, the dimension of language which is strongly related to literacy skills will be termed "context-reduced language proficiency."[11]

In the next section, several theoretical distinctions similar to those developed in the present framework are briefly discussed in order to further elaborate the characteristics of context-reduced language proficiency.

Related Theoretical Frameworks

Several theorists interested primarily in the development of first language academic skills have similarly argued for the necessity to distinguish between the processing of language in informal everyday interpersonal situations and the language processing required in most academic situations (Bereiter and Scardamalia, 1981; Donaldson, 1978; Olson, 1977). In concrete terms, it is argued that reading a difficult text or writing an essay make fundamentally different information processing

---

[10] Wells (1979), in a ten-year longitudinal study, has identified two broad types of home communicative activities that strongly predict the acquisition of reading skills in school. One is the extent to which there is "negotiation of meaning" (i.e., quality and quantity of communication) between adults and children, the other is the extent to which literacy-related activities are promoted in the home, e.g., reading to children). There is no clear-cut relationship between socio-economic status (SES) and the former, but a strong relationship between SES and the latter.

[11] In previous articles I have contrasted cognitive/academic language proficiency (CALP) with basic interpersonal communicative skills (BICS) in order to make the same point; namely, academic deficits are often created by teachers and psychologists who fail to realize that it takes language minority students considerably longer to attain grade/age-appropriate levels in English academic skills than it does in English face-to-face communicative skills. However, because this distinction was not explicitly integrated into a more general theoretical framework, misinterpretation occurred. Hence, the attempt to define such a framework in this paper.

demands on the individual compared to engaging in a casual conversation with a friend.

Embedded and Disembedded Thought and Language. Donaldson (1978) distinguishes between embedded and disembedded thought and language from a developmental perspective and is especially concerned with the implications for children's adjustment to formal schooling. She points out that young children's early thought processes and use of language develop within a "flow of meaningful context" in which the logic of words is subjugated to perception of the speaker's intentions and salient features of the situation. Thus, children's (and adults') normal productive speech is embedded within a context of fairly immediate goals, intentions, and familiar patterns of events. However, thinking and language, which move beyond the bounds of meaningful interpersonal context, make entirely different demands on the individual in that it is necessary to focus on the linguistic forms themselves for meaning rather than on the intentions.

Donaldson (1978) offers a re-interpretation of Piaget's theory of cognitive development from this perspective and reviews a large body of research that supports the distinction between embedded and disembedded thought and language. Her description of pre-school children's comprehension and production of language in embedded contexts is especially relevant to current practices in language proficiency assessment in bilingual programs. She points out that:

> ...*the ease with which preschool children often seem to understand what is said to them is misleading if we take it as an indication of skill with language* per se. *Certainly they commonly understand us, but surely it is not our words alone that they are understanding—for they may be shown to be relying heavily on cues of other kinds. (Donaldson, 1978, p. 72)*

Donaldson goes on to argue that children's facility in producing language that is meaningful and appropriate in interpersonal contexts can also give a misleading impression of overall language proficiency:

> *When you produce language, you are in control: you need only talk about what you choose to talk about...[the child] is never required, when he is himself producing language, to go counter to his own preferred reading of the situation—to the way in which he himself spontaneously sees it. But this is no longer necessarily true when he becomes the listener. And it is frequently not true when he is the listener in the formal situation of a psychological experiment or indeed when he becomes a learner at school. (1978, pp. 73-74)*

The practical implications of this view will be discussed in the context of current assessment practices in bilingual education.

Utterance and Text. Olson's (1977) distinction between "utterance" and "text" relates to whether meaning is largely extrinsic to language (utterance) or intrinsic to language (text). In interpersonal oral situations, the listener has access to a wide range of contextual and paralinguistic information with which to interpret the speaker's intentions; and, in this sense, the meaning is only partially dependent upon the specific linguistic forms used by the speaker. However, in contrast to utterance, written text:

> ...*is an autonomous representation of meaning. Ideally, the printed reader depends on no cues other than linguistic cues; it represents no intentions other than those represented in the text; it is addressed to no one in particular; its author is essentially anonymous; and its meaning is precisely that represented by the sentence meaning. (Olson, 1977, p. 276)*

Olson explicitly differentiates the development of the ability to process text from the development of the mother tongue (utterance) in the preschool years:

> *But language development is not simply a matter of progressively elaborating the oral mother tongue as a means of sharing intentions. The developmental hypothesis offered here is that the ability to assign a meaning to the sentence per se, independent of its nonlinguistic interpretive context, is achieved only well into the school years. (Olson, 1977, p. 275)*

Conversation and Composition. Bereiter and Scardamalia (1981) have analyzed the problems of learning to write as problems of converting a language production system geared to conversation over to a language production system capable of functioning by itself. Their studies suggest that some major difficulties involved in this process are the following: (1) learning to continue producing language without prompting from conversational partners; (2) learning to search one's own memory instead of having memories triggered by what other people say; (3) planning large units of discourse instead of only what will be said next; and (4) learning to function as both sender and receiver, the latter function being necessary for revision.

Bereiter and Scardamalia (1980) argue that the absence of normal conversational supports makes writing a radically different kind of task from conversation.

> *We are proposing instead that the oral language production system cannot be carried over intact into written composition, that it must, in some way, be reconstructed to function autonomously instead of interactively. (p. 3)*

Although the distinctions between "embedded-disembedded," "utterance-text," and "conversation-composition" were developed independently and in relation to a different set of data, they share the essential characteristics of the distinctions outlined in the present theoretical framework. The major difference is that the failure of other frameworks to distinguish explicitly between the cognitive and contextual aspects of communicative activities might incorrectly suggest that context-reduced communication (literate tradition) is *intrinsically* more cognitively demanding than context-embedded communication (oral tradition).

Having described in some detail the nature of the academic tasks students encounter in school, it is now possible to discuss the development of bilingual proficiency among language minority students within this context.

The Nature of Bilingual Proficiency

The Myth of Bilingual Handicaps

The image of bilingualism as a negative force in children's development was especially common in the early part of this century when most teachers of language minority children saw bilingualism almost as a disease that not only caused confusion in children's thinking but also prevented them from becoming "good Americans." Therefore, they felt that a pre-condition for teaching children the school language was the eradication of their bilingualism. Thus, children were often punished for speaking their first language in school and were made to feel ashamed of their own language and cultural background. It is not surprising that research studies conducted during this period (Darcy, 1953) often found that bilingual children did poorly at school, many experiencing emotional conflicts. Children were made to feel that it was necessary to reject the home culture in order to belong to the majority culture, often ending up unable to identify fully with either cultural group.

However, rather than considering the possibility that the school's treatment of minority children might be a cause of their failure, teachers, researchers, and administrators seized on the obvious scapegoat and blamed the children's bilingualism. The research findings were interpreted to mean that there is only so much space or capacity available in our brains for language; therefore, if we divide that space between two languages, neither language will develop properly and intellectual confusion will result (Jensen, 1962). Table 1 outlines the interplay between socio-political and psycho-educational considerations in establishing the myth of bilingual handicaps and the role of "scientific studies" in perpetuating it.

The socio-political and psycho-educational assumptions illustrated in Table 1 are very much in evidence in the current bilingual education debate. The popular press frequently warns that bilingual education will lead to social fragmentation and Quebec-style separatist movements. This fear of bilingual education is often rationalized in psycho-educational terms; namely, that if minority children are deficient in English, then they need instruction in English, not in their first language.

Table 1

BLAMING THE VICTIM IN MINORITY LANGUAGE EDUCATION*

A. *Overt aim*	*Covert aim*	D. *Outcomes*	
Teach English to minority children in order to create a harmonious society with equal opportunity for all.	Anglicize minority children because linguistic and cultural diversity are seen as a threat to social cohesion.	Even more intense efforts by the school to eradicate the deficiencies inherent in minority children.	The failure of these efforts only serves to reinforce the myth of minority group deficiencies.
B. *Method*	*Justification*	C. *Results*	*"Scientific" explanation*
Prohibit use of L1 in schools and make children reject their own culture and language in order to identify with majority English group.	1. L1 should be eradicated because it will interfere with the learning of English. 2. Identification with L1 culture will reduce child's ability to identify with English-speaking culture.	1. Shame in L1 language and culture. 2. Replacement of L1 by L2. 3. School failure among many children.	1. Bilingualism causes confusion in thinking, emotional insecurity, and school failures. 2. Minority group children are "culturally deprived" (almost by definition since they are not Anglos). 3. Some minority language groups are genetically inferior (common theory in the United States in the 1920s and 1930s).

* This table reflects the assumptions of North American school systems in the first half of this century. However, similar assumptions have been made about minority language children in the school systems of many other countries.

Consider, for example, the view expressed by Bethell (1979):

> *Bilingual education is an idea that appeals to teachers of Spanish and other tongues, but also to those who never did think that another idea, the United States of America, was a particularly good one to begin with, and that the sooner it is restored to its component "ethnic" parts the better off we shall all be. Such people have been welcomed with open arms into the upper reaches of the federal government in recent years, giving rise to the suspicion of a death wish. (p. 30)*

The psycho-educational argument appears later when Bethell (1979) approvingly quotes Congressman John Ashbrook's opposition to bilingual education:

> *The program is actually preventing children from learning English. Someday somebody is going to have to teach those young people to speak English or else they are going to become public charges. Our educational system is finding it increasingly difficult today to teach English-speaking children to read their own language. When children come out of the Spanish-language schools or Choctaw-language schools which call themselves bilingual, how is our educational system going to make them literate in what will still be a completely alien tongue...? (pp. 32-33)*

The argument that deficiencies in English should be remediated by intensive instruction in English appears at first sight much more intuitively appealing than the alternative argument that instruction in L1 will be more effective than instruction in English in promoting English skills. This latter argument appears to invoke a "less equals more" type of logic that is unlikely to convince skeptics. In order to evaluate these alternative positions, it is necessary to make their propositions more explicit and make empirical evidence rather than "common sense" the criterion of validity. The issues revolve around two alternative conceptions of bilingual proficiency, termed the Separate Underlying Proficiency (SUP) and Common Underlying Proficiency (CUP) models.

The SUP and CUP Models of Bilingual Proficiency

The argument that if minority children are deficient in English, then they need instruction in English, not in their L1, implies: (a) that proficiency in L1 is separate from proficiency in English, and (b) that there is a direct relationship between exposure to a language (in home or school) and achievement in that language. The SUP model is illustrated in Figure 4.

Figure 4

THE SEPARATE UNDERLYING PROFICIENCY (SUP) MODEL
OF BILINGUAL PROFICIENCY

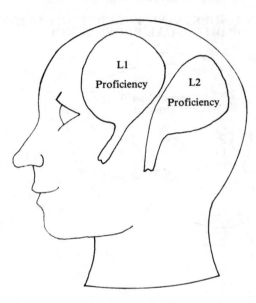

The second implication of the SUP model follows from the first, that if L1 and L2 proficiency are separate, then content and skills learned through L1 cannot transfer to L2 and vice versa. In terms of the balloon metaphor illustrated in Figure 4, blowing into the L1 balloon will succeed in inflating L1 but not L2. When bilingual education is approached with these "common-sense" assumptions about bilingual proficiency, it is not at all surprising that it appears illogical to argue that one can better inflate the L2 balloon by blowing into the L1 balloon.

However, despite its intuitive appeal, there is not one shred of evidence to support the SUP model.[12] In order to account for the evidence reviewed, we must posit a CUP model in which the literacy-related aspects

[12] Macnamara (1970) points out that a strict interpretation of a SUP model would leave the bilingual in a curious predicament in that "...he would have great difficulty in 'communicating' with himself. Whenever he switched languages he would have difficulty in explaining in L2 what he had heard or said in L1" (pp. 25-26). It is not surprising that the SUP model is not seriously proposed by any researcher. Nevertheless, it is important to examine the research evidence in relation to this model, since many educators and policy-makers espouse positions in regard to bilingual education which derive directly from this implicit model.

of a bilingual's proficiency in L1 and L2 are seen as common or interdependent across languages. Two ways of illustrating the CUP model (the Interdependence Hypothesis) are shown in Figures 5 and 6.

Figure 5

THE COMMON UNDERLYING PROFICIENCY MODEL (CUP) OF BILINGUAL PROFICIENCY

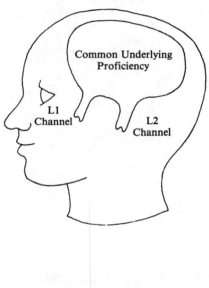

Figure 6

THE "DUAL-ICEBERG" REPRESENTATION OF BILINGUAL PROFICIENCY

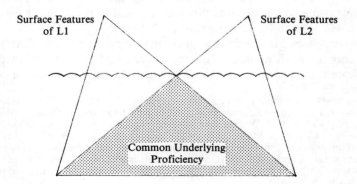

Figure 5 expresses the point that experience with either language can promote development of the proficiency underlying both languages, given adequate motivation and exposure to both either in school or in the wider environment. In Figure 6 bilingual proficiency is represented by means of a "dual iceberg" in which common cross-lingual proficiencies underlie the obviously different surface manifestations of each language. In general the surface features of L1 and L2 are those that have become relatively automatized or less cognitively demanding whereas the underlying proficiency is that involved in cognitively demanding communicative tasks.[13]

There are five major sources of evidence for the CUP model: (1) results of bilingual education programs, (2) studies relating age on arrival and immigrant students' L2 acquisition, (3) studies relating bilingual language use in the home to academic achievement, (4) studies of the relationship between L1 and L2 proficiency, and (5) experimental studies of bilingual information processing. The first three sources will be considered in more detail than the latter two because of their direct relevance to current concerns of bilingual educators in the United States.

Evaluations of Bilingual Programs

Although there is a widespread perception that bilingual education has yet to prove its effectiveness (Trombley, 1980), findings of the available, well-controlled research are strongly supportive of the basic principle underlying bilingual education, i.e., the CUP model of bilingual proficiency. For example, Troike (1978) reviewed 12 evaluations and several research studies in which bilingual instruction was found to be more effective than English-only instruction in promoting English academic skills. Two of these evaluations are outlined here as well as several other evaluations in the United States and elsewhere that clearly refute the SUP model.

Rock Point Navajo Study. Before the bilingual program was started in 1971, children were two years behind United States norms in

---

[13] The data used to support the CUP model primarily involve "context-reduced language proficiency" because the model is developed explicitly in relation to the development of bilingual academic skills. It is probable, however, that many aspects of "context-embedded language proficiency" may also be interdependent across languages. As far as context-reduced language proficiency is concerned, the transferability across languages of the proficiencies involved in reading (e.g., inferring and predicting meaning based on sampling from the text) and writing (e.g., planning large chunks of discourse) is obvious. However, even where the task demands are language specific (e. g., decoding or spelling), a strong relationship may be obtained between skills in L1 and L2 as a result of a more generalized proficiency (and motivation) to handle cognitively demanding context-reduced language tasks. Similarly, on the context-embedded side, many sociolinguistic rules of face-to-face communication are language-specific, but L1 and L2 sociolinguistic skills may be related as a result of a possible generalized sensitivity to sociolinguistic rules of discourse.

English reading by the end of sixth grade despite intensive teaching of English as a second language. The bilingual program used Navajo as the major initial medium of instruction and continued its use throughout elementary school. English reading instruction was delayed until Navajo reading skills were well established (mid-second grade). By the end of the sixth grade, children in the bilingual program were performing slightly *above* United States grade norms in English reading despite considerably less exposure to English than previously (Rosier and Farella, 1976).

Santa Fe Bilingual Program. In the schools involved in this program, Spanish was used for between 30 and 50 percent of the school day throughout elementary school. It was found that children enrolled in the bilingual program consistently performed significantly better than the control group (in an English-only program) in both reading and mathematics. Children enrolled continuously in the bilingual program from second grade caught up with United States norms in English reading by fifth grade and stayed close in sixth grade. In math this group surpassed the national average in fourth grade and maintained an equal or superior status through sixth grade (Leyba, 1978).

Legarreta Study: Direct ESL-Bilingual Comparison. A study carried out by Legarreta (1979) in California compared the effectiveness of three types of bilingual treatments with two types of English-only treatments in facilitating the development of English communicative competence in Spanish-background kindergarten children. The three bilingual treatments were found to be significantly superior to the two English-only treatments in developing English language skills. The most effective program was one with balanced bilingual usage (50 percent English, 50 percent Spanish).

Nestor School Bilingual Program Evaluation. The Nestor program in San Diego involved both Spanish- and English-background students and used a team teaching approach in which instruction in the early grades was primarily through the children's L1. The proportion of instruction in L2 was gradually increased until, by fourth grade, approximately 50 percent of instruction was through each language. The evaluation of the program (Evaluation Associates, 1978) showed that Spanish-background students gained *an additional* .36 of a year's growth in English reading for each successive year they spent in the bilingual program. Spanish-background students who had spent five years or more in the bilingual program at the elementary level tended to perform slightly better in English reading than the school average at the junior high school level, despite the fact that at least 37 percent of the comparison group were originally native English speakers. In mathematics, the sixth grade

Spanish-background children in the program were over a year ahead of the Spanish speakers in the comparison district and only one month behind grade level. The English-background participants in the Nestor bilingual program performed at a higher level than the comparison groups on a large majority of measures; however, this may be due to a selection bias.

The Colorado Bilingual Programs Evaluation. Egan and Goldsmith (1981) and Egan (1981) report on the "overwhelming success" of bilingual programs in Colorado for both language minority and Anglo students. Over 90 percent of the 39 programs for which data were available reported that "limited-English-proficient" students showed a rate of academic progress at least as good as that normally expected for all students. More surprising, however, was the fact that 50 percent of the programs showed growth rates in English academic skills for language minority students well beyond the normal expected growth rates for all students. These results are especially significant in view of previous research in Colorado (Egan and Goldsmith, 1981) showing that Hispanic students tended to fall progressively further behind grade norms during the elementary school years.

Sodertalje Program for Finnish Immigrant Children in Sweden. The findings of this evaluation are very similar to those of the Rock Point Navajo evaluation. Finnish children in Swedish-only programs were found to perform worse in Finnish than 90 percent of equivalent socio-economic status Finnish children in Finland and worse in Swedish than about 90 percent of Swedish children (Skutnabb-Kangas and Toukomaa, 1976). The Sodertalje program, however, used Finnish as the major initial language of instruction and continued its use throughout elementary school. Swedish became the major language of instruction from third grade. By sixth grade, children's performances in this program in both Finnish and Swedish were almost at the same level as that of Swedish-speaking children in Finland, a considerable improvement in both languages compared to their performances in Swedish-only programs (Hanson, 1979).

Manitoba-Francophone Study. A large-scale study carried out by Hébert *et al.* (1976) among third, sixth, and ninth grades, in which minority francophone students in Manitoba were receiving varying amounts of instruction through the medium of French, found that the amount of French-medium instruction showed no relationship to children's achievement in English. In other words, francophone students receiving 80 percent instruction in French and 20 percent instruction in English did just as well in English as students receiving 80 percent instruction in English and 20 percent instruction in French. However, amount of instruction in French was positively related to achievement in French. In other words, students' French benefited at no cost to their progress in English.

Edmonton Ukrainian-English Bilingual Program. This program has existed in eight Edmonton elementary schools since 1972 and is financially supported by the Alberta government. In 1978-1979 there were 697 students enrolled between kindergarten and fifth grades. Ukrainian is used as a medium of instruction for 50 percent of the regular school day throughout elementary school. Only about 15 percent of the students are fluent in Ukrainian on entry to the program. A study carried out with first and third grade students (Cummins and Mulcahy, 1978) found that students who were relatively fluent in Ukrainian as a result of parents using it consistently in the home were significantly better able to detect ambiguities in *English* sentence structure than either equivalent monolingual English-speaking children not in the program or children in the program who came from predominantly English-speaking homes. The evaluations of the program have shown no detrimental effects on the development of children's English or other academic skills. In fact, by the end of fifth grade children in the program had pulled ahead of the comparison group in English reading comprehension skills (Edmonton Public School Board, 1979).

In summary, the results of research on bilingual programs show that minority children's L1 can be promoted in school at no cost to the development of proficiency in the majority language. In other words, the educational argument against bilingual education is invalid; in order to explain the findings, it is necessary to posit a common proficiency dimension that underlies the development of academic skills in both languages. The data clearly show that well-implemented bilingual programs have had remarkable success in developing English academic skills and have proved superior to ESL-only programs in situations where direct comparisons have been carried out.

How do we reconcile the success of L1-medium programs for minority children with the fact that majority language children fare very well academically in French or Spanish immersion programs (Cummins, 1979b; Swain, 1978)?[14] There are many differences between these situations, e.g., prestige of L1, security of children's identity and self-concept, and level of support for L1 development in home and environ-

---

[14] A French immersion program involves teaching students from English home backgrounds through the medium of French for a major part of the school day from kindergarten through high school. The goal is bilingualism in French and English. These programs are now extremely common in Canada, and evaluations show that students gain high levels of French proficiency at no cost to proficiency in English (Swain, 1978).

ment. Thus, it is not surprising that different forms of educational programs should be appropriate for children with very different background characteristics. The apparent contradiction between findings in minority and majority contexts completely disappears when we stop thinking in terms of "linguistic mismatch" or "home-school language switch." In immersion programs for majority language children, as well as in bilingual programs for minority children, instruction through the *minority* language has been effective in promoting proficiency in *both* languages. These findings, which have been replicated in an enormous number of studies, support the following "Interdependence" Hypothesis: *To the extent that instruction in L_x is effective in promoting proficiency in L_x, transfer of this proficiency to L_y will occur provided there is adequate exposure to L_y (either in school or environment) and adequate motivation to learn L_y.* In other words, far from being contradictory, the same theoretical principle, the CUP model, underlies immersion programs for majority language students as well as bilingual programs for language minority students.

Age on Arrival and L2 Acquisition

It would be predicted on the basis of the Interdependence Hypothesis that older learners who are more cognitively mature and whose L1 proficiency is better developed would acquire cognitively demanding aspects of L2 proficiency more rapidly than younger learners. Recent reviews of research on the age issue confirm this prediction (Cummins, 1980a; Cummins, 1981; Ekstrand, 1977; Genesee, 1978; Krashen *et al.*, 1979). The only area where research suggests older learners may not have an advantage is pronunciation, which, significantly, appears to be one of the least cognitively demanding aspects of both L1 and L2 proficiency. In terms of the model presented in Figure 3, we would expect the advantage of older learners to be especially apparent in context-reduced aspects of L2 proficiency because of their greater amount of experience in processing context-reduced aspects of L1.

The extent of the advantage older learners have in acquiring context-reduced cognitively demanding aspects of L2 is illustrated by the data in Figure 7. The test, a group adaptation of the *Ammons Picture Vocabulary Test* (Ramsey and Wright, 1972), and subjects (1,210 fifth, seventh, and ninth grade immigrant students in the Toronto Board of Education) are the same as in Figure 1. However, the data are presented in terms of absolute scores on the test rather than in terms of grade norms. In Figure 1, older and younger L2 learners appeared to approach grade norms at a generally comparable rate. However, because older learners have further to go in order to reach grade-appropriate levels of

Figure 7

AGE ON ARRIVAL, LENGTH OF RESIDENCE, AND PVT RAW SCORES

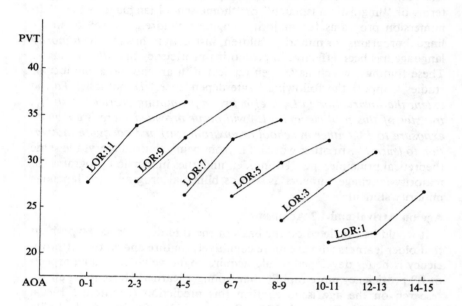

L2 academic proficiency (consider, for example, the difference between the vocabulary knowledge of a twelve- and six-year-old monolingual English child), we would expect them to acquire more L2 than younger learners in absolute terms in the same amount of time. This is clearly the case in Figure 7. In this study, it was possible to make 90 comparisons between older and younger learners on context-reduced cognitively demanding aspects of L2. In 89 of these, older learners performed better.[15]

---

[15] It may appear surprising that older learners make more rapid progress in acquiring L2 in view of the popular myth that there is an optimal pre-pubertal age for L2 acquisition. However, a major reason for the advantage is obvious when the data are viewed from within the context of the CUP model. For example, in learning the term "democracy" the task for a 14-year-old immigrant child consists of acquiring a new label for a concept already developed in L1; for a 6-year-old immigrant child the term will not be acquired until the concept has been developed. The advantage of older learners lies in the interdependence of conceptual knowledge across languages.

The relationship between L1 and L2 proficiency in immigrant students was explicitly investigated in two studies. Cummins *et al.* (1981) reported that older Japanese immigrant students, whose L1 literacy skills were better developed, acquired English proficiency significantly faster than younger immigrant students. It was also found that students who immigrated at younger ages developed significantly lower proficiency in Japanese compared to students who immigrated at older ages and who had been in Canada for the same amount of time. All the students in this study were from upper-class backgrounds.

Skutnabb-Kangas and Toukomaa (1976) also report that among Finnish immigrant children in Sweden, the extent to which L1 had been developed prior to contact with Swedish was strongly related to how well Swedish was learned. Children who migrated at age 10-12 maintained a level of Finnish close to Finnish students in Finland and achieved Swedish language skills comparable to those of Swedes. By contrast, children who migrated at younger age levels or who were born in Sweden tended to reach a developmental plateau at a low level in both Finnish and Swedish academic proficiency.

Consistent with the Skutnabb-Kangas and Toukomaa findings (1976), there is considerable anecdotal evidence that immigrant students from Mexico fare better educationally than native-born Mexican-Americans. For example, Troike (1978) stated that:

> It is a common experience that...children who immigrate to the United States...after grade six...rather quickly acquire English and soon out-perform Chicano students who have been in United States schools since grade one. (p. 15)

Based on a survey of school personnel in four southwestern states, Carter (1970) similarly reported that many teachers and administrators believe that older immigrant students achieved better than native-born Chicano students.[16]

In summary, considerable research supports the prediction derived from the Interdependence Hypothesis that older immigrant children

---

[16] Two empirical studies (Kimball, 1968; Anderson and Johnson, 1971) support these teacher perceptions. However, a recent study (Baral, 1979) reports that immigrant students who had had at least two years of schooling in Mexico performed significantly lower in academic skills than native-born Mexican students. Two factors are important in interpreting these results: first, the immigrant students came from significantly lower socio-economic backgrounds than the native-born students; second, they had been in United States schools only between two and five years. The Canadian findings reported earlier (Cummins, 1981) suggest that it can take up to seven years for immigrant students to approach grade norms in English academic skills. Students who were in Canada for three years were still approximately one standard deviation below grade norms. Thus, the relatively short length of residence and the socio-economic differences between immigrant and native-born students can account for Baral's (1979) findings.

make more rapid progress than younger children in acquiring L2 proficiency. It should be noted that these relationships between L1 and L2 do not operate in a sociocultural vacuum. The role of sociocultural factors in relation to cognitive and linguistic factors will be considered in a later section.

Primary Language Development in the Home

Several studies show that the use of a minority language in the home is not a handicap to children's academic progress.[17] This was evident in the Cummins and Mulcahy (1978) study of the Ukrainian bilingual program where first and third grade students who used Ukrainian consistently in the home were better able to detect ambiguities in English sentence structure. Two other studies (Bhatnager, 1980; Chesarek, 1981) suggest that, under certain conditions, a switch to the use of the majority language in the home is associated with poor academic progress in the majority language.

Chesarek (1981) carried out a longitudinal study among elementary students on a Crow reservation in Montana in which he identified a subgroup of students who had one or more Crow-speaking parents but were raised as English speakers. This group of students scored significantly lower on a non-verbal ability test at school entry than either native Crow-speaking children or English-speaking children of two English-speaking parents. In a longitudinal follow-up at third grade in one of the reservation schools that utilized a bilingual instructional program, it was found that this group performed worse on several aspects of English achievement than the native Crow-speaking group.[18] Chesarek (1981) sums up these findings as follows:

> In other words, children who had only three years exposure to English in a bilingual program context were surpassing children for whom English was the only language. (p. 14)

A very similar pattern of findings emerges from a recent study carried out by Bhatnager (1980) in Montreal, Canada. In this study, the

---

[17] In addition to the studies considered in the text, studies carried out by Carey and Cummins (1979), Ramirez and Politzer (1976), and Yee and La Forge (1974) with minority francophone, Hispanic, and Chinese students, respectively, show that, in itself, the use of a minority L1 in the home is not an impediment to the acquisition of L2 academic skills in school. These findings, of course, create problems of the "linguistic mismatch" rationale for bilingual education, namely, that minority students fail in school because their home language is different from that of the school.

[18] Chesarek (1981) points out there was very little bilingual activity in the classroom since the major efforts were being devoted to developing an orthography and teaching materials as well as training aides to assume instructional activities.

academic progress of 171 Italian immigrant children in English language elementary schools and 102 in French language schools was examined in relation to language spoken at home and with friends and siblings. Bhatnager sums up his findings as follows:

> *The results reported here do not support the popular assumption that the more immigrant children speak the local language the better their adjustment to the host culture. It is interesting to note that immigrant children who used Italian and a Canadian language interchangeably were better even at English or French, of both the spoken and written variety, than children who used English or French all the time....Language retention...should lead to higher academic adjustment, better facility in the host language, and better social relations of immigrant children. (1980, pp. 153-155)*[19]

In all these instances, the SUP model would have predicted that students exposed exclusively to the majority language at home would perform better than students who used a minority language at home. This prediction receives no support from the research findings; instead, the research supports the prediction derived from the CUP model, that experience with either language is capable of promoting the proficiency that underlies the development of academic skills in both languages.

Thus, whether English or a minority language is used in the home is, in itself, relatively unimportant for students' academic development. As Wells' (1979) study has shown, what is important for future academic success is the quality of interaction children experience with adults. Viewed from this perspective, encouraging minority parents to communicate in English with their children in the home can have very detrimental consequences. If parents are not comfortable in English, the quality of their interaction with their children in English is likely to be less than in L1. Thus, the lower academic achievement of minority children who used L2 exclusively with their parents and friends in Bhatnagar's (1980) and Chesarek's (1981) studies may be attributable to the lower quality of communication their parents were capable of providing in their second language.[20]

---

[19] Bhatnager (1980) reports that immigrant students who used L1 exclusively with parents and siblings also performed significantly worse than those who used both L1 and L2. However, it seems likely that this finding can be attributed to the fact that only those students who had immigrated relatively recently would use L1 exclusively. Length of residence is not considered in Bhatnager's study, but the data in Figure 1 suggest that it takes immigrant students at least five years to approach grade norms in L2 academic skills.

[20] Data from two other sources also support the CUP model. These are correlational studies of the relationship between L1 and L2 proficiency and experimental studies of bilingual information processing.

In summary, the research findings from evaluations of bilingual programs, studies of immigrant children's academic progress, and studies that examined the consequences of different patterns of home language use, are consistent with predictions derived from the CUP model. However, the observed relationships between L1 and L2 do not operate independently of the sociocultural context. In the next section the role of sociocultural factors in determining minority students' academic development is considered.

Sociocultural Determinants of Minority Students' Achievement

Linguistic, cognitive, or educational factors by themselves cannot account for the school failure of minority students because there are large individual and group differences in academic achievement of minority students exposed to the same educational conditions (e.g., home-school language switch). Consider, for example, the fact that immigrant students who arrived in Canada before age six achieved grade norms in L2 academic skills (see Figure 1), whereas Finnish students who immigrated to Sweden at an early age attained only a low level plateau in Swedish academic skills. This latter pattern also appears to characterize Hispanic students who immigrate at an early age or who are born in the United States.

What sociocultural factors account for this pattern of *differential* achievement by minority students in different contexts? Socio-economic status (SES) cannot account for the differences because all groups were low SES. Acculturation, or the degree to which minority students adopt the language and cultural values of the majority, likewise fails to account for the data. If acculturation were the major factor at work, we would expect those minority students who used only English at home to perform better academically than those who maintained the use of L1 at home. In fact, as the studies by Chesarek (1981) and Bhatnagar (1980) demonstrate, such "acculturated" students often (but not necessarily

---

Many studies have shown highly significant correlations between L1 and L2 proficiency (Cummins, 1979a) and it has been reported that Spanish reading proficiency developed in a bilingual program is the most stable predictor of English reading proficiency levels students develop after transferring from the bilingual program (Fischer and Cabello, 1978).

Experimental studies of bilingual information processing have consistently shown that bilinguals process semantic memory information in the same way in their two languages and in the same way as monolinguals (Caramazza and Brones, 1980; Enriquez, 1980; Kolers, 1968; Landry, 1978, 1980; McCormack, 1974). In other words, bilinguals have only one semantic memory system that can be accessed via two languages. The studies cited above have been carried out with adult bilinguals; however, a recent study (Chu-Chang, 1981) carried out with Chinese elementary school students has reported similar results. She concludes that, at the input and conceptual level, the two languages of the bilingual are in one storage.

always) show lower levels of English academic achievement than students who continue to use their L1 at home and maintain their allegiance to the home culture.[21]

An examination of the sociocultural characteristics of minority groups that tend to perform poorly in L2-only school situations suggests that the attitudes of these groups towards their own identity may be an important factor in interaction with educational treatment. Specifically, groups such as Finns in Sweden, North American Indians, Spanish-speakers in the U.S., and Franco-Ontarians in Canada all tend to have ambivalent or negative feelings towards the majority culture and often also towards their own culture. This pattern has been clearly documented for Finnish immigrants in Sweden by Skutnabb-Kangas and Toukomaa (1976). For example, Heyman (1973) concludes:

> *Many Finns in Sweden feel an aversion, and sometimes even hostility, towards the Swedish language and refuse to learn it...under protest. There is repeated evidence of this, as there is, on the other hand, of Finnish people—children and adults—who are ashamed of their Finnish language and do not allow it to live and develop. (p. 131)*

The same pattern of ambivalence or hostility towards the majority cultural group and insecurity about one's own language and culture is found, to a greater or lesser extent, in other minority groups that have tended to perform poorly in school. For example, many Franco-Ontarians tend to regard their own dialect of French as inferior and to show low aspirations for social and economic mobility in the majority anglophone culture. In contrast, minority groups that do well in school tend to be highly motivated to learn the majority language and often (though not always) have a strong sense of pride in their own cultural backgrounds.

According to this interpretation, part of the reason bilingual education is successful in promoting minority students' academic progress is that by validating the cultural identity of the students (as well as that of the community), it reduces their ambivalence towards the majority language and culture. Older immigrant students often fare better than minority students born in the host country because they have not been subject to the same ambivalence towards both cultural groups in their pre-school and early school years and, hence, approach the task of learning L2 with a secure identity and academic self-concept. Similarly, the exclusive use of L2 rather than L1 in the home is likely both to reflect and contribute to minority students' ambivalence towards L2.

---

[21] I am grateful to Steve Chesarek for pointing this out to me.

Clearly, at this stage, these suggestions in regard to the operation of "bicultural ambivalence" are speculative. However, they appear to account for the data better than a simple "acculturation" explanation and also provide the basis for a more adequate rationale for bilingual education than "linguistic mismatch" between home and school.

How does the operation of sociocultural factors relate to the linguistic factors (e.g., interdependence between L1 and L2) described earlier? The development of communicative proficiency in L1 and L2 can be regarded as an intervening variable mediating the effects of the sociocultural context on achievement. For example, sociocultural factors are likely to affect patterns of parent/child interaction that will influence the development of communicative proficiency (as described in Figure 2) in L1 and/or L2 that will, in turn, influence children's ability to benefit from instruction. Thus, if parents are ambivalent about the value of their cultural background or feel that they speak an inferior dialect of L1, they may not strongly encourage children to develop L1 skills in the home. They may tolerate (or even encourage) children to watch television for a considerable portion of the day on the grounds that this will help them to learn English and do well at school. This attitude may be encouraged by some teachers who believe that children should be exposed to as little L1 as possible.

Compare this situation to that of language minority parents who feel a strong sense of pride in their cultural background and are eager to transmit this cultural heritage to their children. They are likely to spend more time "negotiating meaning" (in L1) with their children, which according to Wells' (1979) findings, is a strong predictor of future academic success. If we assume that those aspects of communicative proficiency most relevant to academic success develop largely as a result of quality and quantity of communication with adults, then children in the second situation will come to school better prepared to handle the context-reduced communicative demands of school than children in the first situation, despite the fact that they may know little or no English (Chesarek, 1981). As the research reviewed in the context of the CUP model clearly shows, communicative proficiency already developed in L1 can readily be transferred to L2, given motivation to learn L2 and exposure to L2.

How do school programs interact with sociocultural and linguistic factors? As outlined in Table 1, schools have contributed directly to minority children's academic difficulties by undermining their cultural identity, attempting to eradicate their L1, and exposing them to incomprehensible context-reduced input in English. Recent evaluations of bilingual education, however, have shown that when schools reinforce minority children's cultural identity, promote the development of the L1 communicative proficiency children bring to school, and make instruction in English comprehensible by embedding it in a context that is meaningful in relation to students' previous experience, then minority students experience academic success and develop high English literacy skills, in spite of sociocultural impediments.

In summary, although both sociocultural and educational factors contribute directly to the development of communicative proficiency in minority students, a large majority of academic and communicative *deficits* (e.g., low reading achievement) are developed in these students only as a result of failure by educators to respond appropriately to the sociocultural and communicative characteristics children bring to school.

In this section, bilingual communicative proficiency has been considered as a dependent variable in relation to sociocultural and educational factors. Bilingual communicative proficiency can also be regarded as an intervening variable, which in turn influences the further development of cognitive and academic skills. In other words, how do different patterns of bilingual proficiency influence students' ability to benefit from interaction with their scholastic environment? This issue is considered in the next section.

Bilingual Proficiency as Educational Enrichment: The Threshold Hypothesis

It was pointed out in a previous section that because bilingual children performed more poorly than monolingual children on a variety of verbal-academic tasks in early studies, bilingualism was often regarded as a cause of language handicaps and cognitive confusion. However, more recent findings refute this interpretation. A large number of studies have reported that bilingual children are more cognitively flexible in certain respects and better able to analyze linguistic meaning than are monolingual children (Cummins, 1979b). Albert and Obler (1978) conclude on the basis of neuropsychological research findings that:

> *Bilinguals mature earlier than monolinguals both in terms of cerebral lateralization for language and in acquiring skills for linguistic abstraction. Bilinguals have better developed auditory language skills than monolinguals, but there is no clear evidence that they differ from monolinguals in written skills. (p. 248)*

These findings are not at all surprising when one considers that bilingual children have been exposed to considerably more "training" in analyzing and interpreting language than monolingual children.

The greater analytic orientation to language of bilingual children is consistent with the view of Vigotskiĭ (1962), who argues that being able to express the same thought in different languages will enable the child to "see his language as one particular system among many, to view its phenomena under more general categories, and this leads to awareness of his linguistic operations" (p. 110). Lambert and Tucker (1972) argued that a similar process was likely to operate among children in bilingual programs. They suggested that, as children develop high level bilingual skills, they are likely to practice a form of "incipient contrastive linguistics" by comparing the syntax and vocabulary of their two languages.

How do we resolve the apparent inconsistency that bilingualism is associated with both positive and negative cognitive and academic effects? An analysis of the characteristics of subjects in these two types of studies suggests that the level of bilingualism children attain is an important factor in mediating the effects of bilingualism on their educational development (Cummins, 1979b). Specifically, a large majority of the "negative" studies were carried out with language minority children whose L1 was gradually being replaced by a more dominant and prestigious L2. Under these conditions, these children developed relatively low levels of academic proficiency in both languages. In contrast, the majority of studies that have reported cognitive advantages associated with bilingualism have involved students whose L1 proficiency has continued to develop while L2 is being acquired. Consequently, these students have been characterized by relatively high levels of proficiency in both languages.

These data have led to the hypothesis that there may be threshold levels of linguistic proficiency bilingual children must attain in order to avoid cognitive deficits and allow the potentially beneficial aspects of becoming bilingual to influence cognitive growth. The Threshold Hypothesis assumes that those aspects of bilingualism that might positively influence cognitive growth are unlikely to come into effect until children have attained a certain minimum or threshold level of proficiency in the second language. Similarly, if bilingual children attain only a very low level of proficiency in one or both of their languages, their interaction with the environment through these languages both in terms of input and output, is likely to be impoverished.

The form of the Threshold Hypothesis that seems to be most consistent with the available data is that there are two thresholds (Cummins, 1976; Toukomaa and Skutnabb-Kangas, 1977). The attainment of a lower threshold level of bilingual proficiency would be sufficient to avoid any negative cognitive effects; but the attainment of a second, higher level of bilingual proficiency might be necessary to lead to accelerated cognitive growth. The Threshold Hypothesis is illustrated in Figure 8.

Since this hypothesis was originally formulated (Cummins, 1976), several studies have reported findings consistent with its general tenets (Cummins and Mulcahy, 1978; Duncan and DeAvila, 1979; Kessler and Quinn, 1980). Duncan and DeAvila (1979), for example, found that language minority students who had developed high levels of L1 and L2 proficiency (proficient bilinguals) performed significantly better than monolinguals and other sub-groups of bilinguals (partial and limited bilinguals) on a battery of cognitive tasks. Kessler and Quinn (1980) found that Hispanic bilingual students who had been in a bilingual program performed significantly better than monolinguals on a science problem-solving task, while Cummins and Mulcahy (1978) found that Ukrainian-English bilingual students who spoke Ukrainian at home and received 50 percent instruction through Ukrainian were better able to detect ambiguities in English sentence structure than were monolingual English-speaking students.

Figure 8

COGNITIVE EFFECTS OF DIFFERENT TYPES OF BILINGUALISM*

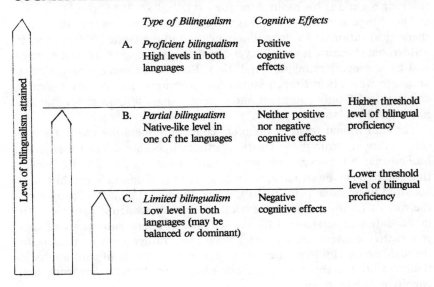

*Adapted from Toukomaa and Skutnabb-Kangas, 1977, p. 29.

In summary, far from impeding English language and general academic skills development, as the SUP model would predict, bilingual instruction appears to offer students a potentially enriching educational environment. For language minority students, this potential appears to be realized only when their L1 continues to develop as they are acquiring L2.

Application of Theoretical Analysis to Bilingual Education

In this section, the implications for bilingual education of the research and theory outlined earlier will be made explicit. The four major implications relate to the rationale for bilingual education, entry criteria, reclassification and exit criteria, and assessment considerations.

The Rationale for Bilingual Education

The failure of L2-only programs to promote L2 literacy skills effectively among some groups of language minority children was interpreted by many academics as support for the hypothesis that mismatch between the language of home and language of school is a major cause of academic retardation among minority children (Downing, 1978; UNESCO, 1953; United States Commission on Civil Rights, 1975). This Linguistic Mismatch Hypothesis is exemplified in the well-known UNESCO statement that "it is axiomatic that the best medium for teaching a child is his mother tongue" (UNESCO, 1953, p. 11).

The Linguistic Mismatch Hypothesis has come to be the main theoretical rationale for bilingual education in the United States. This is unfortunate because it greatly over-simplifies the complexity of the issues and as a general principle has little validity. The success of majority language students in French immersion programs and of some minority children in L2-only programs show clearly that "linguistic mismatch" has limited explanatory power.

The transitional form of bilingual education operating in most states derives directly from the linguistic mismatch hypothesis. The focus on *initial* mismatch between the "visible" surface forms of L1 and L2 implies that children can be switched to an English-only program when they have acquired basic fluency in English. Thus, in most transitional programs, the role of L1 instruction in developing English academic proficiency is inadequately understood. L1 is viewed only as an interim carrier of subject matter content until L2 can take over, rather than as the means through which children "negotiate meaning" with significant adults in their world, thereby laying the foundation for overall academic and cognitive development.

There are several major differences between the linguistic mismatch rationale and that developed in this paper. First, the present rationale emphasizes the sociocultural determinants of minority students' academic difficulties. A major reason for the success of quality bilingual programs is that they encourage minority students (and probably the minority community) to take pride in their cultural background. A program that continues to promote students' L1 throughout elementary school is much more likely to reinforce children's cultural identity than one that aims to remove children as quickly as possible from any contact with, or use of, L1 in school.

A second way in which the present rationale differs from the linguistic mismatch rationale is that it takes account of the difference between context-embedded and context-reduced communicative proficiency. The linguistic mismatch rationale leaves undefined the nature of the "English proficiency" required to survive in an all-English classroom; but by default, relatively superficial aspects of context-embedded communicative proficiency have usually been regarded as adequate. This assumption ignores the fact that it takes L2 learners considerably longer to achieve grade-appropriate levels of L2 context-reduced communicative proficiency than it does to achieve peer-appropriate levels of face-to-face context-embedded communicative proficiency. Thus, the present analysis suggests that a realistic reclassification threshold of "English proficiency" is unlikely to be attained by most language minority students until the later grades of elementary school.

A third difference between the linguistic mismatch rationale and that developed in this paper relates to the role assigned to minority students' L1 proficiency in the acquisition of English academic skills. Instruction through L1 is regarded as much more than an interim carrier of subject matter content; rather, it is the means through which the conceptual and communicative proficiency that underlies *both* L1 and English literacy is developed. The elaboration of the CUP model provides a rationale for continuing the promotion of L1 literacy development throughout elementary school as a means of simultaneously contributing to the development of both English and L1 literacy skills.

A fourth difference is the fact that, unlike the linguistic mismatch rationale, the present rationale emphasizes the additional cognitive and linguistic advantages (beyond the obvious advantage of being bilingual) that research suggests are associated with the attainment of proficient bilingual skills.

Finally, within the present framework, the language spoken by the child in the home is, in itself, essentially irrelevant. What should be much more important in determining the response of the school are the sociocultural characteristics and overall level of communicative proficiency of children on entry. The school program should in every case attempt to build on (rather than replace) the entry characteristics of children.

Who Should Enter Bilingual Programs?

The research evidence reviewed above strongly suggests that programs that aim to develop a high level of proficiency in two languages provide greater potential for academic development for *all* children than education through the medium of only one language. Whether or not this greater potential is realized in any particular bilingual program will, of course, depend on the quality of the program. Research has failed to identify any category of student for whom a bilingual education would be less suitable than a monolingual education. This issue has been extensively researched in Canada in the context of French/English bilingual programs. Students with learning disabilities, low academic ability, and non-English or non-French home backgrounds have all been found to perform at least as well in French/English bilingual programs as equivalent students in English-only programs (Cummins, 1980b). In other words, the enrichment potential of bilingual education is accessible to all students.

This conclusion is also clearly supported by the recent large-scale evaluation of bilingual education programs in the state of Colorado (Egan and Goldsmith, 1981), which found that students from English language backgrounds gained just as much from bilingual education as "linguistically different" students. Both groups of students are reported to have made significant gains in bilingual programs compared to what would have been expected in regular English programs. For language minority students who fail in L2-only school programs, bilingual education offers a very basic form of enrichment, i.e., the possibility of educational survival.

There has been considerable debate in recent years about which categories of language minority students should enter bilingual programs. Much of this debate has been political in nature and only Dulay and Burt (1980) have advanced any serious educational argument in favor of limiting access to bilingual education by Limited English Proficient (LEP) students. Arguing on the basis of the Linguistic Mismatch Hypothesis, Dulay and Burt suggest that "English-superior" LEP students should receive instruction primarily through English, "primary-language superior" LEP students should receive bilingual education, while "limited balanced" (i.e., equally limited in L1 and L2) students should be taught through whichever language is spoken at home. The analysis and research reviewed in this paper shows that this suggestion has no educational support, either empirical or theoretical.

Reclassification and Exiting Considerations

It should be clear by now that there is no educational justification for exiting students from a successful bilingual program. The CUP model provides an interpretation of why students in bilingual programs perform well in English academic skills despite much less instruction through English. Furthermore, many studies show cognitive and academic advantages as a result of attaining literacy and fluency in two languages. Exiting students from bilingual programs in the early grades of elementary school is likely to short-circuit these academic advantages; the rationale for a quick-exit policy is either socio-political in nature or else based on an ill-conceived SUP model of bilingual proficiency.

It is instructive to examine the confused logic of transitional bilingual education as currently practiced in many school districts. Minority students in transitional programs are expected to make so much progress in the cognitive and academic skills underlying English literacy in the early grades that after two or three years they should be able to compete on an equal footing with their monolingual English-speaking peers. In other words, a CUP model of bilingual proficiency is implicitly endorsed in the early grades. Yet proponents of a quick-exit policy revert to a SUP model by assuming (contrary to their earlier assumption and the research data) that children's English skills will not develop adequately unless they are mainstreamed as soon as possible to an English-only program. It is ironic that the earlier they want the child mainstreamed, the more effective they must assume the L1 instruction to have been in promoting L2 proficiency (Cummins, 1980d).

Assessment Considerations

The lack of a theoretical framework that would allow the relationship between "communicative competence" and academic achievement to be considered is especially obvious in the confusion surrounding appropriate ways of assessing language proficiency and dominance for entry and exit purposes in bilingual education. Some measures are intended specifically *not* to relate to academic achievement [e.g., the *Bilingual Syntax Measure* (Burt *et al.,* 1975)], while others are intended to show a moderate relationship [e.g., the *Language Assessment Scales* (DeAvila and Duncan, 1976)].

Given that the purpose of language proficiency assessment is *placement* of students in classes taught through the language which, it is assumed, will best promote the development of academic skills, it is imperative that the test have predictive validity for academic achievement. In other words, the test must assess aspects of language proficiency related to the development of literacy. If it does not, then its relevance to the placement of bilingual students is highly questionable (Cummins, 1980b).

For entry at the kindergarten level, assessment should probably involve cognitively demanding context-embedded measures, while for exit purposes, cognitively demanding context-reduced measures should be used (see Figure 3). The rationale for this suggestion is that context-embedded measures are necessary to reflect children's pre-school language experiences, but context-reduced measures are more appropriate for reclassification purposes because they more accurately reflect the communicative demands of an all-English classroom.

Conclusion

Although further research is required to specify in detail what constitutes "sufficient" English proficiency for reclassification purposes, there is considerable evidence regarding conditions necessary for English literacy development among students traditionally performing poorly in English-only school programs. The research suggests that achievement in English literacy skills is strongly related to the extent of development of L1 literacy skills. Thus, rather than reclassifying and exiting minority students as soon as possible, teachers and administrators should be concerned with providing students with sufficient time in the bilingual program to develop "threshold" levels of biliteracy.

How much time is sufficient? The evidence reviewed earlier suggests that school districts should aim to provide at least 50 percent of instruction in the early grades through the child's L1, and instruction in and through the L1 should be continued throughout elementary school. Although there are no exact formulas as to how much L1 and L2 instruction ought to be provided at any particular grade level, it seems reasonable to suggest that it would be appropriate to provide more English input in school in situations where exposure to English outside school is limited. However, this increased exposure should *not* come in the early grades where the instructional emphasis should be on L1 in order to develop the conceptual apparatus required to make English context-reduced input comprehensible. Where there is little or no exposure to English outside school, between 50 and 75 percent of the instructional time could be through English from third grade.

It is critically important, however, that decisions made by teachers, administrators, and policy-makers regarding bilingual education take account of the nature of language proficiency and its cross-lingual dimensions. The rationale for bilingual education and the specific program suggestions made in this paper and others in this volume can be appreciated only when it is realized that context-reduced communicative proficiency is different from context-embedded communicative proficiency and that most academically important aspects of L1 and L2 proficiency are manifestations of the same underlying dimension.

REFERENCES

Albert, Martin L., and Loraine K. Obler. *The Bilingual Brain.* New York: Academic Press, 1978.

Anderson, James G., and William H. Johnson. "Stability and Change Among Three Generations of Mexican-Americans: Factors Affecting Achievement," *American Educational Research Journal*, VIII, No. 2 (March, 1971), 285-309.

Baral, David P. "Academic Achievement of Recent Immigrants from Mexico," *NABE Journal*, III (1979), 1-13.

Bereiter, Carl, and Marlene Scardamalia. "Does Learning to Write Have to Be So Difficult?" Unpublished manuscript. Ontario Institute for Studies in Education, 1980.

————, and ————. "From Conversation to Composition: The Role of Instruction in a Developmental Process," *Advances in Instructional Psychology*, ed. Robert Glaser. Vol. 2. Hillsdale, New Jersey: Lawrence Erlbaum Associates, 1981.

Bethell, Tom. "Against Bilingual Education: Why Johnny Can't Speak English," *Harper's*, CCLVIII, (February, 1979), 30-33.

Bhatnager, Joti. "Linguistic Behavior and Adjustment of Immigrant Children in French and English Schools in Montreal," *International Journal of Applied Psychology*, XXIX (1980), 141-158.

Bruner, Jerome Seymour. "Language as an Instrument of Thought," *Problems of Language and Learning*, ed. A. Davies. London, England: Heinmann, 1975.

Burt, Marina K., Heidi C. Dulay, and Eduardo Hernandez-Chavez. *Bilingual Syntax Measure (BSM).* New York: The Psychological Corporation, 1975.

Canale, Michael. "From Communicative Competence to Communicative Language Pedagogy," *Language and Communication*, eds., J. Richard, and R. Schmidt. New York: Longman, 1981.

————, and Merrill Swain. "Theoretical Bases of Communicative Approaches to Second Language Teaching and Testing," *Applied Linguistics,* I (1980), 1-47.

Caramazza, Alfonso, and Isabel Brones. "Semantic Classification By Bilinguals," *Canadian Journal of Psychology*, XXXIV, No. 1 (March, 1980), 77-81.

Carey, Steven T., and James Cummins. "English and French Achievement of Grade 5 Children from English, French and Mixed French-English Home Backgrounds Attending the Edmonton Separate School System English-French Immersion Program." Report submitted to the Edmonton Separate School System, 1979.

Carter, Thomas P. *Mexican-Americans in School: A History of Educational Neglect.* New York: College Entrance Examination Board, 1970.

Chesarek, Steve. "Cognitive Consequences of Home or School Education in a Limited Second Language: A Case Study in the Crow Indian Bilingual Community." Paper presented at the Language Proficiency Assessment Symposium, Airlie House, Virginia, March, 1981.

Chomsky, Carol. "Stages in Language Development and Reading Exposure," *Harvard Educational Review*, XLII, No. 1 (February, 1972), 1-32.

Chu-Chang, Mae. "The Dependency Relation Between Oral Language and Reading in Bilingual Education," *Journal of Education*, CLXIII (1981), 30-57.

Cummins, James. "Age on Arrival and Immigrant Second Language Learning in Canada: A Reassessment." *Applied Linguistics,* II, No. 2 (1981), 132-149.

_____. "Cognitive/Academic Language Proficiency, Linguistic Interdependence, the Optimal Age Question and Some Other Matters," *Working Papers on Bilingualism,* No. 19 (1979a).

_____. "The Cross-Lingual Dimensions of Language Proficiency: Implications for Bilingual Education and the Optimal Age Issue," *TESOL Quarterly,* XIV, No. 2 (June, 1980a), 175-187.

_____. "The Exit and Entry Fallacy in Bilingual Education," *NABE Journal,* IV (1980d), 25-60.

_____. "The Influence of Bilingualism on Cognitive Growth: A Synthesis of Research Findings and Explanatory Hypothesis," *Working Papers on Bilingualism,* No. 9 (1976), 1-43.

_____. "Language Proficiency, Biliteracy, and French Immersion," *Canadian Journal of Education,* in press.

_____. "Linguistic Interdependence and the Educational Development of Bilingual Children," *Bilingual Education Paper Series,* Vol. 3, No. 2. Los Angeles, California: National Dissemination and Assessment Center, California State University, Los Angeles, September, 1979b.

_____. "Psychological Assessment of Immigrant Children: Logic or Intuition?" *Journal of Multilingual and Multicultural Development,* I (1980c), 97-111.

_____, and Robert Mulcahy. "Orientation to Language in Ukrainian-English Bilingual Children," *Child Development,* XLIX, No. 4 (December, 1978), 1,239-1,242.

_____, Merrill Swain, Kazuko Nakajima, Jean Handscombe, and Daina Green. "Linguistic Interdependence Among Japanese Immigrant Students." Paper presented at the Language Proficiency Assessment Symposium, Airlie House, Virginia, March, 1981.

Darcy, Natalie T. "A Review of the Literature on the Effects of Bilingualism Upon the Measurement of Intelligence," *Journal of Genetic Psychology,* LXXXII (March, 1953), 21-57.

DeAvila, Edward A., and Sharon E. Duncan. *Language Assessment Scales (LAS).* Corte Madera, California: Linguametrics Groups, 1976.

Donaldson, Margaret. *Children's Minds.* Glasgow: Collins, 1978.

Downing, John. "Strategies of Bilingual Teaching," *International Review of Education,* XXIV, No. 3 (1978), 329-346.

Dulay, Heidi C., and Marina K. Burt. "The Relative Proficiency of Limited English Proficient Students," *NABE Journal,* IV (1980), 1-23.

Duncan, Sharon E., and Edward A. DeAvila. "Bilingualism and Cognition: Some Recent Findings," *NABE Journal,* IV (1979), 15-50.

Edmonton Public School Board. "Evaluation of the Bilingual (English-Ukrainian) Program, Fifth Year." Research report. 1979.

Egan, Lawrence A. "Bilingual Education: A Challenge for the Future," *NABE News,* (March, 1981).

_____, and Ross Goldsmith. "Bilingual-Bicultural Education: The Colorado Success Story," *NABE News,* (January 1981).

Ekstrand, Lars Henri. "Social and Individual Frame Factors in L2 Learning: Comparative Aspects," *Papers from the First Nordic Conference on Bilingualism,* ed., Tove Skutnabb-Kangas. Helsinki, Finland: Helsinfors Universitetet, 1977.

Enriquez, Miguel. "Semantic Integration in Bilingual Language Processing." Paper presented at the Summer Institute on Bilingual Education, University of Arizona, 1980.

Evaluation Associates. "Nestor School Bilingual Education Program Evaluation." Unpublished research report, San Diego, California, 1978.

Fillmore, Lily Wong. "Individual Differences in Second Language Acquisition," *Individual Differences in Language Ability and Language Behavior,* eds., Charles J. Fillmore, Daniel Kempler, and William S-Y. Wang. New York: Academic Press, 1979, pp. 203-228.

Fischer, K. B., and B. Cabello. "Predicting Student Success Following Transition from Bilingual Programs." Paper presented at AERA Meeting, Toronto, Canada. Los Angeles: University of California, Los Angeles, Center for the Study of Evaluation, 1978.

Genesee, Fred. "Is There an Optimal Age for Starting Second Language Instruction?" *McGill Journal of Education*, XIII (1978), 145-154.

Hanson, Göte. "The Position of the Second Generation of Finnish Immigrants in Sweden: The Importance of Education in the Home Language to the Welfare of Second Generation Immigrants." Paper presented at a symposium on the position of the second generation of Yugoslav immigrants in Sweden, Split, Yugoslavia, October, 1979.

Hébert, Raymond *et al. Rendement Academique et Langue D'enseignement chez les Eleves Franco-Manitobains.* Saint Boniface, Manitoba: Centre de Recherches du College Universitaire de Saint-Boniface, 1976.

Hernandez-Chavez, Eduardo, Marina K. Burt, and Heidi C. Dulay. "Language Dominance and Proficiency Testing: Some General Considerations," *NABE Journal*, III (1978), 41-54.

Heyman, Anna-Gretta. *Invandrarbarn: Slutrapport.* Stockholm, Sweden: Stockholms Invandrarnamd, 1973.

Jensen, J. Vernon. "Effects of Childhood Bilingualism, I," *Elementary English*, XXXIX (February, 1962), 132-143.

Kessler, Carolyn, and Mary Ellen Quinn. "Positive Effects of Bilingualism on Science Problem-Solving Abilities," *31st Annual Georgetown University Round Table on Languages and Linguistics,* ed., James E. Alatis. Washington, D.C.: Georgetown University Press, 1980, pp. 295-308.

Kimball, W. J. "Parental and Family Influences on Academic Achievement Among Mexican-American Students." Unpublished PhD dissertation, University of California at Los Angeles, 1968.

Kolers, Paul A. "Bilingualism and Information Processing," *Scientific American,* CCXVII, No. 3 (March, 1968), 78-86.

Krashen, Stephen D. "Bilingual Education and Second Language Acquisition Theory," *Schooling and Language Minority Students: A Theoretical Framework.* Los Angeles, California: Evaluation, Dissemination and Assessment Center, California State University, Los Angeles, 1981.

_____, Michael A. Long, and Robin C. Scarcella. "Age, Rate and Eventual Attainment in Second Language Acquisition." *TESOL Quarterly*, XIII, No. 4 (December, 1979), 573-582.

Lambert, Wallace E., and G. Richard Tucker. *Bilingual Education of Children: The St. Lambert Experiment.* Rowley, Massachusetts: Newbury House, 1972.

Landry, Rodrigue J. "Apprentissage dans des Contextes Bilingues." Unpublished research report. University of Moncton, New Brunswick, Canada, 1980.

_____. "Le Bilinguisme: Le Facteur Répétition," *Canadian Modern Language Review,* XXXIV (1978), 548-576.

Legarreta, Dorothy. "The Effects of Program Models on Language Acquisition by Spanish Speaking Children," *TESOL Quarterly*, XIII, No. 4 (December, 1979), 521-534.

Leyba, Charles F. *Longitudinal Study, Title VII Bilingual Program, Santa Fe Public Schools, Santa Fe, New Mexico.* Los Angeles, California: National Dissemination and Assessment Center, California State University, Los Angeles, 1978.

Macnamara, John. "Bilingualism and Thought," *21st Annual Round Table on Languages and Linguistics, 1970,* ed., James E. Alatis. Washington, D.C.: Georgetown University Press, 1970, pp. 25-45.

McCormack, Peter D. "Bilingual Linguistic Memory: Independence or Interdependence?" *Bilingualism, Biculturalism and Education,* ed., S. T. Carey. Edmonton, Alberta, Canada: University of Alberta Press, 1974.

Mercer, Jane R. *Labeling the Mentally Retarded: Clinical and Social System Perspectives on Mental Retardation.* Berkeley, California: University of California Press, 1973.

Oller, John W., Jr. "The Language Factor in the Evaluation of Bilingual Education," *Georgetown University Round Table on Languages and Linguistics 1978,* ed., James E. Alatis. Washington, D.C.: Georgetown University Press, 1978, pp. 410-422.

_____. *Language Tests at School: A Pragmatic Approach.* New York: Longman, 1979.

Olson, David R. "From Utterance to Text: The Bias of Language in Speech and Writing," *Harvard Educational Review,* XLVII, No. 3 (August, 1977), 257-281.

Ramirez, Arnulfo G., and Robert L. Politzer. "The Acquisition of English and Maintenance of Spanish in a Bilingual Education Program," *English as a Second Language in Bilingual Education,* eds., James E. Alatis, and K. Twaddell. Washington, D. C.: TESOL, 1976.

Ramsey, Craig A., and Edward N. Wright. "A Group, English Language Vocabulary Knowledge Test Derived from the Ammons Full-Range Picture Vocabulary Test," *Psychological Reports,* XXXI (1972), 103-109.

Rosier, Paul, and Merilyn Farella. "Bilingual Education at Rock Point—Some Early Results," *TESOL Quarterly,* X, No. 4 (December, 1976), 379-388.

Shuy, Roger W. "How Misconceptions About Language Affect Judgments About Intelligence," *Issues in Evaluating Reading,* ed., S. F. Wanat. Arlington, Virginia: Center for Applied Linguistics, 1977.

Singer, Harry. "IQ Is and Is Not Related to Reading," *Issues in Evaluating Reading,* ed., S. F. Wanat. Arlington, Virginia: Center for Applied Linguistics, 1977.

Skutnabb-Kangas, Tove, and Pertti Toukomaa. *Teaching Migrant Children's Mother Tongue and Learning the Language of the Host Country in the Context of the Socio-Cultural Situation of the Migrant Family.* Helsinki: The Finnish National Commission for UNESCO, 1976.

Smith, Frank. *Understanding Reading: A Psycholinguistic Analysis of Reading and Learning to Read.* New York: Holt, Rinehart and Winston, 1978.

Swain, Merrill. "French Immersion: Early, Late or Partial?" *The Canadian Modern Language Review,* ed., S. T. Carey, XXXIV (May, 1978), 577-585.

Tannen, Deborah. "Implications of the Oral/Literate Continuum for Cross-Cultural Communication," *Georgetown University Round Table on Languages and Linguistics, 1980,* ed., James E. Alatis. Washington, D.C.: Georgetown University Press, 1980.

Terrell, Tracy D. "The Natural Approach in Bilingual Education," *Schooling and Language Minority Students: A Theoretical Framework.* Los Angeles, California: Evaluation, Dissemination and Assessment Center, California State University, Los Angeles, 1981.

Toukomaa, Pertti, and Tove Skutnabb-Kangas. *The Intensive Teaching of the Mother Tongue to Migrant Children of Preschool Age and Children in the Lower Level of Comprehensive School.* Research Reports 26. Tampere: Department of Sociology and Social Psychology, University of Tampere, Finland, 1977.

Troike, Rudolph C. "Research Evidence for the Effectiveness of Bilingual Education," *Bilingual Education Paper Series,* Vol. 2, No. 5. Los Angeles, California: National Dissemination and Assessment Center, California State University, Los Angeles, December, 1978.

Trombley, William. "Is Bilingual Education Able to Do Its Job?" *Los Angeles Times*, September 4, 1980.

UNESCO. *The Use of Vernacular Languages in Education.* Monographs of fundamental education. No. 8. Paris: UNESCO, 1953.

United States Commission on Civil Rights. *A Better Chance to Learn: Bilingual Bicultural Education.* Clearinghouse Publication No. 51. Washington, D.C.: Government Printing Office, 1975.

Vigotskiĭ, Lev Semonovich. *Thought and Language.* Cambridge, Massachusetts: M.I.T. Press, 1962.

Wells, Gordon. "Describing Children's Linguistic Development at Home and at School," *British Educational Research Journal*, V (1979), 75-89.

Yee, Leland Y., and Rolfe La Forge. "Relationship Between Mental Abilities, Social Class, and Exposure to English in Chinese Fourth Graders," *Journal of Educational Psychology,* LXVI, No. 6 (December, 1974), 826-834.

Bilingual Education and Second Language Acquisition Theory*

Stephen D. Krashen

Introduction

THE IMPRESSION ONE GETS from the popular press is that bilingual education is a mess. We are told that "basic disagreements range across the entire field of bilingual education" (Trombley, 1980a), that the experts disagree on which programs are best, that those who are supposed to benefit from bilingual education often oppose it, that there is little information about how second languages are acquired, and that basic research on all of these issues is either contradictory or lacking.

While we cannot cover the entire field of bilingual education, we will examine some of these disagreements, certain central issues in bilingual education that appear to be unresolved. In the first section, we will briefly describe the issues, the points of contention. Following this, we will review what is known today about the process of second language acquisition. A third section will show how this new information, along with a considerable amount of excellent thinking and research in bilingualism and bilingual education, helps to reslove some of the issues facing parents and educators today. We will see that while bilingual education does have many unresolved problems, the situation is not nearly as bad as it may appear. Basic research and theory already exist that speak to many of the issues in the field today.

The Issues

The aim of this section is merely to present the issues. This is no easy task. There appear to be a bewildering variety of options and programs, each with its supporters and detractors. I will try to present some of these options and some of the points of debate. This will not be a complete survey; it will, however, cover those questions upon which current research and theory can shed some light. The presentation is in the form of definitions, done in the hope that consistent use of terms will alleviate at least some of the confusion that exists in bilingual education today.

---

*This paper owes a tremendous debt to the research and thinking of James Cummins. I would also like to thank Professors Merrill Swain and John Oller for a very helpful discussion of Professor Cummins' ideas and their relationship to second language acquisition theory, and to Robin Scarcella for her comments.

Bilingual Education Programs

While we could use bilingual education as a cover term for practically all of the programs described below, it will be useful to limit it here. Bilingual education refers to situations in which students are able to study subject matter in their first language (L1) while their weaker language skills catch up. This is Trombley's view of bilingual education: "Bilingual Education is intended to permit students who speak little or no English to learn reading, writing, arithmetic and other basic subjects in their primary language while they are acquiring proficiency in English" (September 4, 1980b, p. 1). The theory behind bilingual education is that it allows non-English proficient (NEP) children to keep up in subject matter while acquiring English as a second language.

There are, of course, many varieties of bilingual education. Bilingual education programs vary in at least four ways:

1. Language use (manner). It is possible to present subject matter in the first language and leave it up to the English as a Second Language (ESL) component to provide practice in English (bilingual education + ESL). Most programs provide at least some subject matter in both languages, and there are several ways this can be done. Some provide some subjects in English and others in the first language; others use both languages for the same subject. Here again, there are several possibilities. A common method is speaking in first one language and then the other; an explanation is given in both the first language and in English during the same class hour. This is known as *concurrent translation*.

2. Amount of each language used. Not all programs provide exactly 50 percent exposure to each language. Legarreta (1979) informs us, for example, that in one concurrent translation class, Spanish was used 28 percent of the time and English 72 percent, while in a balanced bilingual class (some subjects in Spanish and others in English), the percentage was 50 percent Spanish and 50 percent English.

3. Type of ESL. There are many ways of teaching the second language. Methods include the still popular audiolingual system, which emphasizes repetition and memorization of phrases and sentences, as well as other grammar-oriented aproaches, which stress the conscious understanding of rules of grammar, and more conversational methods.

4. Purpose. Bilingual programs vary with respect to whether they are intended to maintain the children's first language indefinitely (maintenance) or are only to help them ultimately adjust to an all-English program (transitional). It is important to note that the announced goals of both transitional and maintenance programs always include acquisition of the second language and subject matter education.

Alternatives to Bilingual Education

1. Submersion or "Sink or Swim"

In submersion programs, NEP children are simply placed in the same classroom as native English speakers and the regular curriculum is followed. There is no organized attempt to provide any special instruction or extra help for these children. Although sympathetic teachers often try to do something, all instruction is in English.

Many people feel that "Sink or Swim" is the best solution. Here are the two most commonly heard arguments for "Sink or Swim," as opposed to bilingual education:

a. Clearly, "Sink or Swim" provides more exposure to English, and the more exposure to English received, the better off children are. In recent letters to the *Los Angeles Times,* several writers claimed that bilingual education condemns children to second-class status since it fails to provide a full exposure to English, thus denying immigrant students full economic and social opportunity (September 19, 1980).

b. Many people, it is maintained, succeeded via "Sink or Swim." Since they had to learn English, and were surrounded by it, they learned, or so the argument goes.

We will return to these points of view later, after looking at theory and the empirical research.

2. Submersion + ESL

This option is often referred to simply as "ESL," which is a misnomer, since ESL in some form is nearly always a part of bilingual education programs. In submersion plus ESL, NEP children are usually given a separate ESL class for some prescribed period of time, usually an hour per day (termed "pull-out"). The rest of the day is spent in classes with native English speakers, and the NEP students attempt to follow the all-English curriculum.

Those who favor "Sink or Swim" usually support this program as well, on the grounds that it provides more English; more time spent exposed to English; the motivation to learn, since subject matter is taught in English; and the advantages of formal instruction. Lopez, in a letter to the *Los Angeles Times,* speaks for those who hold this view:

> *Bilingual classes segregate these [non-English-speaking] students and thus seriously reduce their contact with [the] English speakers and, even more importantly, weaken their drive to communicate with others in English. If you have ever taught a class of immigrants, you know that only the most highly motivated will consistently respond in English if they know you speak their native language....You cannot learn*

*English well if you do not have the opportunity to interact
with English speakers in thousands of varied situations over a
period of years. This should take place not only in special
classes (English-as-a-second-language classes are the right
idea for immigrant students, but only for a limited time) but
also in regular classes as well as extra-class situations.
(September 19, 1980)*

Lopez describes herself as one who had to learn English herself as a
young immigrant and as a bilingual teacher. Her view is shared by some
legislators and some members of the communities who are supposedly
served by bilingual education. According to Trombley:

*Many parents think the key to success in the United States is
to learn English, and they do not believe the educators who
tell them their children will learn to speak English better in
bilingual classes. (September 4, 1980b)*

Of course, many legislators, immigrants, and members of minority
language communities support bilingual education enthusiastically. We
will evaluate these arguments in a later section of this paper.

3. *Immersion*

"Immersion" is often used as a synonym for "Sink or Swim," but this
term has been used in the professional literature to refer to a very different kind of program. Immersion typically refers to programs in which
majority language children (e. g., English-speaking children in the
United States and Canada) are instructed in a second language, that is,
programs in which subject matter is taught in a second language such as
Spanish or French. This need not always be the case, however; and
theoretically immersion programs are possible for minority children as
well.

Typically, immersion students receive all instruction in the second
language, with the exception of language arts in the first language. Many
programs, however, increase the amount of subject matter instruction in
the first language as children progress. Immersion students are also
"segregated," that is, native speakers of the second language are not
usually included in these programs; and immersion students do not
usually receive formal instruction in the second language.

In early immersion, the second language is used in kindergarten and
for most subjects starting from the first grade. In late immersion,
students may receive one or two years of formal instruction in the second
language before starting subject matter instruction in the L2. Late immersion programs begin around sixth grade, but here again there is variation. There are also partial immersion programs in which some subjects

are taught in the L2 and some in the L1 (Swain, 1978).

Immersion programs in Canada using French as the second language have been in operation for the last decade and have been carefully followed by researchers. More recently, American immersion programs have been developed using Spanish and other languages.

With this definition of immersion, there really can be no conflict between bilingual education and immersion, since they are aimed at different populations. Nevertheless, immersion is a logical possibility for NEP children (i. e., subject matter instruction in English, segregated from native speakers with L1 language arts), a possibility discussed later. We also see that immersion research is a rich source of information about second language acquisition for bilingual education specialists.

Table 1 reviews the differences between submersion programs and majority child immersion programs.

Table 1

COMPARISON OF SUBMERSION AND IMMERSION PROGRAMS

Submersion	(Majority child) Immersion
Children are mixed with native speakers of the L2.	Children are linguistically segregated.
Language of instruction is the majority language.	Language of instruction is a minority language.
Instruction in L1 language arts is not provided.	Instruction in L1 language arts is provided.

Summary of the Issues

The issues, then, are these:

1. Does bilingual education retard the development of English as a second language?
2. Are "Sink or Swim" (submersion) and/or ESL methods better than bilingual education?
3. How should ESL be taught?
4. Is there a place for "immersion" for the NEP child?
5. Which bilingual education options are better for language acquisition?

The answers to these questions, contrary to much popular opinion, are not obvious, and not merely a matter of common sense. They should not be resolved by vote but by consideration of empirically based theory and research. In the following section, we will review current second language acquisition theory, an exercise that will be of great use in discussing the issues listed above.

Second Language Acquisition Theory

Current second language acquisition theory will be discussed in terms of five hypotheses about second language acquisition:

1. The Acquisition-Learning Hypothesis
2. The Natural Order Hypothesis
3. The Monitor Hypothesis
4. The Input Hypothesis
5. The Affective Filter Hypothesis

These hypotheses are presented here without extensive supporting evidence, as this evidence has been published elsewhere [Krashen, 1981, in press (b); Dulay *et al.*, in press].

The Acquisition-Learning Hypothesis

According to this hypothesis, second language acquirers have two distinct ways of developing ability in second languages. Language *acquisition* is similar to the way children develop first language competence. Language acquisition is a subconscious process in two senses: people are often not aware that they are acquiring a language while they are doing so. What they are aware of is using the language for some communicative purpose. Also, they are often not aware of what they have acquired; they usually cannot describe or talk about the rules they have acquired but they have a "feel" for the language. Language *learning* is different. It is knowing about language or formal knowledge of a language. Language learning is thought to profit from explicit presentation of rules and from error correction. Error correction, supposedly, helps the learner come to the correct conscious mental representation of a rule. There is good evidence, however, that error correction does not help subconscious acquisition (Brown *et al.*, 1973).

In everyday terms, *acquisition* is picking up a language. Ordinary equivalents for *learning* include grammar and rules.

The Natural Order Hypothesis

The Natural Order Hypothesis states that students acquire (not learn) grammatical structures in a predictable order; that is, certain grammatical structures tend to be acquired early and others, late. For English, a very well-studied language, function words (grammatical morphemes) such as -*ing* (as in: John is going to work now.) and plural /s/ (as in: two boy*s*) are among the earliest acquired. The third person singular ending /s/ (as in: He live*s* in New Jersey.) and the possessive /s/ (as in: John'*s* hat) are acquired much later (in children's first language acquisition, possessive and third person endings may come as much as one year later).

It appears that the order of acquisition for first language acquisition is not identical to the order of acquisition for second language acquisition, but there are some similarities. For grammatical morphemes in English, children's second language order is similar to adult second language order. There is thus a "first language order" and a "second language order" (Krashen, 1981).

Two disclaimers about order of acquisition and the Natural Order Hypothesis are necessary. First, linguists do not have information about the order of acquisition of every structure in every language. In fact, we have information only about a few structures in a few languages. As we shall see below, this does not present a practical problem. Also, the order is not rigidly obeyed by every acquirer; there is some individual variation. There is significant agreement among acquirers, however, and we can definitely speak of an average order of acquisition.

As we shall see later, the existence of the natural order does *not* imply that we should teach second languages along this order, focusing on earlier acquired items first and later acquired items later. Indeed, there is good evidence that language teaching aimed at acquisition should not employ a grammatical syllabus.

The Monitor Hypothesis

The Acquisition-Learning Hypothesis merely stated that two separate processes for the development of ability in the second language exist. The Monitor Hypothesis states the relationship between acquisition and learning. It seems that acquisition is far more important. It is responsible for our fluency in a second language, our ability to use it easily and comfortably. Conscious learning is not at all responsible for our fluency but has only one function: it can be used as an editor or monitor. This is illustrated in Figure 1.

Figure 1

ACQUISITION AND LEARNING IN SECOND LANGUAGE PRODUCTION

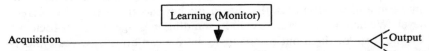

We use conscious learning to make corrections, to change the output of the acquired system before we speak or write, or sometimes after we speak or write (as in self-correction).

Studies done over the last few years (reviewed in Krashen, 1981) suggest that it is not easy to use the Monitor efficiently. In order to use the Monitor Hypothesis, three *necessary* conditions need to be met. These conditions are *necessary* but not sufficient; that is, even if they are met, second language users may not use the monitor very well.

(1) *Time.* In order to use conscious rules, the performer has to have enough time. In normal conversation, there is rarely enough time to consult conscious rules.

(2) *Focus on form.* In order to use conscious rules, just having time is not enough. The second language performer must also be focused on form (Dulay and Burt, 1978) or thinking about correctness. Research has indicated that even when performers have time, as when they are writing, they may not fully use the conscious grammar, since they are more concerned with what they are expressing rather than how they are expressing it.

(3) *Know the rule.* This is a formidable condition, considering our incomplete knowledge of the structure of language. Linguists concede that they have described only fragments of natural languages, and only a few languages have been worked on to any extent. Teachers and students, of course, have access to only a fraction of the linguists' descriptions.

These three conditions place tremendous limits on the use of conscious grammar—and, again, all three must be met to allow effective grammar use—but even this is no guarantee. Research strongly suggests [Krashen, 1981; in press (b)] that conscious grammar use is surprisingly light on anything short of a grammar test.

The Input Hypothesis

According to the first three hypotheses, acquisition has the central role in second language performance. If this is so, the crucial question becomes: How do we acquire? Stated in terms of the Natural Order Hypothesis, we can ask how we move from one stage to another, from stage 3, for example, to stage 4 (or more generally from stage i, our current level of competence, to i + 1, the next stage that the acquirer is due to acquire, or ready to acquire).

The Input Hypothesis postulates that we acquire by understanding input containing i + 1; that is, by understanding language that contains input containing structures that are a bit beyond the acquirer's current level. We acquire structure by understanding messages and not focusing on the form of the input or analyzing it. We can do this, we can understand language that contains structures we do not "know" by utilizing context, extra-linguistic information, and our knowledge of the world. In second language classrooms, for example, context is often provided via visual aids (pictures) and discussion of familiar topics.

Our usual approach to second language teaching is very different from the Input Hypothesis. As Hatch (1978) has pointed out, we assume the opposite: We first teach students structures and then try to give them practice in "using" them in communication. According to the Input Hypothesis, on the other hand, we acquire structure not by focusing on structure but by understanding messages containing new structure.

The Input Hypothesis also claims that we do not teach speaking directly. Rather, speaking fluency emerges on its own over time. The best way to "teach" speaking, according to this view, is simply to provide "comprehensible input." Speech will come when the acquirer feels ready. This readiness state arrives at different times for different people, however. Also, early speech is typically not accurate; grammatical accuracy develops over time as the acquirer hears and understands more input.

A third part of the Input Hypothesis is the claim that the "best" input should not be "grammatically sequenced," that is, it should not deliberately aim at i + 1. We are all familiar with language classes that attempt to do this; there is a "structure of the day" (e. g., the aim of today's lesson is to "learn" the past tense), and both teacher and students feel that the aim of the lesson is to learn and practice this structure. Once the day's structure is mastered, we proceed on to the next. The Input Hypothesis claims that such deliberate sequencing is not necessary and may even be harmful! Specifically, it hypothesizes that if there is successful communication, if the acquirer indeed understands the message contained in the input, i + 1 will automatically be provided in just the right quantities. Acquirers will receive comprehensible input containing structures just beyond them if they are in situations involving genuine communication, and these structures will be constantly provided and automatically reviewed.

It may be useful to detail some of the disadvantages of grammatical syllabi, even those that present structures along the natural order. They assume, first of all, that all of our students are at the same level in a given class, that they are all ready for the same i + 1. This is hardly ever true. In most classes, a substantial percentage of students will have already acquired the structure of the day, while another large sub-group is nowhere near ready for it. Thus, a teacher's audience for any given structure is usually a small part of the class. Even if the structure of the day is the appropriate one, how do we know when we have provided enough practice? And what about students who miss the structure due to absence? Under current procedures, they often have to wait until the following year. A third problem is perhaps the most serious: It is practically impossible to discuss any topic of real interest in any depth when the hidden agenda is practice of a structure.

Genuinely interesting and comprehensible input solves these problems. According to the Input Hypothesis, if students can follow the general meaning of a discussion, i + 1 will be provided for all of them, different i + 1 for different students. With natural comprehensible input, students need not worry about missing a class and thereby missing the past tense forever. It will come up again and again, both in class discussion and in reading. Finally, there is no need to worry about contextualizing a different structure every unit. The focus, at all times, is on helping students understand messages and not rules of grammar.

In other words, input for acquisition need not focus only on i + 1, it only needs to contain it. Thus, i + 1 will be supplied, and naturally reviewed, when the acquirer obtains enough "comprehensible input."

Evidence supporting the Input Hypothesis is given in some detail in other publications [Krashen, 1981; in press (b)] but it is useful to briefly mention two phenomena in second language acquisition that are consistent with this hypothesis. The first is the presence of the *silent period,* a period of time before the acquirer actually starts to speak. The silent period is very noticeable in children's second language acquisition; six- and seven-year-olds, for example, in a new country, may not say anything (except for some memorized sentences and phrases) for several months. According to the Input Hypothesis, this is a time during which they are building up competence via input, by listening. When they are ready, they start to talk.

We generally do not allow adults to have a silent period but insist on production right away. When adults have to talk "too early," before they really have the acquired competence to support production, they have only one choice, and that is to fall back on their first language, an idea first proposed by Newmark (1966). Here is how this works: performers will "think" in their first language, that is, mentally produce the desired sentence in the first language and then fill in the words with second language vocabulary. If time permits, performers will note where the syntax or grammar of the sentence in L1 differs from how this sentence should look in the second language and will use the conscious monitor to make changes. For example, if one wishes to say in French:

(1) The dog ate them.

The learner would mentally produce a sentence similar to (1). Step (2) would be to simply plug in French words, giving:

(2) *Le chien a mangé les.*

Some acquirers may consciously know that sentences like (2) are not correct and, given time, can make the necessary correction, giving:

(3) *Les chien les a mangé.*

According to this view, first language "interference" is not something "getting in the way." It is not interference at all but is the result of falling back on old knowledge. Its cure is more acquisition, or more comprehensible input. It is not restricted to adults but will happen in situations where production demands exceed current competence. It is a fairly common occurrence, and we occasionally see it even in acquisition-rich environments, although the number of first language-influenced errors is generally a small minority of the total number of errors children produce. Sentence (2), in fact, was observed in a child second language acquisition situation in an immersion class in Toronto (Selinker *et al.*, 1975).

Table 2 summarizes the Input Hypothesis:

Table 2
THE INPUT HYPOTHESIS

1. We acquire (not learn) language by understanding input that contains structures that are just beyond our current level of competence (i + 1).
2. Speech is not taught directly, but "emerges" on its own. Early speech is typically not grammatically accurate.
3. If input is understood, and there is enough of it, i + 1 is automatically provided. We do not have to deliberately program grammatical structures into the input.

The Affective Filter Hypothesis

The fifth and final hypothesis deals with the role of "affect," that is, the effect of personality, motivation, and other "affective variables" on second language acquisition. Briefly, the research literature in second language acquisition tells us that the following affective variables are related to success in second language acquisition:

1. *Anxiety. Low* anxiety relates to second language acquisition. The more the students are "off the defensive" (Stevick, 1976), the better the acquisition.

2. *Motivation.* Higher motivation predicts more second language acquisition. Certain kinds of motivation are more effective in certain situations, moreover. In situations where acquisition of the second language is a practical necessity, "instrumental" motivation relates to second language acquisition; in many other situations, such as those where acquisition of the second language is more of a luxury, "integrative" motivation predicts success in second language acquisition (Gardner and Lambert, 1972).[1]

---

[1] "Instrumental" motivation is defined as wanting to acquire another language for some practical purpose, e. g., for a profession. "Integrative" motivation occurs when the language is acquired in order to feel a closer sense of identity with another group.

3. *Self-confidence.* The acquirer with more self-esteem and self-confidence tends to do better in second language acquisition (Krashen,1981).

I have hypothesized that these affective factors relate more directly to subconscious language acquisition than to conscious learning, because we see stronger relationships between these affective variables when communicative-type tests are used (tests that require the use of the acquired system) and when we test students who have had a chance to *acquire* the language and not just learn it in foreign language classes. Dulay and Burt (1977) have made this relationship more explicit and clear by positing the presence of an "affective filter." According to the Affective Filter Hypothesis, acquirers in a less than optimal affective state will have a filter, or mental block, preventing them from utilizing input fully for further language acquisition. If they are anxious, "on the defensive," or not motivated, they may understand the input, but the input will not enter the "language acquisition device." Figure 2 illustrates the operation of the filter.

Figure 2

THE AFFECTIVE FILTER

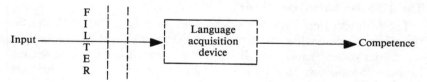

When the filter is "up," input may be understood but will not reach the language acquisition device; it will not strike "deeply" (Stevick, 1976).

The Causative Variable in Second Language Acquisition

We can summarize the five hypotheses with a single claim: People acquire second languages when they obtain comprehensible input and when their affective filters are low enough to allow the input in. In other words, comprehensible input is the only causative variable in second language acquisition. All other factors thought to encourage or cause second language acquisition only work when they are related to comprehensible input.

This hypothesis resolves many problems in the professional literature. For example, some studies seem to show that language teaching is beneficial, while others show that real-world use of the second language is superior [for a review, see Krashen, in press (b)]. This conflict is resolved by positing that language teaching helps second language acquisition by providing comprehensible input. It seems that language teaching is most efficient for students who have no other source of comprehensible input, that is, foreign language students who have no chance to interact with speakers of the target language and beginners who are not yet advanced enough to understand natural second language input outside class. Language teaching is of less value when rich sources of comprehensible input are available, e. g., for the intermediate student living in the country where the language is spoken.

The effects of *age* on second language acquisition also reduce down to comprehensible input plus the affective filter. The professional literature consistently supports these generalizations about age and second language acquisition: (1) Older acquirers progress faster in earlier stages (adults are faster than children; older children acquire faster than younger children), but (2) children outperform adults in the long run (Krashen *et al.*, 1979). It usually takes children about six months to one year to catch up to older acquirers (Snow and Hoefnagel-Hohle, 1978).

A possible explanation for these findings is as follows: Older acquirers are faster because they can use production strategies younger acquirers do not usually have. Specifically, older acquirers are able to "beat the system" and perform using a combination of the first language and the conscious grammar, as described earlier. While children also show occasional first language interference, adults appear to be more able to use the first language syntax as a strategy, and with their superior cognitive development, are better able to use the conscious grammar to bring their sentences into conformity with second language patterns. A good "learner" can use a combination of the first language and monitor to begin speaking fairly complex sentences very early, in a matter of hours. While this system has real drawbacks, i. e., it requires constant monitoring and vigilance, it allows the older acquirer to participate in conversation early and obtain more input.

Recent evidence also suggests (Scarcella and Higa, in press) that older acquirers are more proficient at conversational management. While younger acquirers get what looks like simpler input, older performers are better able to make the input comprehensible; they ask native speakers for more help, are better at keeping the conversation going, etc.

Older acquirers also have the advantage of greater knowledge of the world—greater cognitive/academic language proficiency (CALP) (Cummins, 1980). This additional extralinguistic information gives older acquirers a greater chance to understand what they hear, both in and out of school.

An explanation for children's superiority in ultimate attainment is simply that the strength of the affective filter is sharply increased at puberty; adults may get sufficient quantities of input, but it does not all get in. The increase in filter strength at this time is due to the biological and cognitive changes the adolescent is going through at puberty [Elkind, 1970; Krashen, in press (a)].

Table 3 summarizes explanations for age differences in second language acquisition.

Table 3
AGE DIFFERENCES IN SECOND LANGUAGE ACQUISITION

1. Older acquirers are faster in the early stages of second language acquisition because:
   a. They are better at obtaining comprehensible input (conversational management).
   b. They have superior knowledge of the world, which helps to make input comprehensible.
   c. They can participate in conversation earlier, via use of first language syntax.
2. Younger acquirers tend to attain higher levels of proficiency in second languages than adults in the long run due to a lower affective filter.

Second Language Teaching

Before proceeding on to the implications of second language theory for bilingual education, it will be useful to examine the implications of theory for language teaching, since language teaching is usually considered one of the goals of bilingual education. While theory should not be the only element considered in language teaching practice [Krashen, in press (b)], the five hypotheses given in the previous section have some very clear implications. They predict that any successful second language teaching program will have these characteristics:

1. It will supply input in the second language that is, first of all, comprehensible and, second, interesting and relevant to students. As discussed earlier, the goal of this input will not be to provide practice on specific points of grammar but to transmit messages of interest.

2. It will not force students to speak before they are ready and will be tolerant of errors in early speech. The theory implies that we improve in grammatical accuracy by obtaining more input, not by error correction. [Although error correction will work for some people (monitor users) some of the time (when they have time to think about form) and for some easy-to-learn rules.]

3. It will put grammar in its proper place. Some adults, and very few children, are able to use conscious grammar rules to increase the grammatical accuracy of their output; and even for these people, very strict conditions need to be met before the conscious knowledge of grammar can be applied, given the Monitor Hypothesis presented above. Children have very little capacity for conscious language learning and may also have little need for conscious learning, since they can come close to native speaker preformance standards using acquisition alone.

Many different methods come very close to meeting these requirements. Asher's Total Physical Response Approach, Lozanov's Suggestopedia, Terrell's Natural Approach, and recent materials developed by Winitz are some examples [Stevick, 1980; Krashen, in press (b)]. In addition, several non-methods also meet these requirements. For example, successful *conversation* with a speaker of the language you are trying to acquire may be the best lesson of all, as long as the speaker succeeds in modifying his or her speech so that you understand. According to the theory, acquirers profit directly not from what they themselves say, but from what native speakers say. Acquirer output makes an *indirect* contribution to acquisition by inviting comprehensible input. Also, pleasure reading or reading for content and intrinsic interest has the potential for supplying the necessary input for acquisition.

Subject Matter Teaching and Second Language Acquisition

Another clear potential source of comprehensible input is the subject matter classroom itself in which subject matter is taught using the second language as a medium of instruction (immersion classes).

Simply, the theory predicts that second language acquisition will occur in subject matter classes taught in the second language if the child can follow and understand the lesson. Language levels necessary for comprehension will differ, of course, for different subjects. It has been suggested, for example, that arithmetic does not require as much control of the second language as science. In the former, there is considerable extralinguistic help in understanding, fewer demands on students in terms of verbal responses, and a more restricted vocabulary (Cazden, 1979).

Applied linguistics research confirms this prediction and helps us see both the advantages and limitations of subject matter teaching as a means of encouraging second language acquisition. English-speaking immersion students, both in the United States and Canada, are in general able to follow the curriculum in a second language, that is, they learn subject matter as well as monolinguals do. Research has shown that they also do far better in acquiring the second language than students who study the second language only in formal classes. Researchers are careful to point out, however, that immersion students do not reach native-like levels in speaking and writing. Also, it takes several years for immersion students to attain these high levels of competence in the second language (see e. g., Lambert and Tucker, 1972; Swain, 1978, 1979). The classroom, thus, has its limits. Immersion students hear the language only from the teacher and not from peers. This may mean both a lack of certain kinds of input (conversational) and the existence of an affective filter.

Subject matter teaching, thus, has both advantages and limitations. It can provide comprehensible input and help second language acquisition; students exposed to the subject matter alone can achieve high levels of proficiency in certain kinds of second language usage. This takes time, however, and such students do not typically reach the native speaker level.

Before proceeding to implications, one major point about the success of immersion programs needs to be made. Cohen and Swain (1976) point out that one of the reasons immersion programs succeed, where some kinds of bilingual programs fail, is because the immersion students are "segregated." In early immersion, they note, "all kindergarten pupils are unilingual in the L1. In essence, the successful program starts out as a segregated one linguistically" (p. 47). This linguistic segregation raises the chances of students receiving comprehensible input. The presence of native speakers in a class (submersion) ensures that a good percentage of the language heard by the non-native speaker will be incomprehensible, since teachers naturally will gear much of their speech to the native speakers in a native to native rather than a native to non-native speaker register.

Cohen and Swain (1976) point out several other factors that, in our terms, lead to a lower affective filter in immersion programs. The linguistic segregation "eliminates the kind of ridicule that students exert on less proficient performers" (p. 47), teachers have positive expectations, and the program is voluntary. Also, "in kindergarten, the children are permitted to speak in the L1 until they are ready to speak in the L2" (p. 48). Thus, a silent period in L2 is allowed.

Bilingual Education and Second Language Acquisition

We are now prepared to deal with some of the questions and issues raised in the first section. To do this, we first need to consider what requirements any program must meet in order to promote second language acquisition. From what we have learned from second language acquisition theory, there seem to be two major requirements.

I. Provide Comprehensible Input in the Weaker Language

Clearly, this requirement does not mean merely being exposed to the second language. There is a tremendous difference between receiving comprehensible, meaningful input and simply hearing a language one does not understand. The former will help second language acquisition, while the latter is just noise. It remains noise no matter how much exposure is provided. According to the theory, a small amount of comprehensible input, even one hour per day, will do more for second language acquisition than massive amounts of incomprehensible input.

There are several possible sources of comprehensible input for NEP children. The one that we traditionally turn to is classes in ESL. Simply, the theory predicts that ESL will help to the extent that it supplies comprehensible input. Not all teaching methods do this; some, in fact, supply amazingly little comprehensible input in a second language (e. g., grammar-translation and audio-lingual type methods). Both theory and practical experience confirm that repetitive drill does very little for acquisition; and grammar approaches, shown to be ineffective for adults, are even less effective for small children. ESL can make a contribution when it supplies the necessary input to children who have few or no other sources of input (see Terrell, 1977, 1981 for some ideas on how this can be done).

A second source of comprehensible input for NEP children is interaction with other children outside of school, on the playground, and in the neighborhood. This can be an extremely rich source of input, and it may be the case that the availability of this source is responsible for the success of many people who succeeded without ESL or bilingual education.

It should be pointed out that even with informal playground interaction, acquisition of English or of any other language takes time. As mentioned earlier, children in informal environments typically show a silent period and may produce very little for several months. Thus, even under the best conditions, language acquisition is slow.

A third possible source of comprehensible input is subject matter, as discussed in the previous section. It will help second language acquisition if children understand enough of the second language to follow the lesson. Non-English proficient children, however, can make it to this level in "Sink or Swim" programs only if they get the comprehensible input somewhere else or if the linguistic level of the class is somehow lowered.

II. Maintain Subject Matter Education

A bilingual program needs to make sure that NEP children do not fall behind in subject matter. This entails, in many cases, instruction in subject matter using the first language as a medium of instruction. Contrary to the view of critics, this does not necessarily mean less acquisition of English as a second language. In fact, *it may mean more acquisition of English*. To see how this is so, we will describe what observance this requirement can do for NEP children.

First, the school system's basic responsibility is providing subject matter instruction so that NEP children can keep up and obtain the tools they need to live in and contribute to society. Second, subject matter instruction plays an important role in cognitive development. Children who fall behind in subject matter because they do not understand the language of instruction may also be missing the stimulation necessary for normal intellectual development.

The third reason is that subject matter knowledge and the cognitive/academic proficiency it encourages will help second language acquisition. It does this by giving children the context or background needed to understand academic input. In other words, children who are not behind in subject matter and who have normal cognitive development will simply understand more of what they hear, both in English language medium classes and in academic or intellectual discussions outside of class. If children understand more, they will acquire more of the language! Very simply, the more cognitively mature and knowledgeable children are about the *topic* of discussion, the better chance they have to acquire the language.

Anyone who has attempted to acquire a second language has had experiences that illustrate this phenomenon: We find it much easier to understand discussions of topics with which we are familiar and find it difficult to eavesdrop and come into conversations in the middle. (In my own case, I find it easy to read and understand discussions on familiar topics with my intermediate French and German, but I understand very little when I overhear a conversation in these languages.) This illustrates the powerful effect context and background knowledge have on our ability to understand a partially acquired language. The major point here is that understanding is a prerequisite for acquisition. Thus, the more context or background we can provide, the more acquisition will take place.

Children who are behind in subject matter and weak in the second language face double trouble. Their failure to understand will not only cause them to fall further behind but they will also fail to make progress in second language acquisition. Knowledge of subject matter, thus, has an indirect but very powerful effect on second language acquisition despite the fact that it may be provided in the students' first language.

Finally, it can be argued that maintaining subject matter, whether in the first or second language, leads to a better attitude toward school in general and higher self-esteem, factors that contribute to a lower affective filter and better acquisition of English, especially when English is presented in a school situation.

We can also suggest a third requirement for bilingual programs, not one motivated by considerations of second language acquisition but by independent motivations. As we shall see, this requirement may be met by programs that meet the first two requirements, at little or no additional cost.

III. Maintain and Develop Children's First Language

As with nearly all other issues in bilingual education, there is pro and con here as well. Some experts argue that we should make real efforts to maintain the first language. Reasons given include:

1. Speakers of languages other than English make a valuable contribution to our society. Since so few native English speakers successfully acquire a second language, it is foolish to waste this natural resource. Campbell expressed this view in a *Los Angeles Times* (September 5, 1980) interview:

> [*The*] *emphasis on "transition" means we will systematically eradicate foreign languages in elementary school, then spend millions to try to develop these same skills in high school and college....That doesn't make much sense.*

2. Maintaining the first language and culture of NEP children may help to build pride and counter negative attitudes members of a linguistic minority may have. There is evidence, in fact, that strongly suggests that those language acquirers who do not reject their own language and culture succeed better in second language acquisition than those who have negative attitudes toward their own group (Gardner and Lambert, 1972).

3. Cummins (1978; 1980) argues that in order to keep up in subject matter and maintain normal cognitive development, students need to develop high levels of first language competence. Specifically, they need to develop not only basic interpersonal and communicative skills in the first language (termed BICS) but also "cognitive competence," the ability to "use language effectively as an instrument of thought and represent cognitive operations by means of language" (Cummins, 1978, p. 397). A lack of development of this aspect of first language competence may explain problems some minority children have in school. When the first language is not used extensively and promoted at home, and is not supported at school, low first language skills, according to Cummins, can exert "a limiting effect" on the development of the second language. Majority language children in immersion programs do not have this problem, since their language is highly developed outside school (Cummins, 1978).

Cummins argues that education in the first language develops CALP (Cognitive/Academic Language Proficiency). CALP developed in one language contributes to CALP in any other, according to Cummins; that is, someone who is able to use Spanish for academic purposes will have developed an ability that will be useful in using any other language for academic purposes.

Arguments against first language maintenance have, in general, attempted to counter any of the above arguments but usually insist that since English is the official language of the United States, taxpayers should not have to support the maintenance or development of minority languages.

Another Look at the Options

We can now ask to what extent different programs meet the conditions described in the previous section. In this section, we will see that both theoretical predictions and empirical evidence show that some programs do satisfy the requirements while others do not and that this success or the lack of it depends not only on the program but also on the characteristics of the students. Most important, it will show that research exists, is not conflicting, and that real generalizations can be made about what works and what does not work in bilingual education. Table 4 presents this analysis.

1. We first consider submersion, or "Sink or Swim" programs. According to Table 4, "Sink or Swim" will satisfy the first requirement by providing comprehensible input in the weaker language only when extra ESL is provided (assuming a form of ESL that indeed provides comprehensible input) and/or when children have sufficient contact with input from the outside. In and of itself, "Sink or Swim" may not meet the first requirement, and children in such situations are in danger of not getting the input needed to acquire English. Such situations clearly exist in submersion programs that include children living in *barrios* where there is little if any social interaction among NEP and native English-speaking children.

The second requirement can only be met by "Sink or Swim" if the children's linguistic competence in English develops quickly enough. Children in "Sink or Swim" are playing a dangerous game of catch-up, hoping their competence in English will be high enough to do school work before they are hopelessly behind in subject matter. "Sink or Swim," even under the best conditions, is a risk.

No "Sink or Swim" program, by definition, attempts to meet the third requirement, development of the first language.

2. Immersion programs for majority children do meet all conditions. As discussed earlier, immersion programs have a better chance of supplying comprehensible input in subject matter classes than do "Sink or Swim" programs. Since all children are at the same linguistic level, there is less of a tendency to speak over the comprehension level of the

Table 4
REQUIREMENTS TO BE MET BY PROGRAMS FOR NEP CHILDREN AND CURRENT OPTIONS

Requirements for Programs (predicted by theory)	SUBMERSION ("SINK OR SWIM")			IMMERSION		BILINGUAL EDUCATION	
	Only	+ Informal CI	+ ESL	Majority Child	Minority	Concurrent Translation	Ideal Bilingual
1. Comprehensible input in weaker language.	no	yes	yes[b]	yes	yes[c]	no[d]	yes[e]
2. Maintain subject matter.	no	?[a]	?[a]	yes	yes[c]	?[f]	yes
Additional: 3. Maintain and develop first language.	no	no	no	yes	no	?[f]	yes

a: This program will work if second language ability grows fast enough to reach subject matter threshold before children are too far behind.

b: Yes, if the ESL method supplies comprehensible input.

c: *De facto* immersion programs do not succeed as well as bilingual education, however. May be due to attitudes, teacher expectations, low development of first language, and inappropriate materials.

d: Students tune out weaker language in concurrent translation programs (Legarreta, 1979).

e: Yes, if second language skills are adequate for those classes taught in the second language.

f: Will not succeed unless there is adequate input in the second language.

CI = Comprehensible Input

Ideal Bilingual = Subject matter in primary language, plus comprehensible input in English, either as ESL and/or subject matter instruction in comprehensible English.

students. This helps to satisfy the first and second requirements. The empirical evidence from the research programs evaluating immersion classes done over the last decade confirms that immersion children develop high levels of competence in the second language and do as well as monolinguals in subject matter.

Immersion programs for majority students also meet the third requirement through the use of language arts classes in the first language. Also, many programs provide for increasing use of the first language as a medium of instruction as children progress in school. Of great importance in meeting this requirement is that in immersion programs for majority students, children's first language is the language of the country, home, and playground; there is little chance that this language will be assigned a lower status.

One could argue that a solution for NEP children is an adaptation of the immersion model. This would entail a completely separate curriculum, all taught in English, to groups consisting only of NEP children. Assuming all children start at the same time and on an equal footing with respect to English competence, it would appear to have the linguistic advantage of having a better chance of supplying comprehensible input as compared to "Sink or Swim." Thus, theoretically, we could expect progress both in language acquisition (first requirement) and subject matter (second requirement) even if little or no contact with English-speaking children outside of school was possible. Judging from reports from majority immersion, we would not expect completely native-like English.

It can be maintained, however, that many "Sink or Swim" programs are already *de facto* immersion programs in that they often involve a majority of NEP children and, in some cases, are composed entirely of NEP children (e. g., in certain inner city areas and on American Indian reservations). These programs do not report overwhelming success. There may be good reasons why, however, reasons that explain why minority-child immersion may look good on paper but may not always work.

First, NEP students who enter immersion programs late will face nearly the same problems they face in "Sink or Swim"; they will not understand and may thus fall behind in subject matter and not improve in English. (Late entering bilingual education students will not have this problem; they can be taught in the first language at least until their English develops sufficiently.)

Also, minority immersion teachers may not have the same kinds of expectations as do majority immersion teachers. They may be less able or willing to make input comprehensible and may set higher standards for second language acquisition than are possible under the circumstances. As Cohen (1976) points out, we have a double standard:

> *People applaud a majority group child when he can say a few words in the minority language (e. g., at the beginning of an immersion program) and yet they impatiently demand more English from the minority group child. (p. 85)*

Thus, many *de facto* immersion programs look more like "Sink or Swim," with inappropriate materials and input that is too complex and incomprehensible.

3. We turn now to the programs categorized as Bilingual Education in Table 4. Let us first consider the program labeled concurrent translation. In this kind of program, concepts are explained in one language and then repeated in the second. This kind of program may not meet the first requirement for the simple reason that children need not pay attention to the explanation in the second or weaker language, and there is no motivation for teachers to attempt to simplify explanations in the second language. Legarreta (1979) notes that in the concurrent translation program, "Teachers reported that the Hispanic students tune out the English and wait to hear the material explained in Spanish" (p. 533). (This phenomenon also predicts, and correctly I think, the failure of bilingual TV to teach the second language. In many programs, a given character will speak either Spanish or English, but it is quite possible to follow the story line by attending only to one language. Similarly, it predicts that Americans will not acquire centigrade temperature systems from the practice of announcing the temperature in both centigrade and fahrenheit. Most people will simply listen to the version they understand.) Concurrent translation can theoretically meet the second and third requirements, however, since subject matter can be explained in the first language and continued use of the L_1 helps to ensure its maintenance. In practice, however, concurrent translation often fails to meet these requirements. This is because, despite its intentions, concurrent translation input in many programs often is incomprehensible, most materials are in English, and primary language input often is provided by under-trained aides or Anglophone teachers who have not fully mastered the children's first language.

The Ideal Bilingual program, shown in Table 4, is one in which subject matter is taught in the primary language and some source of comprehensible input in the second language is supplied. This can be in the form of ESL or comprehensible subject matter instruction using English (as in the balanced bilingual program discussed earlier). Such programs have the potential for satisfying all three requirements, even for children who have little access to English outside of school. Balanced bilingual programs will be successful according to the predictions of the theory, especially if the subject matter classes given in the second language are those where more extra-linguistic context is available to aid comprehension (e. g., math), while those dealing with more abstract topics—topics that typically employ fewer physical props (e. g., social science and language arts)—are taught at first in the primary language (Cazden, 1979).

Empirical Evidence

Our analysis based on the three requirements derived from language acquisition theory bring us to these conclusions:

1. "Sink or Swim" programs will not be effective for children with no extra source of comprehensible input.
2. Adding ESL to "Sink or Swim" will help but will not be as effective as bilingual education in encouraging acquisition of English.
3. Bilingual programs in which subject matter is taught in the first language, and a source of comprehensible input is provided in the second language, whether ESL or not, will succeed best.

Despite years of discussion of bilingual education in the professional literature and many studies of different aspects of bilingualism, little research speaks directly to these three predictions. The research that is available, however, is fully consistent with them.

Legarreta (1979) examined the acquisition of English in kindergarten children in three kinds of bilingual programs (balanced, concurrent translation, and concurrent translation + ESL) and two kinds of "Sink or Swim" programs [with and without ESL where the ESL component consisted of "daily, sequenced lessons in English structure and use, presented orally to small groups" (p. 523)]. The overall exposure time was seven months—relatively short for this kind of study, as Swain (1979) points out—and the number of subjects involved was not large. The results, however, are very interesting.

1. Children in all bilingual education programs outperformed "Sink or Swim" children in listening comprehension and conversational competence[2] tests of English, despite the fact that the "Sink or Swim" children had more exposure to English.

---

[2]The test of conversational competence asked children to use the language in real communication; it thus demands more than knowledge of vocabulary and grammar but also tests abilities such as "the ability to be only as explicit as a situation demands, to elaborate, to make inferences about a situation, to be sensitive to social rules of discourse..." (Legarreta, 1979, p. 525).

2. The balanced bilingual program produced the greatest overall gains in both the second language and the first language (Spanish).

3. "Sink or Swim" with ESL outperformed "Sink or Swim" without ESL on listening comprehension testing but not on the test of conversational competence.

Legarreta (1979) concludes that the use of audio-lingual style ESL training is "marginally facilitative" (p. 534), while "an alternate immersion bilingual program, with balanced Spanish and English input, really facilitates both Spanish and English acquisition" (p. 534). This appears to be so, but her data support a deeper generalization: Bilingual programs will work when they supply comprehensible input in the second language and adequate, comprehensible subject matter instruction in either language. The balanced program does this, but so do other versions.

Rosier and Farella (1976) report results from a different context that conform to the same underlying principles. They report of the success of bilingual education for Navajo children at the Rock Point Community School in the heart of the Navajo reservation. In 1960, according to Vorih and Rosier (1978), Rock Point ranked at the bottom of eight Indian schools in student achievement. The introduction of intensive ESL in 1963 helped somewhat, but Rock Point sixth graders were still two years behind national norms. In 1967, bilingual education was introduced, with kindergarten children receiving 70 percent of their instruction in Navajo and first and second graders receiving 50 percent in Navajo. Third through sixth graders had 75 percent of their instruction in English. English is taught in early grades "by TESL methods" (Vorih and Rosier, 1978, p. 264). The program can thus be classified as Bilingual Education + ESL.

Analysis of the Rock Point program confirms the validity of our requirements: Students in the bilingual program, with subject matter in the first language, outperformed non-bilingual education students on a reading test of English. Again, the bilingual students actually had *less* exposure to English but apparently acquired more, confirming that it is comprehensible input and not mere exposure that counts.

Some as yet unpublished research, cited by Cummins (1980), provides even more confirmation. As Cummins (1980) reports it:

> *Carey and Cummins (1979) reported that grade 5 children from French-speaking home backgrounds in the Edmonton Catholic School System bilingual program [Canada] (80% French, 20% English from K-12) performed at an equivalent level in English skills to angolphone children of the same IQ*

in either the bilingual or regular English programs. A similar finding is reported in a large-scale study carried out by Hébert et al. (1976) among grades 3, 6 and 9 francophone students in Manitoba. At all grade levels there was a significant positive relationship between percentage of instruction in French (PIF) and French achievement, but no relationship between PIF and English achievement. In other words, francophone students receiving 80% instruction in French and 20% instruction in English did just as well in English as students receiving 80% instruction in English and 20% in French. (p. 184)

Conclusions

We are now ready to return to the issues raised in the first section of this paper and attempt to give some answers.

1. Does Bilingual Education Retard the Development of English as a Second Language?

Both theory and empirical research tell us that proper bilingual education need not retard the development of second language competence and should, in fact, promote it. Classes taught in the first language help children grow in subject matter knowledge and stimulate cognitive development, which in turn helps second language acquisition by providing children with the extra-linguistic context necessary for comprehension.

2. Are "Sink or Swim" (Submersion) and/or ESL Methods Better?

Obviously, "Sink or Swim" children have more exposure to English, but they do not necessarily have more comprehensible input; it is comprehensible input, not merely "heard" language, that makes language acquisition happen. Thus, "Sink or Swim" classes, at worst, may be providing children only with noise. The results of this are doubly tragic: Children will fall behind in subject matter and will not acquire the second language.

"Sink or Swim" with ESL will fare somewhat better but will work only if children acquire English fast enough, before they are hopelessly behind in subject matter. It may be that in most cases where "Sink or Swim" worked, children had rich comprehensible input from playmates outside the classroom.

3. How Should ESL be Taught?

Second language acquisition research strongly suggests that methodology *per se* is not the issue: By whatever name, children need comprehensible input to acquire English. This can come in the form of

ESL classes taught according to a method that provides such input (e. g., Terrell's Natural Approach) or subject matter taught in comprehensible English.

4. Is There a Place for Immersion for NEP Children?

Theoretically, immersion for NEP children appears to meet the three requirements. Yet, results of *de facto* immersion programs in the United States are not encouraging. This could be due to several factors, including inadequate development of the first language, as suggested by Cummins (1978), differing teacher expectations, the failure of late-entering students to obtain comprehensible input, and inappropriate materials.

5. Which Bilingual Education Options are Better for Language Acquisition?

There are several bilingual education options that will satisfy the requirements given in Table 4 and earlier in the paper. Balanced bilingual education programs will do this as long as those subjects taught in the second language are comprehensible. There is nothing magic, however, in the 50 percent figure: It need not be the case that exactly one-half of the program be in one language and one half in the other. What counts is that the requirements are met and that NEP students receive enough comprehensible input to improve in their weaker language. This has happened with as little as 20 percent input in the second language in some programs.

Several issues of course remain unsolved, and in a real sense they always will be. As is typical of scientific reasoning, we have discussed hypotheses and some evidence that supports them. We have not provided proof, nor can we. What we have tried to show is that there is substantial information available about how language is acquired, that it is certainly enough to formulate hypotheses, that these hypotheses shed light on some of the basic issues in bilingual education, and that the field is not in a state of helpless confusion. Researchers are evaluating children's progress, adding to their knowledge of language acquisition, and using this knowledge to better serve the children they study and those who will come after them.

REFERENCES

Brown, R., Courtney Cazden, and U. Bellugi. "The Child's Grammar from I to III," *Studies in Child Language Development,* eds., C. Ferguson, and D. Slobin. New York: Holt, Rinehart and Winston, 1973, pp. 295-333.

Campbell, Russell. *Los Angeles Times*, September 5, 1980.

Cazden, Courtney B. "Curriculum/Language Contexts for Bilingual Education," *Language Development in a Bilingual Setting,* ed., Eugène J. Brière. Los Angeles, California: National Dissemination and Assessment Center, California State University, Los Angeles, 1979, pp. 129-138.

Cohen, Andrew D. "The Case for Partial or Total Immersion Education," *The Bilingual Child,* ed., António Simões. New York: Academic Press, 1976, pp. 65-89.

____, and Merrill Swain. "Bilingual Education: The 'Immersion' Model in the North American Context," *TESOL Quarterly,* X, No. 1 (March, 1976), 45-53.

Cummins, James. "The Cross-Lingual Dimensions of Language Proficiency: Implications for Bilingual Education and the Optimal Age Issue," *TESOL Quarterly,* XIV, No. 2 (June, 1980), 175-187.

____. "Educational Implications of Mother Tongue Maintenance in Minority Language Groups," *The Canadian Modern Language Review,* XXXIV (1978), 395-416.

Dulay, Heidi C., and Marina K. Burt. "Remarks on Creativity in Second Language Acquisition," *Viewpoints on English as a Second Language,* eds., Marina K. Burt, Heidi C. Dulay, and M. Finnochiaro. New York: Regents, 1977, pp. 95-126.

____, and ____. "Some Guidelines for the Assessment of Oral Language Proficiency and Dominance," *TESOL Quarterly,* XII, No. 2 (June, 1978), 177-192.

____, ____, and Stephen Krashen. *The Second Language.* New York: Oxford University Press, in press.

Elkind, David. *Children and Adolescents: Interpretive Essays on Jean Piaget.* New York: Oxford University Press, 1970.

Gardner, Robert C., and Wallace E. Lambert. *Attitudes and Motivation in Second Language Learning.* Rowley, Massachusetts: Newbury House, 1972.

Hatch, Evelyn M. "Discourse Analysis and Second Language Acquisition," *Second Language Acquisition: A Book of Readings,* ed., E. Hatch. Rowley, Massachusetts: Newbury House, 1978.

Krashen, Stephen. "Accounting for Child-Adult Differences in Second Language Rate and Attainment," *Child-Adult Differences in Second Language Acquisition,* eds., Stephen Krashen, R. Scarcella, and M. Long. Rowley, Massachusetts: Newbury House, in press (a).

____. *Second Language Acquisition and Second Language Learning.* London: Pergamon Press, 1981.

____. *Theory and Practice in Second Language Acquisition.* New York: Pergamon Press, in press (b).

____, Michael A. Long, and Robin C. Scarcella. "Age, Rate and Eventual Attainment in Second Language Acquisition," *TESOL Quarterly,* XIII, No. 4 (December, 1979), 573-582.

Lambert, Wallace E., and G. Richard Tucker. *Bilingual Education of Children: The St. Lambert Experiment.* Rowley, Massachusetts: Newbury House, 1972.

Legarreta, Dorothy. "The Effects of Program Models on Language Acquisition by Spanish-Speaking Children," *TESOL Quarterly,* XIII, No. 4 (December, 1979), 521-534.

Lopez, Rosa Maria. *Los Angeles Times,* September 19, 1980.

Los Angeles Times, September 19, 1980.

Newmark, L. "How Not to Interfere With Language Learning," *International Review of American Linguistics,* XL (1966), 77-83.

Rosier, Paul, and Merilyn Farella. "Bilingual Education at Rock Point—Some Early Results," *TESOL Quarterly,* X, No. 4 (December, 1976), 379-388.

Scarcella, Robin, and C. Higa. "Input and Age Differences in Second Language Acquisition," *Child-Adult Differences in Second Language Acquisition,* eds., Stephen Krashen, Robin Scarcella, and Michael A. Long. Rowley, Massachusetts: Newbury House, in press.

Selinker, Larry, Merrill Swain, and Guy Dumas. "The Interlanguage Hypothesis Extended to Children," *Language Learning,* XXV, No. 1 (June, 1975), 139-152.

Snow, Catherine E., and Marian Hoefnagel-Hohle. "The Critical Period for Language Acquisition: Evidence from Second Language Learning," *Child Development,* XLIX, No. 4 (December, 1978), 1114-1128.

Stevick, Earl W. *Memory, Meaning, and Method.* Rowley, Massachusetts: Newbury House, 1976.

Swain, Merrill. "Bilingual Education: Research and Its Implications," *On TESOL '79,* eds., C. Yorio, K. Perkins, and J. Schachter. Washington, D. C.: TESOL, 1979.

_____. "French Immersion: Early, Late or Partial?" *Canadian Modern Language Review,* XXXIV (May, 1978), 577-585.

Terrell, Tracy D. "The Natural Approach in Bilingual Education," *Schooling and Language Minority Students: A Theoretical Framework.* Los Angeles, California: Evaluation, Dissemination and Assessment Center, California State University, Los Angeles, 1981.

_____. "A Natural Approach to Second Language Acquisition and Learning," *Modern Language Journal,* LXI, No. 7 (November, 1977), 325-337.

Trombley, William. "Bilingual Education: Even the Experts are Confused," *Los Angeles Times,* September 7, 1980a.

_____. "Is Bilingual Education Able to Do Its Job?" *Los Angeles Times,* September 4, 1980b.

Vorih, Lillian, and Paul Rosier. "Rock Point Community School: An Example of a Navajo-English Bilingual Elementary School Program," *TESOL Quarterly,* XII, No. 3 (September, 1978), 263-269.

Part Two
Strategies for Implementation

Effective Use of the Primary Language in the Classroom

Dorothy Legarreta-Marcaida

Introduction: Why is the Effective Use of the Primary Language Essential to School Success?

IN THIS SECTION, the historic view in American education that a child's native language, if other than English, is a handicap—a hurdle to be eliminated—will be briefly contrasted with the present view. This view, based on recent research evidence, finds that, in fact, development of the child's language has clearly beneficial effects on school progress (Cummins, 1981). This section will end with material spotlighting the daily difficulties experienced by limited English-proficient (LEP) children in all-English classrooms, which often lead to school failure. School success, however, the goal of *biliterate, bicultural* children, will result when a firm foundation in the home language is laid by school instruction.

How has bilingualism been viewed in America? Clearly, since assimilation of recent immigrants into an English-speaking western culture has been the goal of our public schools, bilingualism had to be viewed as a handicap. This "melting pot" view included even the Native American and Hispanic cultures that predated the colonialization from Northern Europe in the 17th century. Not surprisingly, research evidence from testing bilingual children seemed to prove that these children were less intelligent than native English-speaking children. For example, Darcy (1953) reviewed the literature to date (110 studies) and found either no effect or adverse effect on intelligence associated with bilingualism. Singer (1956) also reviewed the literature and found only four studies that showed no handicap due to bilingualism. He noted:

> There is no study in the literature in which the language ability in the vernacular, and intelligence of the subjects was tested before and after the acquisition of a second language. No one, it seems, has studied the possibility of either an inhibitory or facilitory effect on the thought processes or intelligence test scores in the vernacular when a second language is acquired. (p. 448)

Further, Singer notes (1956) that in every case cited the intelligence test was administered in the second or weaker language. This early research was again critically reviewed by Macnamara (1966) who noted that control of factors such as socio-economic status, sampling, age, and *validity* of instruments, was generally lacking.

Recently, however, a series of well-controlled studies have been conducted in many parts of the world to discover the effects of bilingualism on intelligence, or *cognitive functioning,* with children tested in their early primary language or by using *non-verbal assessment procedures.*

For example, Feldman and Shen (1971) found five-year-old bilinguals more cognitively flexible in three tasks of labeling behavior, since they did not depend on linguistic symbols. Liedtke and Nelson (1968) used Piagetian assessment techniques and found higher levels of cognitive function in bilingual first graders. Nespor (1969) found that third graders in California who studied a second language were facilitated in their development away from ikonicity (thinking the referent of the word somehow resides in the word) and toward greater understanding of the arbitrary nature of language. Ianco-Worrall (1972) used a semantic/phonetic preference test (which is more like "cap," "can" or "hat"?) with children in South Africa, aged four to nine. She found that the bilinguals achieved semantic preference (e. g., choosing "hat") two to three years earlier than the monolinguals who continued to choose phonetically similar words.

Collison (1974) who studied concept formation in Ghanaian children, taught science either in their native languages or English. In the colloquium method of science teaching, children better understood necessary relationships in the experiments they did if their primary language were used, while the children taught in English were not able to exercise their conceptual potential. Kessler and Quinn (1980) found improved science problem solving ability in bilingual children when tested in Spanish.

The issue is not yet definitely settled, but it appears that recent research indicates greater cognitive flexibility, rather than lessened cognitive functioning in bilinguals.

At about the same time that bilingualism was viewed as a handicap in our own nation, the use of the child's primary language for instruction was gaining support throughout much of the rest of the world. Even in the United States, over 50 years ago, Teacher's College, Columbia University (New York Bureau of Publications, 1926) studied Puerto Rican education by testing thousands of children in English *and* Spanish. Puerto Rican children were markedly behind in achievement on the English *Stanford Achievement Test* but markedly *superior* to United States' children's norms when tested in Spanish. They concluded that, since Spanish is more easily learned than English and has a better writing system, it should be introduced early and used as a medium of school instruction (Andersson and Boyer, 1970). But the "melting pot" view ignored this early finding.

Nearly 30 years later, the widely cited UNESCO document, *The Use of Vernacular Language in Education* (1953) reported on successful programs throughout the world that utilized the vernacular as the initial medium of instruction through literacy. Its general statement notes a number of compelling reasons for using the native language as the medium of instruction, ranging from the fact that language is the expression of children's culture, to their possible loss of the ability to express themselves in an alien language. More recently, Engle (1973) reviewed 25 studies around the world in which use of the vernacular as the medium of instruction was compared to use of another language. She found that, in general:

> *(1) Teaching second language literacy without oral language training is not likely to succeed. (2) Bilingual programs do not retard the development of the child's native language. (3)* Programs become more effective with years in operation (four years seems to be necessary to show results) [*author's emphasis*]. *(4) Teacher variables as training, ethnicity, are important. (5) Kindergarten experiences, especially oral language training, are related to program effectiveness. (6) The success of a bilingual program is related to a vast complex web of factors that differ in each situation: language use in home, status of each language in the culture, etc. (7)* Hawthorne effect *can radically alter results. (8)* There appears to be a transfer of skills from one language to another [*author's emphasis*], *especially among middle class children. (Engle, 1973, pp. 40-42)*

Points (3) and (8), very important ones for bilingual education today, will come up again later in this paper. Cornejo (1974) prepared an update of exemplary programs in California and the Southwest. During 1975, several of these programs published data indicating that pupils schooled bilingually do as well, and usually better, than children schooled in English only, on both state-mandated tests and assessment instruments developed at the project site (San Francisco Unified, Los Angeles Unified, and Valley Intercultural Project) (Title VII, 1975).

For the past six years, bilingual programs in Navaho at Rock Point (Rosier and Farella, 1976; Krashen, 1981), in Spanish at Santa Fe (Leyba, 1978), San Diego at Nestor School (Evaluation Associates, 1978), Redwood City (Ramirez, 1974), and San Francisco (Legarreta, 1979) show clearly that language minority students are doing *better* in

English language and subject matter as well as better in their primary language than control language minority children educated only in English. In all these bilingual programs, the primary language was used effectively: Meaningful "comprehensible input" was delivered directly and in overall amounts, ranging from half to over three-quarters of classroom time in K-2 and about half in upper elementary grades.

These beneficial results due to effective primary language instruction are best explained by Cummins' brilliant work (1979; 1980), detailed in an earlier chapter of this book, on the linguistic interdependence of language acquisition. Good bilingual programs that develop the child's primary language to threshold levels of CALP: Cognitive Academic Linguistic Proficiency (e. g., to full literacy) enable children to master English and succeed in our schools. Generations of school failure experienced in all-English classrooms by Native American, Hispanic, and other linguistic different children can be reversed by good bilingual education to produce children fully proficient in English and their primary language.

Bilingual education is sound pedagogically since language acquisition skills and concept development in the primary language do transfer to English (Cummins, 1981) and actually facilitate English acquisition by providing a richer experiential base and context for acquiring this new language inside and outside the classroom (Krashen, 1981).

In addition to the educational advantages cited above, bilingual education meets the affective needs of children from the first hour of school. Self-esteem and identification with primary language and culture are enhanced when the child's experiences in the home and community are validated both as a knowledge base and a source of social and interpersonal skills. The child's *cognitive style* (manner of learning) is accepted: Recent ethnographic research shows us that linguistic minority children [Hawaiian (Boggs, 1972), Hispanic (Ramirez, 1964), and Native American (Dumont, 1972; Philips, 1972)] use different strategies for learning than do children from an all-English culture.

There is ample evidence that linguistic minority children feel better about themselves, their language, and their culture in bilingual/bicultural programs (Covey, 1973; Rivera, 1973). One study (Skoczylas, 1972) found that Anglo children in the bilingual program had more favorable attitudes toward Mexican-Americans after bilingual education. This study notes that "Mexican-Americans in the control [all-English] program viewed themselves as less handsome and less fair, and Mexican-Americans as relatively sad and dirty" (p. 148). It is difficult to believe that five-year-old Hispanic children come to school with such attitudes. A better explanation can be found in the work of Morris (1974) showing that the self-concept of Puerto Rican children decreased the longer they attended regular classes in New York City. Finally, there is an economic argument for bilingual education that speaks to a more effective use of our linguistic resources in making public policy to promote the foreign language competence essential to our global interests today. Children have, for generations, been deprived of the opportunity to learn how to read and write in their home language by the all-English policy of our public schools (Leibowitz, 1971). Until 1968, for example, only English could be used for instruction in California's public schools. Then in high school these same home languages are presented as foreign languages, with more than two billion dollars annually being spent to teach Spanish, French, Chinese, etc., with poor results (Andersson and Boyer, 1970).

The best example of the public schools' role in implementing language policy is Israel, where Hebrew, a language never spoken except in religious rituals since Biblical times, has been revived completely due to its official status as the school language at all levels (Hofman and Fisherman, 1972). Thus, the unique role of the public school and bilingual programs in the conservation of primary languages in our own country has economic consequences as well as educational ones.

The educational consequences of teaching linguistic minority children in all-English classrooms can perhaps be seen best by focusing on the actual experiences of children in such regular classrooms. As recently as 1975, *only 2-10 percent* of children eligible for bilingual education were enrolled in such programs (Cornejo, 1974). The greater majority of such children today can still be found in "submersion" (see Glossary) programs, where they are effectively excluded from any participation in the classroom (Carter, 1970).

Consider a few anecdotes from a large Northern California city where Hispanic linguistic-minority children were enrolled in regular kindergarten and taught in English all day. The writer (Legarreta, in press) followed 14 monolingual Spanish-speaking five-year-olds, each for a full day (six percent of the school year) in such classrooms and noted:

1. A Spanish-speaking woman came into the classroom holding the hand of a child about five years of age. The woman said that she had found the child crying at a school bus stop outside on Mission Street. The girl had told her she was named Maria F., and she couldn't find her teacher who was a *rubia* (blonde) and whose name she didn't know. The woman had already taken her to four other primary teachers, but no one knew her at the school. She was told to try the office. Maria looked very frightened. (It was already the eighth week of school.)

2. In this class, each child is expected to participate in "sharing." Maria Elena is chosen; she goes up next to the seated teacher, holding a small calendar in her hand.

Teacher: What is it you have?

Maria Elena: Boy. A girl. (The calendar has a picture of a boy and a girl on the front.)

Teacher: No. What is it, class?

Class: A calendar!

Teacher: Yes, a *calendar*. Sit down, Maria Elena.

3. Luis, a monolingual Spanish-speaking child comes in and joins the circle. He is dressed as he would for church: plaid suit, white shirt, bow tie, and new shoes. He is carrying a permission slip written in English for a field trip.

Teacher: Oh, oh, your mother thinks it's today that we're going on the trip. And you didn't bring any lunch. (The group was going to buy lunch on the trip.) And you brought the lunch money already, too. I'll have to call her if I get time. Don't lose the money—the trip isn't until Wednesday.

(Luis has to keep his new clothes clean all day at school, go without lunch, and not lose his money, plus explain what happened—if he understands—to his mother.)

4. Teresa is wiggling in circle time and raising her hand: "*Permiso, permiso.*"

Teacher: Where's Karen?

Children: She has to pee (i. e., *Teresa* has to.)

Teacher: Oh, did Karen use the bathroom? Go down and wait for her, Teresa. (She misunderstands, thinking the children are referring to her question about Karen.)

Teresa wets herself. She is sent to the office with an aide and her mother is called by a Spanish-speaking secretary.

Teacher: Well, was *that* what you were trying to tell me?

This same group of 14 Hispanic children tested significantly lower in measures of both English and Spanish proficiency than did Hispanic children in bilingual programs, after six months of kindergarten.

Good educational practices such as providing "comprehensible input" in English and developing the child's primary language to foster academic learning were not happening: The school program was eradicting Spanish and teaching very little English—though children were "exposed" to it all day long.

State of the Art: How Can Bilingual Programs Facilitate Primary Language and Concept Development?

Today, publicly funded bilingual programs carry the major responsibility for developing and maintaining high levels of proficiency and literacy in the primary language of the linguistic-minority children they serve. Research (Leibowitz, 1971; Andersson and Boyer, 1970; Hofman and Fisherman, 1972; Fishman, 1970) indicates that, historically and currently, the linguistic-minority child's school is not only the major socializing agent to the dominant culture but also provides the crucial impetus to conservation or loss of the native language.

When we also consider Cummins' work (1979, 1980, 1981) on the facilitative role of the primary language in generalized language ability, including acquisition of English and higher order academic abilities, we can be quite confident that bilingual education, making full use of the primary language, is an effective teaching model for linguistic-minority children.

When we turn to the bilingual classroom—the day-by-day pedagogy, lesson plans, continua in language arts, reading, mathematics, etc.—we need to point our own teaching and use of resources in and out of the classroom toward the goal of excellent primary language proficiency, concept development, and literacy in all linguistic-minority children.

This section will focus on five questions central to the effective use of the primary language in the bilingual classroom:

1. To what *extent* should the child's primary language be used overall in grades K-6?
2. In what *manner* should primary language instruction be delivered:
   a. Concurrent translation?
   b. Alternate immersion (direct method) usually through language dominant groupings?
3. What *variety* of the primary language should be used in the classroom?
4. How can we ensure the *prestige* of the primary language *vis-à-vis* the dominant language, English?
5. How can primary language use be *monitored:* a formative evaluation process?

These questions will be answered below, based on recent empirical evidence and/or the published material of professionals knowledgeable in practice and theory of bilingual/bicultural education.

1. To what extent should the child's primary language be used in the bilingual classroom?

Many involved today in bilingual education remember that, as recently as a dozen or so years ago, the public schools in California and the Southwest prohibited the use of the children's home language—unless it was English—even at recess time (Lesley, 1972). Children were frequently kept after school or punished physically (e. g., by spankings, having their mouths taped, etc.) and were even suspended, just for speaking their home language, any time during the school day. Today, some of these same children, now adults, are teaching in bilingual classrooms. They are providing the all-important *primary language model* to a new generation of children, children who are being encouraged to speak, read, and learn school subjects presented in their home language.

Most bilingual theorists and educators have consistently stated that the child's primary language and English should be used equally overall (Andersson and Boyer, 1970). Also, we now know that children who are proficient in speaking, reading, and learning in their primary language acquire English more easily. They do not experience the *subtractive bilingualism* or *limited bilingualism* suffered by children who are exited from bilingual programs too early. We also know now that it takes at least four to five years in a bilingual program for children to demonstrate the "threshold level" of primary language facility necessary for academic success (Cummins, 1981). Therefore, an optimal bilingual program can be heavily weighted in the K-3 grade years toward the primary language. Successful bilingual programs in Florida, Arizona, and California have used Spanish or Navajo for over three-quarters of the school day in the primary grades, with more use of English in upper elementary grades. There is no magic formula for creating fully bilingual children; but, in all cases, the primary language must be first developed to a high level of proficiency to include literacy.

This emphasis on primary language proficiency is simply not happening in bilingual programs in California. In a recent overview of bilingual programs that have had quality reviews, about 44 percent displayed "primary language components that are improperly designed, severely underdeveloped, or only marginally implemented" (Dolson, 1980).

The United States General Accounting Office announced similar findings after a language survey of Title VII programs, noting that far more English than Spanish was being used (United States General Accounting Office, 1976). Other research (Bruck *et al* ., 1979) shows that, even as the school year progresses, teachers tend to use more and more English. To counteract these tendencies and to ensure primary language proficiency, subject matter—not just oral language and reading—must be delivered in the primary language.

Teaching subject matter in the primary language is a direct and powerful way to ensure its optimal use in bilingual programs. All subject areas, especially basic skills such as language arts, reading, and mathematics as well as science and social studies should be delivered in the primary language. Such varied contexts and contents will ensure optimal primary language learning.

There is ample time to offer this range of subject areas in the primary language in the average school day of five to six hours (depending on the teacher's contract), excluding lunch and recess. The planned primary language instruction to limited English proficient (LEP) children meeting standards of quality (600 minutes per week) ranges from 40 to 52 percent of such instructional time in grades 1-6 and up to 70 percent of the time in half-day kindergartens.

Furthermore, there is no longer a shortage of teaching materials: Anyone who has attended a bilingual conference in California or visited bilingual materials centers is aware that materials are now available to teach almost any subject in the major primary language groups in California. The publishing industry is producing and marketing huge quantities within the United States and importing literally tons of classroom materials from abroad. The industry still needs the input of bilingual teachers to prepare materials more appropriate to local needs. In addition, for nearly 20 years, ever since the Coral Way bilingual program, local school districts have published materials tailored to primary language groups in the United States: Native American, various Hispanic groups, Portuguese, Asian, and others. The shortage of materials is over. Invariably, any purchased materials need to be adapted to the levels of language minority children in the classroom. And, as always, the hallmark of an excellent bilingual teacher is the quantity and variety of teacher-made and class-produced materials used in teaching. There can never be too many. In some schools, teacher-made materials, perfectly adapted to the community and the primary language children in it, are the curriculum. For example, the writer has seen outstanding fifth- and sixth-grade science lessons in the primary language developed in rural areas capitalizing on the needs and interests of the communities' children that are far superior to translations of the expensive science "kits" used in regular classrooms. In general, bilingual curriculum materials, now abundantly available, are best used as a basic continuum of skills to which teachers "plug in" their own materials and hourly and daily activities. Whenever purchased materials are too difficult or in a formal standard language variety that children find confusing (e. g., word problems in mathematics), teachers can prepare a more appropriate version tailored to group needs.

Primary language instruction is necessary at all grade levels to achieve the proficiency necessary for academic work, since we have seen that this threshold level is not reached until the upper elementary grades, even under optimal conditions (Skutnabb-Kangas, 1975). Children able to converse fluently in their primary language, e. g., with Basic Interpersonal Communicative Skills (BICS), need formal instruction plus literacy in their primary language to handle academic-cognitive school tasks. Research on first language acquisition (English) clearly indicates that children are still learning more complex syntactic patterns throughout elementary school (Chomsky, 1969). Both technical and literary vocabulary continue to be acquired throughout school; and adolescents add varieties of speech styles, including language mixing, to convey particular intentions.

What this research evidence means, when translated into practice, is that children also need to experience consistency in their bilingual instruction. They should not be shifted in and out of programs or transitioned before their cognitive-academic linguistic proficiency has reached adequate levels.

In every classroom, many levels of primary language will be found. Bilingual programs have been criticized for "being less effective with second or third generation immigrant children than with new immigrants" (Gonzalez, 1977-1978, p. 54). We now know this is probably due to the higher level of language proficiency gained by recent immigrants before their arrival here. Even when United States-born linguistic minority children apparently retain relatively little primary language, it is preferable to restore and develop this language before the child is expected to function totally in English, since the child's experiential base is in the primary language. Furthermore, language assessment instruments used at present to place children are not always accurate. Teachers can accommodate varying levels of primary language proficiency in the classroom by offering a range of curriculum materials, spanning several grade levels. Language-dominant groupings need not be based on a strict equating of linguistic proficiency, as learning proceeds better with redundant input. Children who are more proficient are reinforced in their knowledge, and even learn more profoundly, by helping demonstrate their newly acquired skills to students at less proficient levels (Thonis, 1980). Pairing proficient new immigrants with less proficient children or those in the process of primary language restoration has also been found an effective way to provide meaningful input in real communicative situations and expand relative proficiency. Vocabulary is learned rapidly, and anxiety about making mistakes is low in peer situations. Some migrant programs are on a staggered school year, and fluent primary language cross-age tutors can be enlisted as classroom partners for low proficiency children.

The school day must be structured to allow much primary language used for communicative intent: planning plays, parties, field trips, and other activities; sharing real experiences; and discussing real events, inside and outside the classroom (discussed in the last section). Children acquiring their primary language need non-threatening opportunities to practice it, not teacher correction! Talking to dolls, classroom pets, or younger children is most comfortable.

Bilingual teachers need to develop richer gestural systems and simple ways to code recurrent events in the class schedule so all children, whatever their linguistic background, can participate from their first day of school—especially if they enroll late. Cards with symbols representing milk money, circle time, library time, and learning center time can be used to signal transitions. Since children learn from the total school program, the teaching staff must plan ample opportunities daily for spontaneous primary language use by the children, in the classroom and on the playground. Using the primary language needs to be a happy experience. Filmstrips, jokes, riddles, folk sayings, songs, dances, poems, and family stories can be shared indoors; jump rope, rhymes, games, rhymes children make while singing, swinging, and jumping can be noted; exchange visits to bilingual classrooms on the site made; and enlisting of newly arrived primary language speakers as resource persons can enrich the joy of children learning more about their home language. However, it is obvious that bilingual curricula offered at the school site level must be redesigned to offer substantially greater primary language input.

Though there is no single optimal amount appropriate for every school in California, some generalizations can be made from examining exemplary programs. One frequent option, particularly useful with children who have minimal or no English proficiency, is to offer instruction about 70 percent in the primary language in grades K-2, with the balance of the day in English, emphasizing ESL planned instruction and using highly contextualized materials such as manipulatives for mathematics. Pairing children with bilingual or fluent-English speakers for electives, recess, etc., will also help English acquisition. Normally, children will be reading in their primary language by the second grade. Gradually, more instruction in English will be given in grades 2-6, and introduction to English reading will normally occur, usually with little help, by the third grade. Instruction will now be about 50 percent in each language. In grades 4-6, this ratio will continue, for continued growth in primary language and English skills. Children in such a program will not experience the *subtractive bilingualism* or *limited bilingualism* suffered by children who are exited from bilingual programs too early: Those with less than the four or more years of formal instruction in the primary language needed to reach the threshold of cognitive-academic linguistic proficiency (CALP) (Cummins, 1981). To assess whether or not CALP in the primary language is present, tests of reading are appropriate measures.

2. How should primary language instruction be delivered?

One of two methods of lesson delivery is usually found in bilingual classrooms: (1) Concurrent use of primary language and English; or (2) Alternate L_1/L_2 use, usually with language dominant groupings.

Concurrent translation is used in many bilingual programs today. It is operationally defined by the Office of Bilingual-Bicultural Education thus: "During lessons, two languages are used interchangeably. Special care is taken to avoid direct translation. One person may deliver the lessons using both languages or two teachers/aides may be utilized, each modeling a different language" (Office of Bilingual-Bicultural Education, 1979, p. 4). Although the guidelines specify that direct translation is discouraged, in actual bilingual classrooms, this usually is not the case. Much material is presented in direct translation, with mid-sentence switching of languages, or mid-phrase mixing:

"You're resting nicely—*sin movar los brazos.*"
"I squeeze the glue bottle *despacio.*"
If two persons team-teach, every part of the lesson may be repeated.

Recent research evidence indicates that use of the concurrent method seems to be less effective in developing primary language, and in acquiring English, than the alternate L_1/L_2 method of lesson delivery (Mackey, 1972; Cohen, 1973; Legarreta, 1979). In the Mackey (1972) program (the John F. Kennedy School, Berlin), teachers reported that the bilingual approach used a "mixed" or concurrent use of languages, slowed down both learning and their teaching, and that "many of the American students spoke a type of mixed language, more akin to the Pennsylvania-Dutch than German" (McLaughlin, 1978, p. 158).

In the Cohen study (1973), the teaching staff mixed the primary language and English to provide a concept-by-concept translation, which was frequently sentence-by-sentence throughout the day. In this approach, the Anglo students learned almost none of the primary language of the non-English proficient (NEP) children, simply because they could use English as fully as the teaching staff did. Students mixed languages more than did the Mexican-American children in all-English programs. In general, this method of language delivery was ineffective with Anglo students and only partly effective for the Mexican-Americans (Cohen, 1973).

The writer studied six bilingual classrooms, five of which used the concurrent method, and one that used an alternate L_1/L_2 (direct) AM/PM switch. The Hispanic students were monolingual Spanish speakers at the beginning of the kindergarten year. They were pre-tested by peer testers on comprehension, vocabulary, production, and *communicative competence* in both Spanish and English, and posttested six months later by the same peer testers, native speakers of Spanish or English, to find out how much they had learned. The testing situation was modified so children felt comfortable: Fruit and sweets were served, games were first played with the young testers, and testing was done in familiar settings (Legarreta, 1979). When scores were analyzed, it was found that the Concurrent Translation approach was significantly less effective than the alternate L_1/L_2 approach in producing gains in oral comprehension of English and in communicative competence in both Spanish and English.

During this past year, Wong-Fillmore (1980) has done extensive videotaping in Spanish and Chinese bilingual programs, using the "concurrent translation" and "alternate L_1/L_2 (direct)" delivery method. She noted:

> *Miss C relied on a [concurrent] "translation approach" toward language use as her primary instructional strategy. Miss C almost always said things twice, first in one language, and then, exactly translated, in the other. At times, Miss C used only English in her group lessons, but, by agreement, her aide would repeat each sentence immediately in Spanish. Thus, in a kind of bilingual pas de deux, Miss C and her aide maintained the translation format in their teaching....However, this does not seem to work well, at least where language learning is concerned, since students apparently learn to ignore the language they do not understand. They know they can count on the message being given in the language they know, and hence, there is no motivation to try to figure out what is being said in English. We have numerous video-record observations of the students [Hispanic and Anglo] in this classroom alternately being attentive and inattentive as the teachers switch between languages in their lessons. During the times the language they do not understand is being spoken, the students simply stop listening. (Wong-Fillmore, 1980, pp. 28-29)*

Teachers using the "concurrent translation" delivery method also commented that they were always "switching gears linguistically" and found that teaching much like professional simultaneous translators do is very tiring. Sometimes teachers would say things that were idiomatically incorrect in their primary language because they were translating directly from English (Cohen, 1973).

This language delivery method has other drawbacks: "It tends to be boring, the child just waits to hear the lesson in the known language, and lessons are unicultural" (Andersson and Boyer, 1970, p. 102). Wong-Fillmore (1980) notes that teachers using this method tend not to modify their translation to the level of the child's proficiency in the primary language, nor do they feel it is necessary to use a rich gestural system or concrete visual demonstrations to help the child's comprehension. It's enough that everything is being translated! But such translation does not serve as "comprehensible input" to language learners new to either language.

The Alternate L_1/L_2 (direct) model may be either an:

(a) Alternate days approach, based on the Philippine model (Tucker *et al.*, 1970). Here, the classroom language and curriculum shift daily between two languages, so that language use was 50/50.

(b) Morning-afternoon switch, as exemplified in the Coral Way-Miami Schools (de Inclan, 1971), which relies on team teaching, with each member stronger in one language. Concepts and instruction utilize one language in the morning, the other in the afternoon.

(c) "Preview-Review" technique (Krear, 1977), in which material is previewed in one language and presented in the other. Later, the class reviews the materials in the preview language. The two languages are thus used about equally.

(d) "Language dominant groupings" in subject matter also utilize the alternate L_1/L_2 (direct) method of lesson delivery. In this fourth method, the most popular variant of this model, children are grouped by language dominance, and instructed in discrete groups, with appropriate materials in that language. The writer has seen all four variants in bilingual classrooms being effectively used, with each choice reflecting staffing patterns, classroom ethnicity, and language dominance at the site. Research findings from programs using this lesson delivery approach are positive, as noted above. Another example from the early '60s, well before bilingual education became popular, is in the Miami schools, which became inundated with Cuban refugee children. The first full bilingual program in the United States was initiated in 1963 at the Coral Way School, using the alternate L_1/L_2 lesson delivery approach. By sixth grade, both Spanish- and English-dominant children in this program scored as well in English subjects as children taught only in English. The Spanish-dominant children read equally well in Spanish or English; the English-dominant children were somewhat weaker in

Spanish reading but all were fully bilingual speakers and readers (Richardson, 1968; de Inclan, 1971, 1977).

What appears to be happening in the bilingual alternate L_1/L_2 approaches, with balanced input of Spanish and English, is that children are really beginning to learn to understand and use English, while also developing their primary language and academic skills. Since they are alternately immersed in their primary language and then in the second language, they are forced to begin to sort out the English input they hear, using context and other cues. They then begin to construct hypotheses about its form and their functions, just as they did in acquiring their primary language. This method also has almost no language mixing on the part of the staff or children. Wong-Fillmore (1980) comments on the alternate L_1/L_2 (direct) approach:

> This is the method by which each lesson is taught directly, either in English or in the home language, with the use of translation kept to a minimum. This ordinarily works in such a way that lessons in a particular subject area are given in English on certain days, and in the other languages at other times, with no repeats given of the same lesson. This method seems clearly the best, but it obviously puts a heavy burden on both the students and the teacher. The teachers have to figure out how the materials to be taught can be communicated to those students who do not understand the language of instruction well enough to know what is being said, and the students need to be more than ordinarily attentive to what the teacher is doing and saying during the lesson. This means that the lesson must involve enough of the kinds of experiences (e. g., demonstrations, participation in ongoing activities) which permit the children to figure out what the point of the lesson is even if they do not understand what is being said, or could not understand it out of context. This kind of approach requires a lot of planning, preparation and imagination on the part of the teacher. Our current research, however, indicates that it is worth the effort. In contrast to the translation method, the direct approach seems to work well both for subject matter learning and for second language learning. (p. 9)

The work of the teaching staff in any variant of alternate L_1/L_2 (by days, AM/PM switch, preview-review, or language dominant groupings) may be greater, as Wong-Fillmore notes; but teachers are not feeling exhausted from "switching gears linguistically" or uneasy from non-idiomatic translating, as in the Concurrent Translation approach. Nor are they mixing languages. The language models, primary language and English, are clear. Since teachers cannot "fall back" on English for enrichment materials in a school subject, children will benefit from more complete presentations of subject matter in their primary language. The requisite addition of cognitive-competence (Cognitive/Academic Language Proficiency) to the linguistic competence (Basic Interpersonal Communicative Skills) primary language speakers bring to formal schooling will be facilitated by the alternate L_1/L_2 method of lesson delivery.

3. What variety of the primary language should the teaching staff use?

Unless the bilingual community and parents of the children involved decide otherwise, the bilingual program teaching staff should speak an informal standard variety of the primary language: one that reflects their country of origin, if they are native speakers, or their training, if their second language is the minority language. Every language, of course, includes specific manners of speaking, or "registers" which differ, for example, when educated adults are speaking to each other or when educated adults are teaching children. Every language also has certain ways to signal affection, acceptance, or closeness; and the primary language teacher must freely speak this way to the children. Frequently, teacher aides will be drawn from the minority language community and will naturally speak the local variety used in the children's homes. This is always an asset for the bilingual program. Teachers need to reflect their professional training in their use of the primary language; but this must never be done at the expense of their students' self-image, which is based on the language variety they bring to school. Thus, primary language teaching must be based in the variety the children bring from their homes based on the local adult speech. If this variety contains forms different from that of some of the teaching staff, and it invariably will, these should not be "marked" by singling them out for correction. The American Association of Teachers of Spanish and Portuguese recommends that:

> Especially in the case of learners whose dialect differs markedly from world standard Spanish, the first weeks, months, or even the entire first year—should focus patiently on developing their self-confidence as speakers and writers of their own kind of Spanish. (Gaardner, 1971, p. 5)

All studies of non-standard varieties of language or "social dialects" demonstrate very clearly that the number and frequency of non-standard forms spoken is very small, and these do not interfere with communicative intent. The primary language, and any and all languages that are "alive" (i.e., spoken), are rich in varieties or dialects: Central Standard Mexican Spanish, that spoken in Jalisco, Michoacan, and

Mexico City, is different from the Spanish of LaHabaña, Cuba; the "*Carioca*" of Rio de Janeiro is different from the Portuguese of the Azore Islands; and the Cantonese of Canton is different from that of San Francisco. These differences (or "non-standard" forms) in phonology, vocabulary, and intonation patterns do not make the language varieties mutually unintelligible, since the underlying semantics as well as the syntax are rarely at variance. A recent example is the showing of old American western television programs, e. g., "*Bonanza,*" "*Gunsmoke,*" and "*Little House on the Prairie,*" which are very popular in Castilian-speaking Spain. They are telecast with dubbed-in Mexico City Spanish. Everyone in Spain understands and enjoys them in spite of many differences in vocabulary, phonology, intonation patterns, and even grammar or syntax. Unfortunately, there frequently is prejudice against non-standard speakers of any language, and this includes their children. However, formal differences between regional and social language varieties, or "dialects," are really superficial and meaningless when viewed in terms of the basic goals of bilingual classrooms. The sensitive bilingual teacher will accept the children's speech patterns, phonology, and vocabulary, and then carefully extend them to demonstrate, over and over again, that there are many different ways to say the same thing. Among any bilingual staff, from disparate primary language backgrounds, a variety of social dialects can be naturally demonstrated to the children. The teacher can also demonstrate the forms most appropriate for various domains of use, e. g., informal joke-telling vs. answering the bishop at confirmation. Children can thereby add social dialects to their primary language repertoire, becoming *additive bilingual* speakers. Frequently, too, purchased primary language reading materials reflect a regional variety of the language, and the teacher can note these variations to the children.

It has been noted by researchers on child language acquisition that many so-called "errors" children make are developmental and will disappear as they mature. Common Spanish language examples, due to children's overgeneralization of regular verb patterns, are "*Yo sabo eso*" and "*Yo lo hazo.*" Such overgeneralization is a language acquisition strategy all children use ("runned" and "feets" are English examples). To correct such "errors" is not useful for two reasons:

(a) Research on child language acquisition shows that children apparently do not process such correction and continue to produce the overgeneralized form until the correct irregular form is internalized naturally as an exception to the pattern: "runned-ran" (Slobin, 1971).

(b) When children are corrected, they may shift to use of a more primitive form, and may even be rewarded for this. Providing a good

primary language model with comprehensive input is a much more productive technique than correction.

Since children live in communities where languages are in contact, very
frequently, English words are mixed into primary language sentences or
anglicized forms are used: *"es un skyscraper"* and *"voy a correctar
eso."* In areas where much Black English is heard, this may also be
mixed in. It has been shown (Hernandez-Chavez, 1980) that these
"borrowings" may serve as initial steps in acquiring a second language,
as "place holders." Again, the bilingual teaching staff need only take
care not to mix languages in their teaching and continue to provide clear
primary language models. Teacher attitudes are important. Many
bilingual teacher trainers, workshop leaders, and researchers in bilingual
classrooms have noted the very apparent prejudice often demonstrated
by bilingual teachers toward a child's use of "non-standard" forms of
the primary language, particularly with middle-class, Mexican-American
teachers or those trained professionally in South American countries.
This attitude clearly negates many of the benefits of bilingual schooling.
Stigmatizing, in any way, a child's home language, always produces bad
effects, lowered self-esteem, lowered motivation to learn the primary
language, sometimes even a disassociation from the family's culture.
Bilingual teachers with negative attitudes toward regional varieties of the
primary language need to re-examine affective aspects of the teaching
process and root out this prejudice. The variety the children use must be
respected and extended in a non-judgmental way.

4. Why and how can we ensure the prestige of the primary language in school settings?

Whenever a primary language or language variety is disvalued by the
dominant culture, its place in a bilingual program is less secure. Con-
versely, certain primary languages (e. g., French and German) confer
prestige upon their users and may serve as a marker of an educated,
cultured person. Andersson (1976) notes that 15 years ago, even "bilingual" had totally negative connotations. Specifically, it "meant Mexican, that is, poor, lower class, uneducated, and, we inferred,
uneducable" (p. 498) to educators in the Southwest. Though such
linguistic prejudices are totally irrational, they still exist; and we cannot
simply ignore them. Rather, professionals in bilingual education need to
demonstrate consciously the prestige of primary languages other than
English.

We know that bilingual children quickly learn the *relative* prestige of
their primary language *vis-à-vis* the dominant language, English. This is
made explicit by bilingual teaching staff in several ways, the major one,

of course, being the proportion of the primary language the teacher uses in formal teaching as well as the choice of language used to talk to aides, student teachers, colleagues, and important visitors from outside the school.

There is also evidence that teachers tend to speak the primary language consciously and deliberately, while using English in a spontaneous and casual (unmarked) manner. This also is communicated to the children (Shultz, 1975). Other unconscious "markers" are found such as bilingual teacher's frequent switch to English for all disciplinary speech, or to signal an important transition in teaching (Legarreta, 1977). Many bilingual programs teach "core" subjects (reading and mathematics) and use the primary language only for electives such as art and music (Lesley, 1972).

To counteract all these practices and thereby raise the status of the primary language, bilingual teachers must first become conscious of their language choices in and out of the bilingual classroom. Then they need to monitor their language choices to ensure that the primary language is accorded prestige. One bilingual program provides these directions:

> *The teacher should address other adults in Spanish in order to show the children that the language has prestige among adults. The teacher should be particularly careful to address outside visitors who know Spanish in this language. (Ramirez, 1974, p. 136)*

It is very important for all children in a bilingual classroom—both minority and majority—to hear the primary language used by classroom teachers and aides, resource teachers, ESL pull-out teachers, cross-age tutors, parent volunteers, and the principal for informal, everyday communication, and for the salute to the flag, a formal event.

Language minority children will feel reassured that the language they speak at home is also a school language, appropriate for educated people to use. The English-speaking children will take notice also that the second language with which they are struggling is used in everyday situations by educated, powerful adults. Frequently, bilingual staff who have acquired their primary language fluency as adults need opportunities to practice some domains of language use not taught in language classes: how to convey acceptance, skepticism, how to joke, gossip, or negotiate, etc. Native speakers can help by providing opportunities for such primary language practice, rather than switch to English, in the teacher's lounge, on the playground, and in social situations such as school events. An excellent opportunity to utilize the primary language is in the inservice training necessary in bilingual programs.

Bilingual teacher trainers report that they personally address colleagues at their universities and colleges in the primary language. They
also help student teachers to become less self-conscious when they use the
primary language in teaching. One professor commented:

> *Student teachers need to hear courses such as "Educational*
> *Psychology" taught in the primary language—theoretical*
> *courses, as well as the practical, methods courses—and more*
> *of us are doing our lectures in the primary language.*

Workshop leaders, too, are presenting many more training sessions in
the primary language.

At the school site or district level, on-going course work in the primary
language can be offered through arrangements with local adult education
programs. Many teachers who are not working in bilingual programs are
anxious to improve their own language skills. Principals, as educational
leaders of a school, can serve as effective models to the school staff by
enrolling, as can school board members. Sometimes, bilingual programs
seem isolated within a school or ignored or envied by non-bilingual staff.
Some teachers' lounges appear almost segregated. To overcome this and
encourage the free flow of information and teaching techniques so vital
to a school, two-way bilingualism would be ideal since all children would
be better served. As a first step, there are useful booklets, e. g., *Spanish
Phrases for Schools* (available from P.O. Box 28, Fullerton, California)
to help all school personnel communicate more effectively with primary
language children. Parent classroom volunteers can be encouraged to
begin the process of becoming bilingual also. One program has a bilingual teacher exchange program with Mexico, which includes sharing
of research information.

For students from English-speaking homes, the second language component in a bilingual program is an excellent vehicle for adding prestige
to the primary language. These lessons need to be planned, of high quality, e. g., comprehensible and personally meaningful to the students.
Their place in the curriculum is analogous to the ESL component, which
invariably commands "prime time" in bilingual programs. Here, again,
opportunities for natural language use abound, with primary language
speakers available for peer tutoring and practice. Outside the classroom,
opportunities for primary language use are endless: mealtime conversations, playground interaction, planned games at recess, music and dance
outdoors, on trips to points of interest in the primary language community, and in sports events. The kind and amount of encouragement L_2
learners receive from their first produced words forward is important.

It has been demonstrated in several research studies that children from
primary language homes almost immediately model their language

choice on that of the teacher (Bruck *et al.*, 1979; Legarreta, 1977). When teachers, as a matter of course, respond in English to students' questions or comments in the minority language, the message is unmistakable. To ensure primary language status, children must hear it being used.

Other ways to enhance the prestige of the primary language include inviting prominent persons who speak this language to talk to the class or to assemblies. Clergymen, businessmen, store owners, professionals, artists, union people, alumni of the school who have gone on to college, and local sports figures, are usually willing to come. In the classroom, the prestige of the primary language is enhanced by using poetry, drama, and literature written in the countries where primary language children have their roots. A good supply of attractive reference books and dictionaries in the primary language that are appropriate to the classroom levels of the children are also essential. Too often, a large and colorful selection of hardcover books for English pleasure reading can be found in bilingual classrooms, contrasting with a much smaller selection of colorless dog-eared paperback books, alphabet level books, and basic reader series in the primary language. More subtle markers to increase primary language status include equality in size and placement of classroom labels in each language, relative importance of posters in each language, student work, instructions on the blackboard, and so on. Stopgaps such as covering the English text on worksheets in mathematics with a xeroxed translation in the primary language also help, though commercial workbooks are better and available. Signs in public areas of the school site in both languages—halls, bathroom, and cafeteria—also signal the relative importance of the languages.

5. How can primary language use be *monitored:* a formative evaluation process?

Monitoring of actual language use is a valuable formative evaluation measure, since bilingual teachers can consciously modify their language choices depending on the results of the monitoring. It is important to note, once again, that language choice for important language functions in the classroom such as "solidarity" and "cooling/disciplining" need to be considered as well. The bilingual teaching staff's choices between the primary language/English are important signals to linguistic minority children.

Is it necessary for teachers in bilingual classrooms to "monitor" their language use? Clearly, research tells us the answer is "yes." Lesley (1972) found that in 21 bilingual programs in California, teachers in six classrooms used English over 75 percent of the time; another 12 used

English from at least 50 to 75 percent of the time, and three used 25 percent English. These results were based on the teacher's self-report, which, unfortunately, is not reliable, since many balanced bilingual speakers are not consciously aware of which language they are using at a given time (Gumperz, 1970). Many bilingual teachers are convinced they are teaching in Spanish much more of the time than a quantitative assessment, an actual count of their Spanish and English talk shows. In the writer's research in bilingual classrooms (Legarreta, 1977), teachers and aides have been confident that they use Spanish and English about equally. When classroom interaction was assessed quantitatively to arrive at actual percentages of Spanish and English used, it was found that in classrooms using Concurrent Translation, English was used by both the teacher and the aide, on an average, nearly three-quarters (72 percent) of the time; and Spanish was being used just over one-quarter (28 percent) of the time.

In this research, a quantitative coding technique, the *Flanders Interaction Analysis Instrument,* was adapted to be used in a bilingual setting; and the functions of talk teachers and children use (warming, amplifying, directing, responding, correcting, and cooling) were noted. Classroom interaction was tallied every three seconds, 100 tallies every five minutes of classroom time. A full class day was coded for the four Concurrent Translation classrooms and two days in the Alternate L_1/L_2 classroom. All bilingual classrooms had native Spanish-speaking teachers and aides.

In the four classrooms utilizing Concurrent Translation as the language model, English was spoken most of the time by teachers and pupils. The range was 59 to 84 percent, with an average of 72 percent of English used during a typical session by teachers.

In contrast, in the Alternate Periods model, teachers produced nearly equal amounts of English and Spanish (53/47). Spanish-speaking children spoke English to the teacher/aide an average of 71 percent of the time in the Concurrent Translation classrooms with the range being 52 to 93 percent. Again, the Alternate Days classroom maintained parity in language choice by pupils (49 percent).

Since there was considerable symmetry between teacher talk and Spanish-speaking pupil talk in all classrooms considered, it appears that Spanish-speaking children reflect the language choices of teacher/aide, regardless of the bilingual model used (Concurrent Translation or Alternate Days).

This represents a dramatic shift in language use by Spanish-speaking five-year-olds in Concurrent Translation classrooms. In the short span of about nine weeks of formal schooling, children who speak only Spanish in their homes, neighborhoods, and churches* are apparently already reflecting the vastly different language input in the schools by bilingual teacher/aides.

The study also showed that bilingual teachers in the Concurrent Translation classrooms used an average 77 percent English for "solidarity" functions (e. g., warming, accepting, or amplifying pupil talk), while the Alternate L_1/L_2 teaching staff used much more Spanish (72 percent) for this function. For giving directions or directing pupil work, Concurrent Translation classrooms averaged 72 percent English and 62 percent Spanish for Alternate L_1/L_2. Interestingly, *all* classrooms, including the Alternate L_1/L_2 classroom, used English well over half the time (58 to 91 percent) to discipline (cool) pupils. In the Concurrent Translation classrooms, there were 189 instances of switching language (70 percent from English to Spanish), since English was used so predominantly. The Alternate L_1/L_2 classroom rarely switched (11 instances), and switching was from Spanish to English to reprimand Black and Anglo children.

Recall that all teaching staff stated that the primary language and English were being used equally. However, this only occurred in the Alternate L_1/L_2 approach. Here, again, solidarity functions of language were generally in the child's vernacular, while cooling and correcting functions were more equal in each language than in the Concurrent Translation classrooms. Additionally, a consistent language model was presented to the pupils, with code-switching occurring *very* infrequently. Since the ethnic mix in the bilingual classrooms was 65 percent Spanish-speaking, with about half of these children being monolingual Spanish, it seems fair to conclude that the language choices of the teachers/aides in the Concurrent Translation model were far from optimal: They did not reflect the classroom ethnic mix, nor the communicative repertoires of the majority of pupils served, nor the goals of bilingual education. Instead of producing bilingual pupils, a language environment so heavily English-dominated discriminates against Spanish-speaking pupils and discourages Anglo pupils from learning Spanish as well. Rather than being bilingual education, capitalizing on the unique linguistic and cultural backgrounds of Latino children, the Concurrent Translation model studied is a rapid transition-to-English program.

Despite teachers/aides' sincere and conscious commitment to bilingual teaching, they seem overwhelmed by the pull of the dominant

---

*"A Pupil's Language Use Inventory" (Fishman *et al.*, 1971), given in Spanish to all Spanish-speaking pupils, indicated that Spanish was spoken overwhelmingly (95 percent) in the domains of home, neighborhood, church, and recess.

language and culture, with the result that English becomes the classroom language. This phenomenon was also noted by Shultz (1975) who saw it as another example of an implicit decision by bilingual staff that English was the "advantageous and natural language of the classroom."

From the above, it is clear that bilingual teachers need to self-monitor their language use. Ways to do this include:

(a) With a tape recorder the staff in each classroom can tape one another randomly over several days, being sure to include all subjects and activities in a typical class day, using a separate tape for each teacher. As the tape is played back, stop the playback at every language choice or change a teacher makes while writing down the number of seconds each language is used, timed with a stopwatch or clock with a second hand.

(b) A simple coding technique can be learned in an hour, and language use of bilingual teachers and aides can be easily monitored by a resource specialist as a means of improving the delivery of bilingual education. (See Appendix 1 for sample coding sheet.)

(c) A classroom language checklist may also be prepared, with a profile of language choice by subject matter, groupings, and activity. Then teaching staff can time, with a stopwatch, their *actual* instruction in the primary language. This "self-coding" is tedious, but results are illuminating.

(d) Videotaping has been used, but it is costly and time consuming. It is an excellent training vehicle and the most complete way to monitor language choice.

Natural Resource for Natural Primary Language Use

As noted in the introduction, research evidence indicates that threshold proficiency in the primary language will assist in academic success and in acquisition of English. To acquire this level of proficiency, the school bilingual program is crucial. Equally important is the home, where linguistic minority children acquire their basic language skills. Encouraging parents, older siblings, relatives, extended family, and honorary family members (godparents, etc.) to use the primary language freely with the child is essential. Families, especially mothers (Cohen, in press) have many misgivings about using the primary language. They sometimes feel a child is wasting time by not studying in an English-only classroom. They need much reassurance that the child learns better in the primary language; that they, the parents, are expected to help with homework and be involved in their child's education and that the child is also learning the English language at school.

The full utilization of family resources must be part of the ongoing parent involvement component. Bilingual staff need to visit homes early in the year to explain bilingual education and its advantages to children. (A suggested diagram to help explain linguistic interdependence to parents will be given in Appendix 2.) The primary language link between home and school can be forged in a wide variety of ways after the initial home visit. Some suggestions to the families can include:

1. Having parents and/or older siblings, literate in the primary language, read stories aloud to the child. Durkin's (1972) study indicates reading aloud to young children is the single most effective key to reading success.

2. Participation in the home-school library program, where children bring primary language stories, magazines, and books home weekly for family use.

3. Encouraging parents, relatives, and honorary family members to tell stories, folk tales, sayings, riddles, jokes, etc., from the primary language culture to the children.

4. Wider use of radio and TV programs and movies in the primary language. Teachers can prepare a monthly list of these and other community cultural events given in the primary language for parents.

5. Flexibly scheduled visits to the classroom, including babies and relatives, to learn about bilingual education firsthand.

6. Request for cooperation of parents when children are preparing assignments. This includes help with homework as well as sharing memories when class is making family trees, writing autobiographies, letters to relatives, etc.

7. Encouraging parents to share records, photos, letters, artisanry, etc., from the primary language culture, with responsible use assured by the teacher.

8. Encouraging parents or relatives to share their cultural knowledge of growing, preparing, and preserving food and medicinal plants, traditional celebrations, music, dance, poetry, clothing, etc., with the school.

9. Providing in-service training in the primary language to parents in how to help with homework, through home visits, meetings, notes home, etc.

Bilingual teachers will also find many resources within the school. Too often, the bilingual program is a separate "island" in a school. This isolation is counterproductive to learning. Bilingual teachers need to reach out to all the school staff, both to reassure them, and to exchange teaching ideas that work for all children. Resources in the district must be located: Sometimes it is a treasure hunt, in that more materials are available than was thought. Community people, including clergymen, professionals, businessmen, athletes, musicians, artists, and union people fluent in the primary language can be good resources.

Recess and lunch period can be used for natural primary language input to informal settings, using teaching staff and groupings of "best friends" to cue primary language use. What follows are practical suggestions for natural language use at school:

1. Language arts, literacy, and creative writing. (Remember that literacy and writing are presented together in the countries of origin of many primary languages.)

2. *Home-School Library Program*—children take home books on a weekly basis written in primary language to read to parents, for parents to read, for references, etc.

3. *Story charts*—of children's stories in primary language to be illustrated by children and parents.

4. *Autobiography*—of each child with family tree and photos (on loan) of family members through grandparents. Make a class book of these and include teaching staff and principal.

5. *Sayings and riddles*—from their parents: books of examples, illustrated by children, in the classroom library.

6. *Recipes*—gathered and illustrated by children, with their comments. Some can be tried out in class cooking projects.

7. *Board games*—in primary language, crossword puzzles, word bingo, and scrabble.

8. *Comics*—write own captions on culturally relevant comics (Hispanic: *Los Agachados, Mafalda,* etc.

9. *Much recognition*—for fluent primary language readers in school and community. Example: Certificate when 10 books in primary language are completed, plus letter in primary language to parents of this achievement.

10. *Class-made books*—on field trips, pets, birthday parties, favorite songs, etc., in primary language.

11. *Dictation*—by teacher.

12. *Teacher and class*—collect menus, newspapers, comics, songs, recipes, filmstrips, fashion-beauty-sports magazines, short books, advertisements, etc., in the primary languages of the children so that the *learning centers* are fresh and interesting. These can be made with individual "carrels" or spaces made with cardboard

boxes. Children can work undisturbed with self-chosen primary language materials.

13. *Language masters*—made from children's language variety, e. g., different ways to say "X." Example: *cacahuate, mani* for *peanut.*

14. *Teacher*—in K-3, and later, the children themselves, can *write down* taped stories in primary language.

15. *Children*—draw and caption pictures to illustrate stories read to them in primary language.

16. *Poetry and rhymes*—in primary language on large charts—children's use of syllabization and recognition; illustrates vocabulary, word patterns, and rhyming words; it's best to use new words right away.

17. *Picture cards for vocabulary*—made by children.

18. *Daily work plan*—in primary language, discuss with class in circle time.

19. *Children write letters to relatives*—take to post office and mail.

20. *Children write captions*—for photos and pictures teacher brings in primary language.

21. *Frequent group discussions*—in primary language on relevant topics, e. g., why people come to the United States, frightening experiences, how people celebrate holidays, etc.

22. *Puppets, doll corner, pets*—are good contexts to encourage informal primary language practice.

23. *Listening post*—stories in primary languages, followed by discussion.

24. *Class produced dialogues, plays, and dramatized stories.*

25. *Published creative writing*—(mimeographed) in school newspaper.

26. *Oral book reports*—weekly, in the primary language to build confidence.

27. *Songbook*—of primary language songs from homes.

28. *Class puzzles*—using a grid (teacher made) for question-asking skills.

29. *Peer tutors*—fluent in the primary language, for informal practice on a regular basis; they can reinforce learning.

30. *Creative writing*—in the primary language can be published in local paper; recognition is important.

31. *Culturally relevant*—art and craft activities encourage natural primary language use and parent involvement.

32. *Music program*—can use the primary language and be based on

culturally-relevant materials.

33. *"Generative Word" literacy method*—(Freire) can be used, eliciting important words in the primary language from the class and illustrating them for personal dictionaries.

By using such resources within the home, classroom, and school, the effective use of the child's primary language will be assured. Cognitive competence and school success will follow, for all children.

REFERENCES

Andersson, Theodore. "Popular and Elite Bilingualism Reconciled," *Hispania,* LIX, No. 3 (September, 1976), 497-499.

____, and Mildred Boyer. *Bilingual Schooling in the United States.* Austin, Texas: Southwest Educational Laboratory Publishers, Inc., 1970.

Boggs, Stephen T. "The Meaning of Questions and Narratives to Hawaiian Children," *Functions of Language in the Classroom,* eds., Courtney B. Cazden, Vera P. John, and Dell Hymes. New York: Teachers College Press, 1972, pp. 299-327.

Bruck, Margaret, Jeffrey Schultz, and Flora V. Rodriguez-Brown. "Assessing Language Use in Bilingual Classrooms: An Ethnographic Analysis," *Papers in Applied Linguistics: Evaluating Evaluation.* Arlington, Virginia: Center for Applied Linguistics, 1979.

Carter, Thomas P. *Mexican-Americans in School: A History of Educational Neglect.* New York: College Entrance Examination Board, 1970.

Chomsky, Carol. *The Acquisition of Syntax in Children from 5 to 10.* Cambridge, Massachusetts: M.I.T. Press, 1969.

Cohen, Andrew D. "Bilingual Education for a Bilingual Community," *Bilingual Education and Public Policy in the USA,* ed., Raymond V. Padilla. Rowley, Massachusetts: Newbury House, in press.

____. "Innovative Education for La Raza, A Sociolinguistic Assessment of a Bilingual Program." Unpublished PhD dissertation, Stanford University, 1973.

Collison, G. Omani. "Concept Formation in a Second Language: A Study of Ghanaian School Children," *Harvard Educational Review,* XLIV, No. 3 (August, 1974), 441-457.

Cornejo, Ricardo. *A Synthesis of Theories and Research on Teaching in First and Second Languages.* Los Angeles, California: University of California, Los Angeles, Center for the Study of Evaluation, 1974.

Covey, D. "An Analytical Study of Secondary Freshmen: Bilingual Education and Its Effect on Academic Achievement and Attitudes of Mexican-American Students." Unpublished PhD dissertation, Arizona State University, 1973.

Cummins, James. "The Construct of Language Proficiency in Bilingual Education." Paper presented at the Georgetown Round Table on Language and Linguistics, Georgetown University, March, 1980.

____. "Linguistic Interdependence and the Educational Development of Bilingual Children," *Bilingual Education Paper Series.* Vol. 3 No. 2. Los Angeles: National Dissemination and Assessment Center, California State University, Los Angeles, September, 1979.

____. "The Role of Primary Language Development in Promoting Educational Success for Language Minority Students," *Schooling and Language Minority Students: A Theoretical Framework.* Los Angeles, California: Evaluation, Dissemination and Assessment Center, California State University, Los Angeles, 1981.

Darcy, Natalie T. "A Review of the Literature on the Effects of Bilingualism Upon the Measurement of Intelligence," *Journal of Genetic Psychology,* LXXXII (March, 1953), 21-57.

de Inclan, Rosa. "Bilingual Schooling in Dade County," *Bilingualism in Early Childhood: Papers from a Conference on Child Language,* eds., William F. Mackey, and Theodore Andersson. Rowley, Massachusetts: Newbury House, 1977.

_____. "An Updated Report of Bilingual Schooling in Dade County." Paper presented at the 1971 Conference on Child Language, Chicago, Illinois, 1971.

Dolson, David. "Bilingual Education Program Standards: Advancement by a State Education Agency." Paper presented at the TESOL Conference, San Francisco, California, March, 1980.

Dumont, Robert V. "Learning English and How to be Silent: Studies in Sioux and Cherokee Classrooms," *Functions of Language in the Classroom,* eds., Courtney B. Cazden, Vera P. John, and Dell Hymes. New York: Teachers College Press, 1972, pp. 344-369.

Durkin, Dolores. *Teaching Young Children to Read.* Boston, Massachusetts: Allyn & Bacon, 1972.

Engle, Patricia. "The Use of the Vernacular Languages in Education: Revisited." University of Chicago, 1973. (Mimeographed.)

Evaluation Associates. "Nestor School Bilingual Education Program Evaluation." Unpublished research report, San Diego, California, 1978.

Feldman, Carol, and Michael Shen. "Some Language-Related Cognitive Advantages of Bilingual Five-Year-Olds," *Journal of Genetic Psychology,* CXVIII (June, 1971), 235-244.

Fishman, Joshua A. "Language Maintenance and Language Shift," *Readings in the Sociology of Language.* Mouton: The Hague, 1970, pp. 585-660.

_____, Robert L. Cooper, and Roxana Ma. *Bilingualism in the Barrio.* Bloomington, Indiana: Indiana University Press, 1971.

Flanders, Ned A. *Analyzing Teacher Behavior.* Reading, Massachusetts: Addison-Wesley Publishing Co., 1970.

Gaardner, Bruce. "Teaching Spanish in Schools and Colleges to Native Speakers of Spanish." 1971. (Mimeographed.)

Gonzalez, Gustavo. "Teaching Bilingual Children," *Bilingual Education: Current Perspectives.* Arlington, Virginia: Center for Applied Linguistics, 1977-1978.

Gumperz, John. "Sociolinguistics and Communication in Small Groups," *Working Paper #33.* Berkeley, California: Language Behavioral Research Laboratory, University of California, Berkeley, 1970.

Hernandez-Chavez, Eduardo. Personal communication. 1980.

Hofman, J., and Haya Fisherman. "Language Shift and Language Maintenance in Israel," *Advances in the Sociology of Language,* ed., Joshua A. Fishman. Vol. II. Mouton: The Hague, 1972.

Ianco-Worrall, Anita D. "Bilingualism and Cognitive Development," *Child Development,* XLIII, No. 44 (December, 1972), 1390-1400.

Kessler, Carolyn, and Mary Ellen Quinn. "Bilingualism and Science Problem-Solving Ability," *Bilingual Education Paper Series.* Vol. 4 No. 1. Los Angeles, California: National Dissemination and Assessment Center, California State University, Los Angeles, August, 1980.

Krashen, Stephen D. "Bilingual Education and Second Language Acquisition," *Schooling and Language Minority Students: A Theoretical Framework.* Los Angeles, California: Evaluation, Dissemination and Assessment Center, California State University, Los Angeles, 1981.

Krear, S. "Pre-Reading Skills in a Second Language of Dialect," *Bilingualism in Early Childhood: Papers from a Conference on Child Language,* eds., William Francis Mackey, and Theodore Andersson. Rowley, Massachusetts: Newbury House, 1977.

Legarreta, Dorothy. "The Effects of Program Models on Language Acquisition by Spanish Speaking Children," *TESOL Quarterly,* XIII, No. 4 (December, 1979), 521-534.

____. "Fourteen Children: Barriers to Spanish-Speaking Children's Success in Traditional Classrooms," in press.

____. "Language Choice in Bilingual Classrooms," *TESOL Quarterly,* XI, No. 1 (March, 1977), 9-16.

Leibowitz, Arnold H. *Educational Policy and Political Acceptance: The Imposition of English as the Language of Instruction in American Schools.* U.S., Educational Resources Information Center, ERIC Document ED 047 321, March, 1971.

Lesley, T. "Bilingual Education in California." Unpublished MA thesis, University of California, Los Angeles, 1972.

Leyba, Charles F. *Longitudinal Study, Title VII Bilingual Program, Santa Fe Public Schools, Santa Fe, New Mexico.* Los Angeles, California: National Dissemination and Assessment Center, California State University, Los Angeles, 1978.

Liedtke, W. W., and L. D. Nelson. *Bilingualism and Conservation.* U.S., Educational Resources Information Center, ERIC Document ED 030 110, 1968.

Mackey, William Francis. *Bilingual Education in a Binational School.* Rowley, Massachusetts: Newbury House, 1972.

Macnamara, John Theodore. *Bilingualism and Primary Education: A Study of Irish Experience.* Edinburgh: Edinburgh University Press, 1966.

McLaughlin, Barry. *Second Language Acquisition in Childhood.* New York: John Wiley & Sons, 1978.

Morris, P. "Self-Concept and Ethnic Group Mixture Among Hispanic Students in Elementary Schools." Unpublished PhD dissertation, Columbia University, 1974.

Nespor, Helen. "The Effect of Foreign Language Training on Expressive Productivity in Oral Native Language." Unpublished PhD dissertation, University of California, Berkeley, 1969.

New York Bureau of Publications. "A Survey of the Public Educational System of Puerto Rico," Teachers College, Columbia University, 1926.

Office of Bilingual-Bicultural Education. *Program Quality Review Instrument.* Sacramento, California: California State Department of Education, 1979.

Philips, Susan U. "Participant Structures and Communicative Competence: Warm Springs Children in Community and Classroom," *Functions of Language in the Classroom,* eds., Courtney B. Cazden, Vera P. John, and Dell Hymes. New York: Teachers College Press, 1972, pp. 370-394.

Ramirez, G. "The Spoken English of Spanish-Speaking Pupils in a Bilingual and Monolingual School Setting." Unpublished PhD dissertation, Stanford University, 1974.

Ramirez, Manuel. "Current Educational Research: The Basis for a New Philosophy for Educating Mexican-Americans." Riverside, California: University of California, Riverside, 1974. (Mimeographed.)

Richardson, Mabel. "An Evaluation of Certain Aspects of Academic Achievement of Elementary Pupils in a Bilingual Program." University of Miami at Coral Gables, Florida, 1968. (Mimeographed.)

Rivera, E. "Academic Achievement, Bicultural Attitudes and Self-Concepts of Pupils in Bilingual and Non-Bilingual Programs." Unpublished PhD dissertation, Fordham University, 1973.

Rosier, Paul, and Merilyn Farella. "Bilingual Education at Rock Point—Some Early Results," *TESOL Quarterly,* X, No. 4 (December, 1976), 379-388.

Shultz, Jeffrey. "Language Use in Bilingual Classrooms." Harvard University, 1975. (Mimeographed.)

Singer, Harry. "Bilingualism and Elementary Education," *Modern Language Journal,* XL, No. 8 (1956), 444-458.

Skoczylas, V. "An Evaluation of Some Cognitive and Affective Aspects of a Spanish-English Bilingual Education Program." Unpublished PhD dissertation, University of New Mexico, 1972.

Skutnabb-Kangas, Tove. "Bilingualism, Semilingualism, and School Achievement." Paper presented at the 4th International Congress of Applied Linguistics, Stuttgart, 1975.

Slobin, Dan Isaac. *Psycholinguistics.* Glenview, Illinois: Scott, Foresman & Co., 1971.

Thonis, Eleanor W. Personal communication. 1980.

Title VII. "Interim Evaluation Reports: Los Angeles City Unified School District, San Francisco Unified School District, Valley Intercultural Programs." Washington, D.C.: Office of Education, 1975.

Tucker, G. Richard, B. P. Sibayan, and F. T. Otanes. "An Alternate Days Approach to Bilingual Education," *Report of the 21st Annual Round Table Meeting on Linguistics and Language Study,* ed., James E. Alatis. Washington, D.C.: Georgetown University Press, 1970, pp. 281-299.

UNESCO. *The Use of Vernacular Languages in Education.* Monographs on fundamental education. No. 8. Paris: UNESCO, 1953.

United States General Accounting Office. *Bilingual Education: An Unmet Need.* Washington, D.C.: Government Printing Office, 1976.

Wong-Fillmore, Lily. "Language Learning Through Bilingual Instruction." University of California, Berkeley, 1980. (Mimeographed.)

Appendix 1

CODING LANGUAGE CHOICE

The writer used a modified interaction analysis instrument, based on work by Flanders (1970). The following categories were used:

1. What language is being used? Spanish or English (in columns).

2. Who is speaking to whom?

    Code 1 = Teacher
    Code 2 = Aide
    Code 3 = Hispanic Student
    Code 4 = Anglo Student
    Code 5 = Group (i. e., whole class)

3. What is the speaker doing? functions of speech:*

    Solidarity functions: 1 = Warms, 2 = Accepts, 3 = Amplifies.
    Others: 4 = Elicits, 5 = Responds, 6 = Initiates, 7 = Directs.
    Distancing functions: 8 = Corrects, 9 = Cools, 10 = Silence or confusion.

---

*1. Warms = praises or encourages student action or behavior.
2. Accepts = uses ideas of students by clarifying or incorporating their ideas.
3. Amplifies = builds upon or develops student ideas.
4. Elicits = asks a question of student.

Appendix 1 (continued)

4.   **What is this event?**
      An event consisted, in this study, of a verbal interaction sequence
      characterized by a stable setting and grouping of pupils, and
      usually, adult initiated. A slash mark (/) indicated a change of
      event. Marginal notes were used to clarify events. Time bounding
      of a series of events (an activity) were also noted.

A sample of coding looks like this:

OBSERVATION TALLY SHEET

OBSERVER: *DL*   DATE: *12/5*   TEACHER CODE: *Aguirre*   TIME: *9:10*

SPAN.	ENG.	NOTES	SPAN.	ENG.	NOTES	SPAN.	ENG.	NOTES
132		Activity: Circle time *Muy bien, Carlos*			9:17 Math Activity			
133		*Quieres decir*						
133		*mas? Pues.../*						
	1G7	O.K., stand up						
	1G7	to play "Simon says"						

to 35   to 70   to 100
tallies   tallies   tallies

The observer codes every five seconds, or 12 times a minute. Marginal notes (Activity,
words, etc.) are optional. Coding should span several segments of different classroom activities to indicate the language choices of the teaching staff.

In this sample, "132" shows that a teacher was accepting what a Hispanic child said at
9:10. The teacher switched to English after 15 seconds to direct the group.

---

5. Responds = answers student question, lectures, etc.
6. Initiates = gives direction or suggestion to someone.
7. Directs = commands or gives order to which student must comply.
8. Corrects = rectifies student answer, justifies authority.
9. Cools = chastise student verbally to change behavior.
10. Silence or confusion = quiet or chaotic time.

Appendix 2

SOME SUGGESTIONS FOR SAMPLE MATERIAL TO INCLUDE ON A HOME VISIT TO FAMILIES OF PRIMARY-LANGUAGE-DOMINANT CHILDREN

1. It's good to bring photos of the children and some work in the primary language they have done to focus the visit on the children at home and at school; it's also a good icebreaker.

2. Be sure to reassure—especially mothers—that children are not "wasting time" by being taught in their primary language and also that the school *is* providing instruction in English everyday.

3. Reassure parents that being bilingual is an asset vocationally today in California, but especially if the children can *read* and *write* in both languages. Also, note that being bilingual aids cognitive ability by showing diagram below.

4. A clear diagram to illustrate the linguistic interdependence of language acquisition by children, which shows that learning in the primary language helps children learn in English.

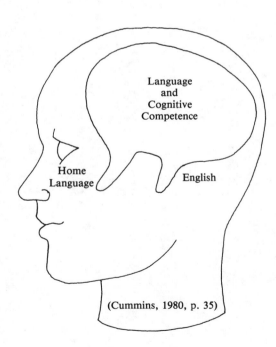

(Cummins, 1980, p. 35)

Appendix 2 (continued)

5. Suggest ways parents can help the child and the bilingual program. Stress *speaking a lot* to the child in the primary language by all the family and other sources of language mentioned earlier.

6. Encourage family to participate in the bilingual program by suggesting specific ways: Be flexible and try to make visits to school possible and convenient.

7. Encourage parents to suggest additional ways they could participate in the bilingual program and their child's education.

8. Try to capitalize on family trips to country of origin or arrival of relatives in the school program.

9. Speak the primary language throughout the home visit: It has prestige in the eyes of the school.

THE NATURAL APPROACH IN BILINGUAL EDUCATION

Tracy D. Terrell

Introduction

APPROACHES TO SECOND LANGUAGE instruction today may be classified as communicative or grammar based. In communicative-based instruction, goals, teaching techniques, and student evaluation are all based on behavioral objectives defined in terms of abilities to communicate messages. For example, can the students describe the place where they live? Or, can they recount an incident that took place before they arrived at school? In grammar-based instruction, goals, teaching techniques, and student evaluation are defined in terms of accuracy in grammar usage; for example, can the students correctly use the two forms of the verb *be* in the past tense? Or, can the students form tag questions?

Grammar-based approaches are most successful in contexts in which the goal is either a knowledge of grammar or the ability to produce grammatically correct sentences in a limited communicative context. Grammar-based approaches such as grammar translation, audio-lingualism, or cognitive-code have been overwhelming failures in preparing students to function in normal communicative contexts. This has led the profession to modify the use of these approaches in the direction of communicative-based approaches, especially when teaching a second language to language minority children. In these cases, English as a second language (ESL) instructors, for example, are aware that the instructional goals must be immediately relevant to the functional language needs of their students in learning to live in a different language environment.

Several communicative approaches have been reported in the professional literature: Lozanov's Suggestopedia (Bancroft, 1978; Lozanov, 1975, 1978), Curran's Community Counseling-Learning (Curran, 1976; LaForge, 1971; Stevick, 1973, 1980), Galyean's Confluent Education (Galyean, 1976; 1977), and Terrell's Natural Approach (Terrell, 1977, 1980, in press; Krashen and Terrell, in press) to mention those most widely used. All are derived from the same philosophical position regarding language instruction: that the ability to communicate messages in spoken or written form is the primary goal of instruction and that classroom activities, textbooks, and other materials (as well as the evaluation of student progress) are formulated in communicative rather than grammatical or structural terms. In addition, they are based implicitly (or sometimes explicitly) on the same theory of second-language acquisition, namely, that in order to acquire language, students need a rich acquisition environment (Blair, in press) in which they are receiving "comprehensible input" in low anxiety situations (Krashen, 1977; 1978; 1979; 1981; in press).

Unfortunately, the specific techniques of both Suggestopedia and Community Counseling-Learning are not easily applicable to normal elementary and secondary classroom situations; and I will not discuss them further here. Galyean's humanistic techniques, on the other hand, are entirely consistent with the philosophy and practice of the Natural Approach. [See Galyean (1976) and Moscowitz (1978) for other sources of communicative-based classroom activities.]

The Natural Approach, however, is not simply a series of specific classroom techniques but also a philosophy of goals in language teaching based on a theory of second-language acquisition, which predicts how these goals might be met. All human beings possess the ability to acquire second languages if they can receive "comprehensible input" in low-anxiety situations. Children acquire second-language competence slowly but in the long run are nearly indistinguishable from native speakers. Adults, if they receive "comprehensible input," acquire language quite rapidly at first but often have far more difficulty interacting within a new culture. This, in turn, increases difficulty in obtaining "comprehensible input" and limits the degree to which native speaker levels of competence can be achieved. This does not mean, however, that adults cannot become quite comfortable in their normal daily functioning in the second language. It does mean that native levels of grammatical accuracy, especially phonological accuracy, with few exceptions, will not be achieved.

The techniques and specific classroom practices of the Natural Approach are designed, then, to facilitate the natural acquisition process. Although there is a basic unity to the approach, there will be some differences in its application to children as opposed to adolescents or adults. We will be concerned specifically in this paper with the application of the Natural Approach to second (as opposed to foreign) language English instruction in bilingual-bicultural education programs, kindergarten through eighth grade.

Principles of the Natural Approach

The evidence from research in second-language acquisition supports the notion that there are two rather different ways of internalizing language. Following the terminology of Krashen (1977; 1978) and others, the term *acquisition* will refer to development of language proficiency without conscious recourse to rules, while the term *learning* will refer to development of language proficiency through the conscious, directly accessible knowledge about language rules. Krashen has hypothesized that those two modes of internalizing language are interrelated in a particular way, i.e., acquired rules are used to initiate utterances, while consciously learned rules are used in a more restricted way to *monitor* for correctness and perhaps appropriateness. Thus, acquired rules occupy a central position in all language use, while consciously learned rules play a more intermittent and peripheral role.

In the Natural Approach, the centrality of the acquisition process is recognized, and the classroom techniques are specifically designed to facilitate this natural process. This is not to say that learning activities are not a part of the approach, but their role is always subordinate to that of acquisition. In the following discussion, I will focus mainly on techniques for encouraging acquisition; it is probable that in most cases some conscious learning also takes place.

For the sake of exposition, language skills may be considered by stages: I. Survival communication skills; II. Extended communication, beginning literacy; and III. Language for academic purposes. Stage I consists of the beginning of Cummins' Basic Interpersonal Communication Skills (BICS), and Stage III corresponds to his Cognitive/Academic Language Proficiency (CALP) (see Cummins, 1978; 1981). Stage II is simply the transition between the two. In this paper, I will concentrate on Stages I and II, since the Natural Approach is concerned mainly with the acquisition of BICS.

There are two basic principles of the Natural Approach in teaching Basic Interpersonal Communication Skills: (1) speech is not taught directly but rather is acquired by means of "comprehensible input" in low-anxiety environments, and (2) speech emerges in natural stages (Terrell, in press; Krashen and Terrell, in press).

The first principle, that the ability to comprehend underlies the ability to speak, stems from observing both children and adults in natural language acquisition situations. It says, essentially, that we need not worry about the neurological mechanism of acquisition, e.g., exactly how each child or adult acquires. If the conditions specified below are met, acquirers will be successful in obtaining competence in Basic Interpersonal Communication Skills.

Following Krashen (1977; 1978; 1979; 1981), there are three important conditions that must be met if acquisition is to occur:

1. *The acquirer must receive "comprehensible input."* Acquirers must hear (or in certain cases, read) language they understand. It is impor-

tant to realize that by *understand* we do not mean that the acquirers recognize the meaning of every word used, can interpret every grammatical structure correctly, nor that they know the meanings of all the morphemes in the sentence. What we do mean is that the acquirer understands the essential meaning of the message communicated.

2. *The speech must contain a message and there must be a need to communicate that message.* Sentences created only for practice of some rules and that do not contain real messages to be communicated may serve some *learning* purpose, but they will not be useful for *acquisition*.

3. Even if these conditions are met, acquisition may not occur if the acquirer is under stress or emotional tension. Therefore, *the "comprehensible input" must be supplied in low-anxiety environments.* Acquirers of all ages need to feel secure *affectively* in order for the acquisition process to take place. We will return in some detail to techniques for guaranteeing that each of these conditions will be met in the language classroom.

The second general principle of the Natural Approach claims that speech will emerge in natural stages during the acquisition process. I will consider briefly these stages and return later to each in more detail.

The first stage consists of a pre-production period labeled the "silent" period or the "pre-speech" stage. In this period, the acquirers are concerned with gaining competence in comprehending messages in the new language. It is the time for getting used to a new phonology (including supersegmentals such as rhythm and intonation), associating new lexical items with familiar concepts (mostly concrete entities, qualities, or events), and with new body language and gestures. Grammatical signals of morphology (word formation) and syntax (sentence formation) are justifiably ignored by the acquirer in this period as irrelevant to basic comprehension. This "pre-speech" period may last from just a few hours to several months. Children acquiring second languages usually need a longer pre-speech stage (three to six months) than adults (several hours to several weeks). (For evidence supporting a pre-production stage, see Asher, 1969; Davies, 1976; Nord, 1980; Postovsky, 1974; Winitz and Reeds, 1973.)

Speech emerges slowly but naturally at different moments for different individuals. The first natural speech to emerge usually consists of single-word responses, of short fixed phrases, or routine expressions. These are usually words and phrases the acquirers have heard and comprehended in many contexts and feel confident enough to produce. It may consist of single-word items such as *yes, no, me, play, go, pencil,* and *paper;* or routine expressions such as *thank you, I'm fine, What you doing?* and so forth. The transition to the single-word production stage from the pre-speech stage to early production should occur spontaneously without any coersion on the part of the instructor. Forcing production before the acquirer is ready will at best delay language acquisition and force reliance on patterns and other learned material, and at worst may create blocks to the acquisition of the new language, blocks which later could prove to be quite difficult to remove.

If the acquirer continues to receive sufficient "comprehensible input" and the affective conditions for acquisition are met, speech will continue to improve in fluency and correctness. Acquirers will slowly expand their lexicon and grammar, producing longer and longer phrases as they begin to acquire the rules of discourse and the broad range of skills we refer to as communicative competence. It should be remembered, however, that forcing students to produce speech that is more complex than their acquired competence will only slow down the process.

The important point is that the instructor's primary responsibility is not to force speech production but rather to create the necessary conditions for acquisition to take place. Speech will emerge when the acquirer is given the opportunity and need to speak in non-coersive, low-anxiety situations.

Natural Language Acquisition Situations

Let us consider briefly informal evidence for the above claims taken from natural language acquisition situations. We will examine children and adults in first- and second-language acquisition contexts.

Children, when acquiring their first language, are in optimal situations for language acquisition. Those who take care of children assume that they will acquire language without any explicit teaching although a few people have the mistaken belief that they teach their children to speak. Children are given a long pre-production period: Caretakers speak to their children seeking to convey messages long before they utter their first words. In addition, all of the conditions for acquisition are met: Caretakers do not speak to children aimlessly but try to convey messages; for the most part, these messages are important to the children in their interactions with their environment and the people in their environment. Caretakers neither drill children nor create grammatical exercises for them. Children's attempts to comprehend, and especially their attempts to produce speech, are greeted with praise; and they are considered to be successful even when they only partially comprehend or make the barest attempt at production. Simply put, caretakers have high expectations for eventual success (all normal children acquire their first language at native levels of basic interpersonal communicative competence) but are accepting of imperfect stages in the process. This acceptance of errors and incomplete utterance encourages children to continue to interact with success in the language they are acquiring. This is the case in spite of the fact that many caretakers mistakenly believe that they indeed do correct children's errors and that it is this correction that leads to language acquisition. Finally, children are immersed in "comprehensible input" from many sources for many hours of the day. It is no wonder that the acquisition process works so well in child first-language acquisition.

In situations of child second-language acquisition, conditions may not be as optimal as in first-language acquisition, since children are usually aware that they cannot interact in the new language as can native speakers of their same age. This can inhibit them, especially in initial stages of seeking and obtaining contacts with other children and adults. However, in most cases, children acquiring second languages are allowed a pre-production period in which they begin to comprehend but are required to say very little. In their early attempts at speech production, children will make many grammatical errors; however, these are normally accepted by native speaker peers and adults without too much fuss. Indeed, since children are usually allowed to respond or even initiate conversations with very short utterances, errors are not as apparent as they might be were the child to be forced to produce large amounts of speech. If the child continues to obtain "comprehensible input," progress in fluency and accuracy in the second language is steady.

Adults in natural second-language acquisition contexts, for example, immigrants to another culture, experience many more difficulties in obtaining "comprehensible input" under optimal conditions. First of all, although we simplify our speech in order to make less competent non-native speakers understand, it is difficult to judge the necessary level of the non-native speakers until we have interacted with them for more than a few initial moments. It is not always easy for non-native speakers to integrate themselves into the new society in such a way as to make friends who will be interested enough in communicating with the acquirers to take the time and trouble to talk to them over extended periods of time, making their speech comprehensible. In addition, the process of speech simplification so necessary for making the input comprehensible is not as easy in the case of adults as it is for children, since adults tend to be interested in more complex topics of conversation and have communicative needs that require much more sophisticated levels of language than do children. Thus, adults who have to deal with the difficulties of living in a new culture will tend to concentrate on being in the company of those who speak their language.

Adults are more aware of correctness in language and find it much more difficult emotionally to speak with reduced structures and a high level of grammatical incorrection. This seems to be a self-generated feeling of inadequacy since, for the most part, native speakers of a language do not overtly correct foreigners who are acquiring the language any more than they do with children.

In conclusion, the same factors that guarantee successful acquisition of a first or second language for children are also necessary for adult language acquisition. But while most adults are successful, if imperfect acquirers, they usually have more difficulty than children.

Teacher Behaviors in the Natural Approach

The primary factor in reaching acceptable levels of competence in basic interpersonal communication is "comprehensible input." Most children in ESL classes have been and are continually exposed to input in English; often, however, much of the input is not comprehended and is therefore useless for acquisition. If the only "comprehensible input" the children receive is in the ESL classroom, they will acquire, but the process can be painfully slow and inadequate to their need for interacting in an English-speaking environment. Thus, the teacher has two primary responsibilities: (1) provide a source of "comprehensible input" such that the acquisition process is begun, and (2) provide for the comprehension of sufficient lexical items (words) in domains outside the classroom so that children can begin to make use of other sources of input. This would include input from older siblings whose English is more advanced, teachers, administrators, and other English-speaking adults, English-speaking peers, and so forth. The more quickly children can take advantage of sources of input other than the ESL instructor, the faster will be the progress in acquisition.

In the classroom, instructors must: (1) create a necessity for communication of some message, (2) communicate a message, and (3) modify (simplify) their speech until the students understand the message. There are several general modifications caretakers make in their speech to children or which native speakers make in their speech to foreigners that are helpful in ensuring comprehension (Hatch, 1979).

Before examining these important speech modification techniques, it should be stressed that translation via the native language of the acquirer is *not* necessary or even desirable, except perhaps in exceptional circumstances. If the instructor has asked a question or given an instruction that has not been understood, it will be necessary to modify speech, repeating the message in several forms until comprehension is achieved. This modification (often simplification) is what ensures that the acquirer will achieve input at the correct (i + 1) level (Krashen, 1981). If instructors resort to translation through their own knowledge of the students' languages or through native speaker teacher's aides, the input has not been made comprehensible; rather, the message has been transmitted via another medium, i. e., the first language. Consequently, the most important part of the input process has been eliminated. Indeed, the process of modification and simplification in order to ensure comprehension of some message is always more important in terms of acquisition than is the message itself. If opportunities for "comprehensible input" are lost because of frequent translation, acquisition will be severely retarded.

What is it, then, that instructors can do to ensure comprehension through speech modification and simplification? First, it should be emphasized that the modifications of speech necessary for comprehension by an acquirer cannot be consciously controlled to a high degree. Thus, the following discussion is meant to be a *description* of what will happen to the speech of an instructor whose central purpose is to convey messages to children with limited English competence. Again, this observation only underscores the importance of maintaining the focus of both instructor and students on the communication of messages rather than linguistic form and correctness of those messages.

Hatch (1979) reports the general modifications to speech that may help acquirers (see also Krashen, 1980). The first is to talk slower to acquirers. This does not mean the speech is distorted nor is it exaggeratedly slow. For English, this means clearer articulation [fewer reduced vowels, fewer consonants deleted, fewer contractions, fewer fused forms (*do you want to* rather than "jew wanna"), longer pauses at natural breaks, etc.]. Also helpful is increased volume on key words and exaggerated intonation accompanied by appropriate body language and movement. Vocabulary can be modified to include high frequency words with fewer idioms and less slang. The use of pronouns can be reduced in favor of using specific names of the intended referents instead of *one, he, her, us, their,* etc. An attempt to clarify the meaning of possibly unfamiliar words within the speech context should be made. For example, a mother might say to a child, *"Where's your new domino game? You know, those little black things with white dots?"* Vocabulary acquisition is aided by the use of visuals, the objects themselves, pictures, and/or gestures that aid in clarification.

The syntax of speech addressed to learners is often simpler. Sentences are usually shorter, with less compounding and subordination of clauses. New information in each sentence is reduced. Often, key topics can be repeated: *Did you have a good weekend, you know, Friday, Saturday?*

Finally, the subject of the communication will be most easily comprehended if it is familiar to listeners. For children, this means little displacement; they should focus on the here and now. For all ages, this means using visual aids: pictures, objects films, slides, acting out, etc. It means avoiding abstractions in beginning stages and using all sorts of extralinguistic means to aid comprehension or carry meaning since often the new words cannot by themselves.

Concentrating on comprehension of real messages also means avoiding the use of language drills and grammar exercises which, by their very nature, are out of context and contain no important message to be conveyed to listeners. (We will return to this position when we discuss the sorts of acceptable acquisition activities to be used in the Natural Approach.) Here, it is enough to note that traditional ESL drills and exercises fail on most accounts to provide "comprehensible input" (no message, no need) and, therefore, also fail as a source for acquisition.

Yet, as we have noted already, it is not enough to give "comprehensible input" with the focus on the message. The acquirers must be in a low-anxiety situation. In Dulay and Burt's (1977) terminology, the instructor must strive at all times to lower students' Affective Filter. There are several guidelines that, if followed, will help create low-anxiety situations: (1) the emphasis should be on the use of language in interpersonal communication, i. e., the focus is on the students and their needs and desires as individuals; (2) all attempts at language use should be accepted and encouraged without overt correction of form; and (3) no attempt should be made to force production before acquirers are ready.

Since it is important to accept positively all attempts by children at communication, all use of the native language should be accepted. If a child's native language is not understood by most of the other children and/or the instructor, the instructor should encourage someone (another speaker of that language, an aide, an older sibling, or friend) to help out by conveying the message in English. Such efforts should always be shown acceptance. After the message is understood, the instructor should take advantage of the communication to teach the necessary lexical items to convey that message in English.

In classes in which there is a common first language also understood by the instructor, children should be encouraged to communicate in that language with the instructor responding positively in English. Such child L1 instructor L2 interchange can be very helpful in encouraging acquisition in the pre-production stage.

In addition to acceptance of the use of the primary language, the instructor must accept all imperfect attempts at expression in English. Speech is not improved by overt error correction. Improvement comes in time if children continue to receive correct input at an appropriate level. However, it is probable that "expansion" is helpful. Expansion means accepting what children have said and incorporating it in correct form in the instructor's response. For example:

Instructor: John, what do you have in your picture?

      John: Have dog.

Instructor: Right. Look at John's picture, class. Does he have a dog? Yes, he does. Do *I* have *a* dog in my picture? No, I have a cat.

Teaching Techniques for Natural Acquisition Stages

Pre-production

I have suggested that all acquirers in natural situations begin the acquisition process by learning first how to comprehend the gist of messages from input. Allowing acquirers this "silent" period simplifies the acquisition process in that it allows them a chance to concentrate completely on decoding without worrying about production skills. In other approaches (grammar translation, audiolingual, etc.), students are forced from the beginning to produce language. They must comprehend what is said (no small task), coordinate pronunciation or spelling, attend to correct grammar, and choose the appropriate words, all in addition to formulating the content of what they are communicating. The complexity of this process forces the instructor to simplify radically the interchange both in content and structure, a simplification that is much more extreme than that required for "comprehensible input." Indeed, the content of the communication is normally so simple in these approaches, it is practically vacuous.

By concentrating on the receptive skills and postponing the production skills, these difficulties can be avoided in initial stages. Acquirers can comprehend complex messages more rapidly than they can produce them. In fact, they need only learn to recognize the meaning of key words and attend to extralinguistic contextual clues to be successful at comprehension and thus begin the acquisition process. It appears that a pre-production period is so programmed into the acquisition process that approaches in which it is not allowed actually slow down the acquisition process.

There are several classroom techniques that can be used in the pre-production stage. They involve relating language to either movement, visuals, or both. Let us consider movement first.

The use of movement in language teaching has been proposed most strongly by Asher (1969; 1977; see also Swan, 1980 for classroom suggestions) in a method called Total Physical Response (TPR). In this approach, the instructor gives a command that the students execute in class as a group. Later, after confidence has been built up, commands are given to individuals.

A sample lesson may include the following general techniques. First, the instructor gives a command such as *stand up* and actually executes the command. Then the command is given again, and both the instructor and the students carry out the command together. The third time the command is given the instructor indicates that the students should carry out the command by themselves. If they do not understand what to do this third try, then the instructor again issues the command and executes it with them. After the command has been successfully carried out, a second command is added, such as *turn around*. The sequence is repeated until the children are successful at carrying out the command without the instructor. A third command is added to the first and second and the sequence is repeated until the participants are successful. Then the three are given in random order until there is no difficulty in carrying out the instructions. Attention span for TPR activities varies according to age. Younger children are easily distracted and often attend only to what their classmates do. Older children must be given a wide variety of activities to maintain interest.

TPR requires no verbal response from children; but some do repeat the commands out loud, others do not. What is important is that the children can be successful with this activity without English speech production. All classroom management language can be taught *via* TPR. The following examples are based on Swan (1980):

1. Movement: stand, sit, walk, turn, stop, sing.
2. Body Parts: touch your shoulders, nose, eyes, ears, head. Sample sequence: touch your mouth, sit, touch your shoulders, smile, turn, touch your head, etc.
3. Classroom: touch (point to) the wall, floor, a desk, a table, a window. Sample: touch the wall, walk, sit, touch your eyes, point to the table, touch a chair, sing, etc.

Although TPR is a logical starting technique for the pre-production stage, it is also valuable even after the children are talking for two reasons: (1) body movement helps to form stronger associations between language and its referents than dealing exclusively in the abstract, and (2) increased opportunities for meaningful listening comprehension allows for the utilization of input for acquisition and should therefore always precede speech production.

There are other activities for the pre-production period that can be done with visuals or objects involving *association* of language with particular children in the classroom, thereby facilitating retention of new meanings. The simplest of these techniques is to name objects from the classroom, passing them out to the children one by one. The key question is *Who has the____?* The following is an example of possible "comprehensible input" for beginners. Recall that the children will not comprehend every word, only the messages. (Words essential for comprehension are emphasized.)

> *This is a* pencil. *It's a* yellow *pencil. Who wants the yellow pencil? [picking student who has raised his/her hand] Do you want the pencil, Melissa? Good, here you are. Thank you. Now, class, who has the pencil? Does* Melissa *have the pencil? [Most of the class will say Melissa.] Yes, that's right.* Melissa *has the* pencil.

Note that to comprehend the activity the children need only to comprehend the words *pencil, yellow, who,* and *you* if they attend to the context provided by the instructor's actions and gestures. The same sequence is then repeated with different objects until everyone in the group has an item. Typical input would sound like this:

> Where's *the* small box? *[Students point.] Now where's the* large *box? [Students point.] That's right,* Jaime *has it. Who has the* plastic pencil sharpener? *[Juan.] And who has the* chalk? *[Ester.] Does* Linda *have a* piece *of* paper? *[Students either nod heads or answer yes/no.]*

This technique with classroom objects can be combined with TPR, as illustrated in the following sequence.

> *Who has the* rubber band? *[Linda.] O.K.,* Linda *give your* rubber band *to* Louis. *Does* Louis *have a* ruler? *[Students nod no.] Does he have a* board eraser? *[Students nod yes.] O.K.,* Louis, *give your* blackboard eraser *to* Linda.

A combination of TPR and the naming technique should be used until the children can recognize all important words used daily in the classroom situation. It is particularly important for the instructor to realize that children can quite quickly acquire enough vocabulary at a recognition level to follow all instructions and even begin to comprehend some peer talk in the classroom without having produced a single word in English.

The first language functions using TPR and the children's names will have as early goals the identification of classroom objects and people, and the performance of actions in the classroom. Other important goals to be included in early TPR/naming activities are descriptions including comparatives: big, smallest, longer, colors; locations: on the table, in the corner, under the window; numbers: *who* has *three pencils?,* and so forth.

After the relevant vocabulary and structures needed to deal with classroom actions, entities, and their descriptions are comprehended, some provision must be made to give input involving other activities and entities not in the classroom, while still remaining in the pre-speaking stage. This is most easily accomplished by visuals, especially pictures cut from magazines and/or slides and filmstrips. In fact, a large picture file encompassing all possible semantic fields (colors, animals, foods, dwellings, landscapes, weather, etc.) is an absolute must for a language teacher at all levels of instruction. Such large files are simply not commercially feasible, and instructors will have to make their own individual collections. This is not really as difficult a task if the teacher requests that students each bring to class a picture to talk about; in a short time the instructor will have amassed a large picture file.

Pictures may be used in much the same way as objects. First, the instructor describes the contents of the picture; the complexity of the description will depend on the level of children's comprehension:

> *Here's a new* picture. What *do we* see *in this picture?* [*without waiting for a response if the students are still pre-production*] A man *and a* woman. *There's a* man *in this picture and a* woman *with him.* Here's *the* man *and* here's *the* woman. [*pointing*] Who wants *the picture of the* man *and the* woman? [*Johnny raises his hand.*] O.K., *here's the picture of the* man *and the* woman. *This picture is for* Johnny. *Now who has the picture of the* man *and the* woman? [*Johnny.*] *Right.* Johnny *has the picture with the* man *and the* woman.

In this particular activity, the instructor might have as a goal to use words relating to identification of human beings: man, woman, boy, girl, baby, and so forth. The same activity can incorporate family relationships: father, mother, son, daughter, and so forth.

As comprehension increases, the instructor expands the activity to include more complex input. For example, the goal might be to teach comprehension of speech describing common recreation activities, especially those in which the students would engage outside the classroom while at school:

> *I have a* new *picture.* What *do we see? A* boy *and a* girl. *The* girl *is playing* baseball. *The* boy *is* watching *her play baseball.* [*Remember, complex words and syntax will not affect the comprehension if the rhythm, intonation, and emphasis coordinate well with the extralinguistic context.*] Who wants *this*

picture of the little girl *playing baseball?* Who has *the picture of the little* boy watching *the little girl play baseball?* Where *is the picture with the* baseball?

This technique is limited only by the teacher's imagination and the students' attention span. In a single session, young children usually pay attention to ten pictures or so. Older children may learn to identify up to 20 before they tire of the activity. Often, adolescents or adults can do 30 or more in a single session. The content is also unlimited. One can give "comprehensible input" in such semantic fields as community professions, clothing, food, geography, and with many other items not easily transportable to the classroom.

The pre-production stage can last as long as is needed. Children should not be forced to speak before the acquisition process has had a chance to begin developing. Earlier, I suggested that with rank beginners, this may take from three to six months. In the case of students who have some competence in English, some responses will be made from the beginning. This is not harmful; it should, however, not be taken as a sign that they do not need to receive the input described in this section but rather that the interchanges may take the form described in the next section.

In summary, I have suggested three primary techniques for the pre-production stage: (1) TPR, (2) TPR combined with naming objects, and (3) pictures. Responses to check on comprehension are: (1) movement, (2) pointing, (3) nodding one's head, and (4) saying the name of a student. In the next section, we will consider how using these same techniques can facilitate the transition into speaking.

Transition into Production

The primary question, of course, is how can the instructor know when children are ready to make the transition into speech production? Theoretically, this question is somewhat difficult to answer; in practice, there are certain techniques that greatly facilitate the instructor's task.

Essentially, the answer is to use the pre-production activities as usual but to integrate slowly two sorts of questions: *yes-no* and *here-there*.

Everyone *look at this* picture. What *do we* see? [*Without waiting for response.*] *There is a* man looking *in the* window. *Is there also a* woman *in this picture? Do you also* see *a* woman? [*Some students will answer yes.*] *Yes, that's right. There is a* man looking *in the* window, *and a* woman. What *is the* woman doing? [*No pause.*] *Is she* looking *at the* man? [*No.*] *No, she's* reading *a* newspaper.

The idea is not to begin suddenly to ask a series of *yes-no* questions but to continue with the pre-production interactions as usual and from time to time insert a *yes-no* question.

The same observations apply to the *here-there* responses. These questions may be used in the three interaction types. First, they may be used referring to descriptions of the students themselves.

> *What is the* name *of the person in our class with* long blond
> hair? [*Melinda.*] Where *is she?* [*There.*] *And* where *is the* boy
> *in the class with* short blond hair? [*There.*] *And* what *is his*
> name? What *is the* name *of the person wearing a* blue and
> white striped shirt *today?* [*Jaime.*] *Is* Jaime *sitting* beside
> Melinda? [*No.*] *No, he's sitting* beside Al. *Does* Al *have on a*
> *pair of* tennis shoes *today?* [*Yes.*] Where *is someone with a*
> *pair of* white socks? [*There.*] *Yes, there and there and there.*
> [*pointing to several*]

When students answer with *here* or *there,* they should point to the object or person being singled out.

Secondly, *here-there* questions may be applied to objects in the classroom or brought to class and passed out to the students.

> Who *has the* eraser? [*Jimmy.*] *And* where *is the* napkin? [*No.*]
> *Does* Lisa *have the* apple? [*No.*] *Does she have the* orange?
> [*No.*] *The* grapes? [*Yes.*] Where *is the* banana? [*Here.*] *Yes, I*
> *have the* banana.

Finally, *here-there* questions may also be used with pictures.

> Who *has the* picture *of the* man washing *the* dog? [*Gilberto.*]
> *And* where *is the* picture *of the* father reading *the* book *to his*
> daughter? [*Here.*] *Does* Luis *have the* picture *of the* little girl
> *and her* dog? [*Yes.*] *And* where *is the* picture *of the* little boy
> *with his* dog? [*Here.*]

With *yes-no* and *here-there* questions, the focus is still primarily on extending their recognition vocabulary, and for the most part the children are still in the pre-production stage. It is also important that the students realize they can say words in English without pressure and without fear of being corrected. If the children are reticent to say *yes-no* or *here-there,* it is probable that the children do not yet feel comfortable responding in English. This may be because they have not yet acquired enough English, i. e., the instructor should continue with pre-production activities and return later to these sorts of questions. Or, the children may have indeed acquired enough to respond, but do not yet feel comfortable doing so. The remedy, of course, is to try to show the children that all attempts at production, regardless of pronunciation or difficulties with possible errors, will be responded to positively exactly as parents respond positively to children's first attempts at production no matter how deformed they may be.

The next step is to give students the opportunity to say some of the words they can recognize. The easiest way to accomplish this is to ask *either-or* questions embedded in the comprehension interchange exactly in the same way that *yes-no* and *here-there* questions were introduced.

> Who *has on a* red jacket *today?* [*Don.*] *And* where *is there a* yellow shirt? [*There.*] *Is this* shirt red? [*No.*] *Is it* blue?[*No.*] *Is it* green? [*Yes.*] Everyone look at Melinda's socks. *Are they* black *or* blue? [*Blue.*] Look at my socks. *Are they* white *or* red? [*Red.*]

The same sorts of questions apply to pictures:

> Look *at this* picture. *Is there an* animal *in this* picture? [*Yes.*] *Is it a* dog *or a* cat? [*Cat.*] *Is the* cat *on the* roof? [*No.*] *Is it on the* porch? [*Yes.*] *Is there a little* boy *or a little* girl *in this picture?* [*Girl.*] *Is she wearing a* sweater? [*No.*] *A* coat? [*Yes.*] *Is she wearing a* coat *because it's* hot? [*No.*] *No, because it's* cold.

If the first time the instructor introduces *either-or* questions the students are reticent about answering, this is simply a signal to the instructor that production pressures have come too soon and that they have not yet had sufficient opportunity to acquire the lexical items they are being called upon to produce. In general, *either-or* questions are relatively simple since they require only the ability to comprehend the questions and a repetition of one of the lexical items the instructor has just mentioned.

The next step is the production of single words that have not been mentioned in the question. There are two techniques. One is simply to ask the question, *What is this (that)?* (Remember that in early production stages, the students will not usually use articles, i. e., *a, an,* and *the.*) The expected answer to an identification question is a single word; the instructor provides the positive expansion.

> Who *has the* plastic pencil sharpener? [*Phil.*] *Is the* ball *in* front *of* Cheryl? [*Yes.*] Where *is the* ruler? [*There.*] John, show *us what you have. Is that a* truck *or a* car? [*Car.*] Jaime, show *us what you have. What does* Jaime, *have, class?* [*Fireman.*] *That's right,* Jaime *has a* fireman.

The other possibility is to begin a statement or a question and indicate by intonation that someone should try to finish it.

> Andy, hold up *your* picture. Everyone look at *Andy's* picture. *Do you* see *a* car? [*Yes.*] *Is it* blue? [*No.*] *No, it is not* blue, *it's...*[*red*]*. Is there a* man *driving the* car? [*No.*] *There's a...*[*woman*]*.*

Usually the instructor will not even have to decide when the children are ready for the transition into these sorts of questions since they will do it automatically themselves when asked questions with negative answers.

> Luis, show *us your* picture. *Is there an* elephant *in Luis' picture?* [*Students will say no and name the correct animal at the same time.*]

The important thing to remember about the transition period is that it should be considered an extension of the pre-production period in the sense that the primary emphasis is still on the development of listening comprehension abilities through recognition of new lexical items. The following is a suggested list of comprehension goals that should be met before production beyond the limited one-word responses described in this section are encouraged.

1. Following commands for classroom management
2. Names of articles in the classroom
3. Colors/description words for articles in the classroom
4. Words for people; family relationships
5. Descriptions of students
6. Clothing
7. School areas
8. Activities associated with school
9. Names of objects in the school outside the classroom
10. Foods (especially those eaten at school)

The goal is that students be brought as quickly as possible to a level of comprehension such that they can begin to get "comprehensible input" outside the language class, in other classes, on the playground, and outside of school hours. The faster the students begin to understand, the faster the acquisition process will develop.

Early Production Techniques

The basis of the transition to early production is to use more and more questions that can be responded to with a single word. Thus, a conversation about foods meant to encourage early conversation might sound like this:

> Everyone look *at* Linda's picture. *Do you know* what *she has?* [*Cake, piece cake, chocolate cake*] *Right. It's a piece of* cake, *a piece of* chocolate cake. *Does everyone* like *cake?* What *do we* eat *with* cake? [*Milk.*] *Milk? A* glass *of* milk? *Yes, I like to* drink *a* glass *of* milk *with my* cake. [*Note that the answer was not quite correct since the question referred to eating, not drinking; the answer was accepted in any case.*] What *do we* eat *with* cake? *Does anyone* like *to* eat ice cream

with their cake? [*Several, if not all, hands will go up.*] Jaime,
do you like ice cream? Who *has a* favorite flavor *of* ice
cream? [*Usually someone will volunteer a flavor.*]

The basic interaction is still oriented to listening comprehension, but
many more opportunities for the creative production of lexical items are
provided.

The transition to two- or three-word phrases is made simply by asking
questions that can be responded to with two- or three-word phrases.

Mark, hold up *your* picture. *Everyone* look *at* Mark's picture.
What *is in the picture?* [*Woman.*] *Yes, there's a woman.*
What *is she* wearing? [*Red dress.*] *Yes, that's right, she has on
a* red dress. *Is she wearing a* hat? [*No.*] *Tell me something
about the woman. For example,* look *at her* hair. *She
has...*[*brown hair*]. What *is she* doing? [*Reading book.*] *Yes,
she's* reading *a* book.

Often, the first two-word phrases produced naturally are adjective-noun
combinations (without the articles) and verb-complement combinations
(without the articles or subject), whereas subject-verb combinations are
normally produced later. Other early two-word combinations include *no*
plus verb, pronouns plus a negative (*no me, me no,* etc.), a subject
followed by a complement without a predicate, especially if the predicate
would be the copula (*that book, chalk* or *table, doll pretty,* etc.). It
should be emphasized that during the early production stages, it is
counterproductive to stress the production of: (1) articles, (2)
demonstratives in correct form (*this, that, these, those*), (3) the copula,
(4) the third person singular -s, (5) most pronouns, (6) most auxiliaries,
and (7) tag answers (*Yes, he is; No, I'm not,* etc.). Such grammatical
items are entirely unnecessary for developing a broad basis for listening
comprehension and can be added to students' production abilities much
easier later. Indeed, an emphasis on their production will necessarily
retard comprehension development.

On the other hand, it is helpful for children to memorize certain patterns or routines without necessarily understanding the meanings of the
individual words or their constituent structure: *How are you?, Excuse
me, May I be excused?,* and so forth.

One production technique that can include simple routines and patterns is the *circle* question. The pattern is given to the first student who
asks a second, the second asking the third, and so forth. Some examples
are:

Hello. My name is ____. What is your name?
Hello. How are you? I'm fine, thank you.

What do you have? I have a ____.
What are you doing? I'm ____.

Such activities should not be pushed too soon. If the students have not had enough "comprehensible input," their acquisition system may not yet be built up enough to feel comfortable with this sort of activity. Also, since every student is required to perform, it is best to wait until even the slowest acquirer in the class is ready for the activity. Again, although the entire pattern is given, not too much importance should be placed on absolute correctness in using the articles and other function words.

Older children can usually work well with short, open-ended dialogs:

I

1.   Hello, my name is _____.
2.   How are you? My name is _____.

II

1.   How are you today?
2.   ____, thanks, and you?
3.   _____.

III

1.   Hi. Where are you going?
2.   I'm going to ____.
3.   What are you going to do?
4.   I'm going to _____.

Also useful with older children are guided interviews. The guidelines are distributed in written form and the students work in pairs.

What is your name? My name is ____.
Where do you live? I live in ____.
What do you study? I study ____.

If so desired, guidelines can be included for reporting the information back to the class:

His/her name is ____.
He/she lives in ____.
He/she studies ____.

The open-ended sentence can elicit a variety of simple responses and provide input for expanded interactions. The instructor selects a sentence with a single word missing. Students are to fill in the blank with a word of their choice. (See Christensen, 1977.)

After school I'm going to ____.
My parents don't want me to ____.
In my refrigerator there is ____.
I like best to play ____.

Encouraging Speech Production

The underlying assumption of the Natural Approach is that it is not necessary to teach students to speak. Speech will emerge, as we have said, when given the need to speak, an opportunity to express oneself in a low-anxiety situation, and "comprehensible input" to develop the acquired system. The important point with activities to encourage speech is that there be a focus other than language form.

There are several techniques that will result in a focus on messages rather than language. One is to teach course content itself, that is, to use the second language to teach academic content such as mathematics, geography, history, etc., or non-academic content such as physical education or driver's education. Such is the approach used in Canadian "immersion" programs. It should be kept in mind, however, that the teaching of content in the target language will be effective only in the case that the students are able to receive "comprehensible input," i. e., the level of input is appropriate to the level of the students' competence in the target language. With homogeneous groups, e. g., a group of non-English speakers, it is a relatively simple task for the instructor to give input that will be comprehensible for all in the group. If the class is made up of individuals with radically different comprehension levels from, say, native speakers to non-English speakers, maintaining an appropriate level of input for all students is practically impossible. In such cases, grouping is essential.

Besides teaching subject matter, there are three general techniques for diverting attention from language form to its use: games, affective-humanistic activities, and problem-solving tasks.

Games are important, not only because they are fun and provide a period of relaxation for both instructor and children, but, more importantly, because they provide an intense point of concentration, the objective of which is not language. In games, more than in any other activity, the language is obviously a tool or a means of achieving another goal: the game playing itself. Teachers of primary children are, of course, fully aware of how many activities must be made at least "game-like" to maintain interest. It is generally conceded that children acquire language best by having fun. On the other hand, too often game-like activities are used with the idea that their only value is to provide a moment of relaxation. Games are valuable in language acquisition if they provide a rich source of "comprehensible input" and/or provide opportunities for children to express themselves in English in low-anxiety situations. I will not dwell on the use of games since the same games used for native speakers are appropriate also for second-language acquirers if the proper level of input is maintained (see Gasser and Waldman, 1978; Hill and Fielden, 1974).

The second general approach to acquisition activities is to focus the children's attention on themselves. The idea is to involve them affectively with each other and the instructor. This is the focus of Christensen's Affective Learning Activities (Christensen, 1975; 1977), Moscowitz's Humanistic Activities (Moscowitz, 1978), and especially Galyean's Confluent Education (Galyean, 1976). Christensen (1977) uses the term affective to mean "the set of personal experiences, values, feelings, opinions, interests, imaginings, fantasies, already stored in an individual's mind" (p. ix). Christensen (1977) suggests eight models for classroom activities: situations, open-ended sentences, preference ranking, interviews, public opinion, crazy sentences, mini-poems, and dialogs. Although not all models are appropriate for all levels, they are definitely worth consideration, since in most cases the models are very adaptable to a wide variety of classroom situations.

Moscowitz (1978) gives 120 humanistic (or awareness) exercises that "attempt to blend what the student feels, thinks, knows with what he is learning in the target language. Rather than self-denial being the accepted way of life, self-actualization and self-esteem are the ideals the exercises pursue" (p. 2). The aim at involving the students in an activity that is intrinsically so interesting that they do not focus on language *per se* and, in addition, are designed to allow students "to be themselves, to accept themselves, and to be proud of themselves" (p. 2).

Not all types of humanistic activities will appeal to all students and instructors. But with some adaptations, most of the suggestions are viable at all levels of instruction. Moscowitz (1978) includes suggestions for activities that lead students to use language in talking about relating to others, discovering myself, my strengths, my self-image, expressing my feelings, my memories, sharing myself, my values, the arts and me, and me and my fantasies. I will describe two such activities as examples of the variety of possibilities:

> Suppose you weren't you. *Tell the children that they are to pretend that they are a member of the category you mention. They are to write down what they are and why they chose that particular thing to be. For example, if you were a season of the year, which one would you like to be? If you were a*

musical instrument, which one would you like to be? Why?
(pp. 68-70)
The gift I've always wanted. *Imagine that it is your birthday.*
You will receive a special gift. You can decide what the gift
will be. Write what you want to have more than anything else
on a slip of paper. You do not have to sign your name, but I
will collect the papers as you enter the classroom tomorrow.
(pp. 148-149)

As the instructor reads the gift suggestions to the class, they are to note down three other gifts from the list they would also like to have. Use group discussions as a follow-up.

Galyean (1976) suggests activities that allow for the sharing of feelings, interests, personal imagery, values, attitudes as well as ideas, opinions, and impersonal descriptions. Her "Confluent Education" techniques are to represent the flowing together of cognitive, affective, and interactive goals and objectives into one learning experience. The following are some suggested activities adapted from Galyean (1976):

Desires. *It's your birthday. Your parents ask you what you*
want. Use the pattern. I want _____.

Preferences. *I will give you several choices and I want you to*
decide which you prefer. I will call out two items and you will
move to the left or right of the room according to which you
like best. Which do you like best?

Right	Left
tacos	*pizza*
hamburgers	*hot dog*
movies	*television*

Abilities. *I will tell you I know how to do certain things. Some*
will be true and some false. You are to guess which I really
know how to do. (Then each child gets to suggest something
he or she knows how to do. The class guesses whether it is
true.)

Feelings. *I will give you a "feeling" word. When I do this, I*
want you to think of where you are when you have this feel-
ing. Use the following pattern: I am (feeling) *when I am*
(place).

My room. *I imagine that you are in your own room. You are*
taking the class on a guided tour of your room at home. You
are telling us what you have there. Here is your model. This is
my room. I have _____.

A third approach to focusing students' attention on content rather than language form involves traditional problem solving. The techniques can range from genuine problem solving to simply consulting tables, graphs, maps, and charts for information. Genuine problem solving involves setting up situations that require students to predict an outcome. Especially popular are short mystery stories of the "Who-done-it" type. Also useful are language riddles.

The use of tables, graphs, charts, and other displays of information is becoming quite popular with textbook writers, and this technique is used in most newer ESL texts (see, for example, Yorkey et al., 1977; Olsen, 1977). The idea is that the students are given a display of information they use to answer questions. With younger children, the charts should be simple, involving primarily pictures and symbols at first. For example, one chart could consist of children wearing different-colored clothing placed on the left side of the page and various colored toys on the right. The idea is to draw a line from a child to a toy whose color matches the children's clothing. The verbal interaction will be similar to the following:

> *What's the* name *of the little* boy *playing with the ball? What* color *is the* ball? *What* color *is the boy's* shirt? *Do they* match? *Is there* anyone *in our group with a red shirt?* [*Paul.*] *Paul, do you have a red ball?* [*No.*] *What color is your ball?*

In all cases, chart work and puzzle solving serves only as an initial focus after which the conversation naturally shifts to the children themselves.

Older children can work with more complicated charts of information. A copy of *TV Guide* could serve as a basis for the following sort of conversation:

> *What* time *is the news on channel* 7? *Find your* favorite *program. What is it? What* time *is your* favorite *program on? What programs are on at 6 p.m.? Which would you* choose? *Why?*

Timetables are also useful. For example, using a bus timetable, appropriate questions might be:

> *When does the first* bus *leave for* Los Angeles? *What bus must I take if I want to be in* San Diego *for a meeting at* 11 *a.m.?*

A major temperature chart with average temperatures of major world cities could be used with questions like:

> *Which city is the best for visiting the* beach *in* January? *Which city is the* coldest *in* March? *Which city would you* like *to live in? Why?*

Also useful are advertisements from newspapers or magazines. One can use advertisements for automobiles, clothing, food, employment, housing, and so forth. The discussion can be oriented factually. For example, looking at a number of automobile ads, the instructor might ask questions like:

> *What is the* most *expensive car for sale? Which is the* least *expensive? Are there more* foreign *or* American *cars for sale under $6,000? Which of these cars would you choose to buy?*

The last question is probably the most important feature since it takes off from the material and focuses on personal reactions or opinions. Again, it should be stressed that all displays of information should be used as a basis for subsequent personalization.

Information displays can also be constructed using the students as sources of information. For example, the goal of the following activity is to construct with the children a chart of daily activities. Each child thinks of one thing he/she does each day. Each activity should be different. The names and the activities are written one by one in chart form on the chalkboard. (Instructor may have the children also copy if appropriate.) After the chart is finished, the instructor asks questions like:

> What *does Melissa do? Who* washes *her* dog? *Who* brushes *his* teeth? *What does* Linda *do?*

The chart could be made more complex by adding a third dimension such as days of the week:

> *What does Mark do on* Mondays? *Does Jane* clean *her room on* Thursdays *or on* Fridays? *Who works* hardest *on Saturday?*

In summary, then, in the Natural Approach we use any sort of activity in which children can focus on something other than language forms. Three main categories of activities that will focus attention on message rather than form have been suggested: games, affective-humanistic activities, and problem-solving tasks.

Reading and Writing in the Natural Approach

I will not discuss the teaching of reading and writing *per se* since these are essentially a part of the development of CALP; instead, I will comment on the integration of reading and writing in the first stages of acquisition, i. e., the pre-production stages.

In the case of full bilingual programs, as students are receiving their first interaction with English, they will also be learning to read in their native language. The listening comprehension and early production skills in English are then, in a sense, a part of a "reading readiness" phase for eventual English reading. During the listening activities, the instructor may, whenever appropriate, write key lexical items on the chalkboard.

However, at no point should the success of the communication depend on the ability to read what has been written on the board. In addition, extensive writing of the target language should probably be delayed until the students are fairly comfortable with the spelling patterns of their native languages. Normally, if the students have learned to read in their native language, simply writing words in English on the board as they are introduced in listening comprehension sections is enough to begin the reading process. Later, of course, it would be appropriate for the instructor to work intensively with reading and spelling skills.

In situations in which the children are not receiving reading instruction in their native language (e. g., because of a number of different native languages in the group), then the pre-production and early production stages serve the same functions as the reading readiness stage for native speakers. However, this listening stage will have to last longer than is necessary with native speakers. During this stage the instructor can, when he/she feels the students are cognitively ready, begin to write key lexical items on the chalkboard. This amounts to simply allowing students to associate written words with the words they are hearing, without trying to work on phonetic skills. At first, this amounts to the "look-see" approach to the teaching of reading. However, this is only true initially; later when the students' comprehension is developed enough, the teacher may begin with normal phonic and syllabic approaches (Hatch, 1978).

The Use of Continua in the Natural Approach

Ideally, the Natural Approach would be used with a pre-planned continuum with the following characteristics: (1) goals are formulated in terms of communicative skills; (2) structure and form are subordinated to the particular communicative and academic goals; (3) the continuum begins with listening comprehension activities; and (4) transitional activities are provided between listening, speaking, reading, and writing. In fact, it should be clear that the Natural Approach cannot be easily used without clearly defined goals for the language course.

Many continua in use today can be adapted for use with the Natural Approach. There are usually two major problems that must be addressed, however: (1) listening and speaking activities are often not separated either in presentation or evaluation; and (2) communicative and grammatical goals are mixed together with no indicated relationship. Thus, the instructor will have to revise the continuum and its evaluation guides so that each goal has a listening phase that begins long before speech production is required. Evaluation also must record three stages: (1) aural comprehension, (2) oral production of utterances that convey messages, and (3) oral production target constructions with grammatical accuracy.

Let us look at an example. The following is a "goal" structure from a continuum used in many California ESL programs:

"Where is the (pet)?"

"Here/there it is."

First, we must determine the communicative goal. In this case, children are to learn to locate animals. This involves two lexical sets: common animals and locative expressions.

The first step is to devise an activity in which the children learn to recognize the names of animals. One way is to use pictures or miniaturized stuffed or plastic animals and pass them out to the children. Then the instructor asks questions such as, "Who has the dog?" and "Who has the cat?" After they recognize the animal words, the instructor can then hide each animal someplace in the room and ask the children to find the animals. When they find one, they must say, *"here* (or *there*) it is."
In a separate activity, the instructor can use *either/or* questions to supply opportunities to distinguish *here/there:* Where is the black kitty? Here or there? [pointing]. Children answer with a single word.

Let us examine a more complex example.

"Do you want any/some (breakfast)?"

"No, I don't want any (breakfast)."

The goal is obviously grammatical: The use of *any/some* in questions with the use of *any* in negative responses. Such a goal *must* be recast into communicative terms before it serves any real purpose. In this case, we could adopt a goal of accepting or refusing offers of food. The instructor can ask the children to pretend to be eating lunch. The instructor offers a picture of food or a plastic replica, asking each child, "Do you want _____?" "Do you want a _____?" "Do you want any _____?" according to the appropriate usage. Each child should respond either, "No, thank you" or "Yes, please." (Note that the response suggested on the continuum is absurd since, "No, I don't want any _____." is *not* a normal response to the question, "Do you want some _____?"

The above activity serves for using *some/any/a* in a form that provides students with "comprehensible input." A similar, but far more complex activity can be devised to elicit production of *some/any/a.* The instructor could, for example, pass out pictures of various foods to each child. The question is, "Do you have any/some/a _____?" If the answer is negative, the student responds, "No, but I have some/a _____."

It is important to realize that the comprehension of the meaning of sentences with *any/some/a* is relatively simple, although their production in correct contexts can be very difficult. This is an excellent example of why evaluation of children's progress must separate comprehension from production skills.

Evaluation in the Natural Approach

Evaluation of second-language students must be based on the previously established goals. It is convenient to focus on two general areas: (1) interpersonal communication skills, which consist of mostly listening and speaking and Cummins' BICS; and (2) academic skills, which consist of all four skills of listening, speaking, reading, and writing and Cummins' CALP. The specific goals may be defined in terms of the students' ages and their immediate needs. In any case, it is important that the skills be evaluated, at least in part, separately. It is especially important that for beginning students the listening comprehension skill be considered the most important for evaluation of students' progress, not the ability to produce.

The following are some sample goals for listening comprehension skills for beginners acquiring BICS:

1. Can follow classroom directions;
2. Can point to classroom items;
3. Can distinguish items according to color, shapes, sizes, and other characteristics;
4. Can point to people (including family relationships);
5. Can distinguish people according to physical and psychological descriptions (sick, happy, sad); and
6. Can act out comon school activities.

Oral production goals for beginners might include the following:

1. Can give classroom commands to peers;
2. Can exchange common greetings;
3. Can name classroom objects;
4. Can describe classroom objects in terms of color, size, etc.;
5. Can describe people, including physical and psychological descriptions; and
6. Given an action picture of a common recreational activity, can describe what is happening.

Oral production goals are always formulated in terms of the ability to communicate messages. However, each production goal usually implies the use of a particular language structure to convey that message. For example, Goal 6 above implies the use of the present progressive, i. e., the auxiliary *be* usually in contracted form followed by a present participle (*-ing*). In the evaluation of speech production, the instructor should note two things: (1) ability to transmit a message, and (2) structural accuracy in transmitting that message. Thus, in this case, the evaluation consists of three sub-parts:

1. Ability to describe common recreational in-progress activities,
2. Ability to use the auxiliary *to be* correctly, and
3. Ability to use the present participle (*-ing*) forms correctly.

Thus, at one stage, students may well be able to transmit the message, but may not yet use either the auxiliary or the participle. Later, they may have acquired the participle but still only use the auxiliary sporadically. Finally, both will be acquired.

Although progress in grammatical accuracy should be noted, the overall evaluation and assessment of students acquiring BICS should be based almost exclusively on the ability to transmit messages. The acquisition of grammar in early stages is so variable from student to student that although progress can be measured, it should not be given central importance. Only in extreme cases (low grammatical accuracy after several years of "comprehensible input") should remedial work be considered.

Conclusion

In conclusion, the Natural Approach is intended as a means of developing high levels of communicative skills among second-language acquirers. The approach contains at least the following features:

1. Behavioral objectives defined in terms of communicative contexts (situational-functional).
2. Activities to meet objectives are presented in two-stage format: comprehension/production.
3. Children are given a pre-production period that is as long as necessary.
4. Language activities focus on content, not form.
5. Children have opportunities to express themselves in low-anxiety situations.

REFERENCES

Asher, James J. *Learning Another Language Through Actions: The Complete Teacher's Guide.* Los Gatos, California: Sky Oaks Productions, 1977.

_____. "The Total Physical Approach to Second Language Learning," *Modern Language Journal,* LIII, No. 1 (January, 1969), 3-17.

Bancroft, W. Jane. "The Lozanov Method and Its American Adaptations," *Modern Language Journal,* LXII, No. 4 (April, 1978), 167-175.

Blair, R., ed. *Innovative Approaches to Language Acquisition and Learning.* Rowley, Massachusetts: Newbury House, in press.

Christensen, Clay Benjamin. "Affective Learning Activities (ALA)," *Foreign Language Annals,* VIII, No. 3 (October, 1975), 211-219.

____. *Explorando: Affective Learning Activities for Intermediate Practice in Spanish.* Englewood Cliffs, New Jersey: Prentice Hall, 1977.

Cummins, James. "Educational Implications of Mother Tongue Maintenance in Minority Language Groups," *The Canadian Modern Language Review,* XXXIV (1978), 395-416.

____. "The Role of Primary Language Development in Promoting Educational Success for Language Minority Students," *Schooling and Language Minority Students: A Theoretical Framework.* Los Angeles, California: Evaluation, Dissemination and Assessment Center, California State University, Los Angeles, 1981.

Curran, Charles Arthur. *Counseling-Learning in Second Languages.* Apple River, Illinois: Apple River Press, 1976.

Davies, Norman F. "Receptive vs. Productive Skills in Foreign Language Learning," *Modern Language Journal,* LX, No. 8 (December, 1976), 440-443.

Dulay, Heidi C., and Marina K. Burt. "Remarks on Creativity in Language Acquisition," *Viewpoints on English as a Second Language,* eds., Marina K. Burt, Heidi C. Dulay, and M. Finnochiaro. New York: Regents, 1977, pp. 95-126.

Galyean, Beverly. "A Confluent Design for Language Teaching," *TESOL Quarterly,* XI, No. 2 (June, 1977), 143-156.

____. *Language From Within.* Long Beach, California: PRISM Research and Development, 1976.

Gasser M., and E. Waldman. "Using Songs and Games in the ESL Classroom," *Teaching English as a Second or Foreign Language,* eds., M. Celce-Murcia, and L. McIntosh. Rowley, Massachusetts: Newbury House, 1978.

Hatch, Evelyn M. "Reading as a Second Language," *Teaching English as a Second or Foreign Language,* eds., M. Celce-Murcia, and L. McIntosh. Rowley, Massachusetts: Newbury House, 1978.

____. "Simplified Input and Second Language Acquisition Theory." Paper presented to the annual meeting of the Linguistics Society of America, Los Angeles, California, 1979.

Hill, Leslie Alexander, and R. D. S. Fielden. *English Language Teaching Games for Adult Students.* Vol. 1: Elementary. Vol. 2: Advanced. London, England: Evans, 1974.

Krashen, Stephen D. "Bilingual Education and Second Language Acquisition Theory," *Schooling and Language Minority Students: A Theoretical Framework.* Los Angeles, California: Evaluation, Dissemination and Assessment Center, California State University, Los Angeles, 1981.

____. "The Monitor Model for Adult Second Language Performance," *Viewpoints on English as a Second Language,* eds., Marina K. Burt, Heidi C. Dulay, and M. Finnochiaro. New York: Regents, 1977.

____. "The Monitor Model for Second Language Acquisition," *Second Language Acquisition and Foreign Language Teaching,* eds., Rosario C. Gingras. Arlington, Virginia: Center for Applied Linguistics, 1978, pp. 1-26.

____. "Relating Theory to Practice in Adult Second Language Acquisition," *Recent Trends in Research on Second Language Acquisition,* ed., S. Felix. Tubingen, Germany: TBL Gunter Narr, 1979.

____. "The Theoretical and Practical Relevance of Simple Codes," *Second Language Acquisition,* eds., R. Scarcella, and Stephen D. Krashen. Rowley, Massachusetts: Newbury House, 1980.

____. *Theory and Practice in Second Language Acquisition.* London: Pergamon Press, in press.

____, and Tracy D. Terrell. *The Natural Approach: Language Acquisition in the Classroom.* London: Pergamon Press, in press.

LaForge, Paul G. "Community Language Learning: A Pilot Study," *Language Learning,* XXI, No. 1 (June, 1971), 45-61.

Lozanov, Georgi. "The Nature and History of the Suggestopaedic System of Teaching Foreign Languages and Its Experimental Aspects," *Suggestology and Suggestopaedia,* I (1975), 5-15.

____. *Suggestology and Outlines of Suggestopaedia.* New York: Gordon and Breach Science Publishers, Inc., 1978.

Moscowitz, G. *Caring and Sharing in the Foreign Language Classroom.* Rowley, Massachusetts: Newbury House, 1978.

Nord, J. R. "Developing Listening Fluency Before Speaking: An Alternative Paradigm," *System,* VIII (1980), 1-22.

Olsen, J. E. *Communication Starters and Other Activities for the ESL Classroom.* San Francisco, California: Alemany Press, 1977.

Postovsky, Valerian A. "Effects of Delay in Oral Practice at the Beginning of Second Language Learning," *Modern Language Journal,* LVIII, No. 5-6 (September-October, 1974), 229-239.

Stevick, Earl W. "Review Article: Counseling-Learning: A Whole-Person Model for Education," *Language Learning,* XXIII, No. 2 (December, 1973), 259-271.

____. *Teaching Languages: A Way and Ways.* Rowley, Massachusetts: Newbury House, 1980.

Swan, B. S. *Teaching English Through Action.* 1749 Eucalyptus, Brea, California, 1980.

Terrell, Tracy D. "The Natural Approach to Language Teaching: An Update," *Modern Language Journal,* in press.

____. "A Natural Approach to Second Language Acquisition and Learning," *Modern Language Journal,* XLI, No. 7 (November, 1977), 325-337.

____. "A Natural Approach to the Teaching of Verb Forms and Function in Spanish," *Foreign Language Annals,* XIII, No. 2 (April, 1980), 129-136.

Winitz, Harris, and James A. Reeds. "Rapid Acquisition of a Foreign Language (German) by the Avoidance of Speaking," *IRAL,* XI, No. 3 (August, 1973), 295-317.

Yorkey, R. C. *et al. Intercom: English for International Communication.* New York: American Book Company, 1977.

Reading Instruction For Language Minority Students

Eleanor W. Thonis

Introduction

GIVEN THE ENORMOUS COMPLICATIONS implicit in attempting to design reading instruction for language minority students, it seems prudent to suggest that there is not a single solution applicable to all students who are not native English speakers. Of primary importance is the natural order and appropriate sequence for skill development. If students cannot speak a language and use its vocabulary, syntax, and functional grammar at the approximate level of a six and one-half year-old child, learning to read that language will be difficult. If they have not been encouraged to develop at least one language fully across all four modalities of listening, speaking, reading, and writing, then a functional illiteracy may be the unfortunate result. If the usual course of language acquisition and language development has not been encouraged as students interact with an environment and use language as an organizer, then ability to mediate meaning at higher levels of cognition may be thwarted. Maturation, language, age, and skill level variables must be considered. In addition, there are social, political, and economic factors that may support or mitigate against the best conditions for learning to read. These many variables have been the subject of research and argument among educators everywhere.

In United States' schools, debate has centered around English-speaking children who are struggling with the capricious nature of the English writing system. Children who speak English advance quite logically to the written language for which they have oral forms. For more than a century, despite voluminous literature in the field of reading instruction, the controversy continues over methods and materials best suited for ensuring literacy in English. For educators interested in the teaching of reading to language minority children, however, there is not such a long history of combat nor as impressive a number of combatants. Recognition of the unique literacy needs of language minority students in classrooms where English is the language of instruction is relatively recent. The research has been controversial and the recommendations, contradictory. Data from investigations of native language literacy as the introductory program have been overruled by data on the success of immersion in second language literacy plans (Bowen, 1977; Tucker, 1977). Findings suggesting early introduction to second language writing systems have been canceled by conclusions on the effectiveness of later introduction. Achievement levels in school subjects have been variously determined as better or worse when offered in native or second language. Most significantly, almost all of the research has been criticized for its lack of rigor (Troike, 1978). The purpose of this paper is to review some of the educational questions about teaching reading to language minority students and to consider the relevant research. Among the several issues are these: (1) constructs relative to reading instruction for language minority students, (2) transferability of reading skills, (3) nature of the reading process, (4) student background factors, (5) methods of instruction, and (6) supportive resources for literacy and biliteracy.

Relevant Constructs

Well-developed speech, functional literacy, and adequate thinking ability are essential for success in school. Teachers at all levels agree that learning can best take place when students speak well, read easily, and think effectively. When all the students in a class are native English speakers, teachers are challenged to provide for *personalized* growth of listening and speaking abilities, for *individualized* literacy skills, and for the *unique* thinking strategies demonstrated by different students with diverse competencies in the *one* language. When students not native to English are in classrooms designed for English speakers, teachers are even more sorely pressed to adapt the educational offerings for students. Among the questions tormenting teachers are: Should the native language be used for instruction? Should reading and writing be introduced in the native language? How does language processing influence thinking? Partial answers to such questions may be found in an appraisal of the underlying assumptions that form the basis of available programs. Teachers should consider the various theoretical positions with a view to the influences each would exert in preserving the vital bond between speech and print in promoting a unity between language (both oral and written) and thinking. If it can be argued that these three elements are essential requirements for optimum school achievement, then it follows that classroom practices must nurture the speech-print-thought triangle in consistent and appropriate ways.

All normal human beings use language in their daily lives. This ability serves individuals in personal and social situations requiring communication. Cummins (1980) calls this universal characteristic the "basic interpersonal communications skills" (BICS). He suggests that these are surface features of language that do not necessarily predict success in school. This construct of BICS as applied to programs of second language instruction in English may account in part for some of the disappointing results in English-as-a-Second Language (ESL) programs.

ESL lessons focus on pronunciation, grammar, structural patterns, and vocabulary—the visible manifestations of language. Teachers are distressed when repeated practice from the language class does not appear to carry over into the content areas where other kinds of language demands are made. While interpersonal communication skills in specific contexts are readily understood from the situation itself, they appear insufficient for problem solving, for reasoning, or for other cognitive processes required for academic achievement in subject matter.

The term "cognitive academic language proficiency" (CALP) is proposed by Cummins (1980) in describing the language abilities needed to go beyond ordinary communication. CALP is considered to be very important in learning to read. Reading is thinking, among other things; and comprehension of a page of print is possible only to the extent that the reader *brings* the concepts encoded in the language to that page. The ability to abstract from the language as written and to reflect further on its contents are dimensions of language proficiency not readily apparent in natural, informal communication. The distinction is an important one when planning English literacy programs for non-native English speakers. The assumption that the communication skills (BICS) acquired in the second language are adequate for reading comprehension is questionable. Many of the school's academic tasks, including reading, demand verbal reasoning that may be independent of specific language skills. As Furth (1966) has pointed out, the deaf reason and they have no language as generally defined. The idea of global language capacity that lies beneath the surface and that serves to support specific visible language appears to be consistent with principles of transfer of learning. Though *specific* languages may differ greatly in their observable forms, students responding to a new language may be able to demonstrate a kind of *general* understanding and make sense of the unfamiliar. They seem to transfer skills across languages with remarkable success. Teachers have noted that this transfer is more likely to be observed among *older* students and among students with solid first language skills.

Cummins (1980) has adapted Shuy's (1976) *iceberg* metaphor to illustrate diagrammatically the distinctions between the visible and underlying language proficiencies. He suggests that for bilingual students a *dual* iceberg tip rests upon the *single* entity of cognitive academic proficiency. The surface features of speech and print, plus the deeper requirements of thought in response to school tasks, may be illustrated below by a further adaptation of Cummins' (1980) adaptation. The dual-iceberg representation of the essential speech-print-thought triangle follows.

ICEBERG METAPHOR

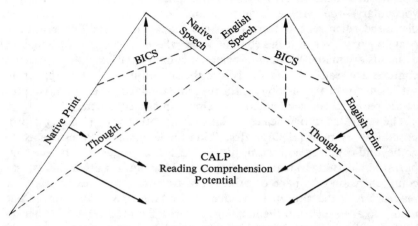

(Adapted from Cummins, 1980; Shuy, 1976; and Thonis.)

The successful development of BICS in one or both languages certainly requires thought. However, the comprehensibility at this level may be found to a great extent in the *specific* context of the interpersonal exchange. On the other hand, the comprehension of written language as found in textbooks and in other classroom materials demands thought that is likely to be out of context for the reader's immediate experience. Cummins refers to the decontextualized dimension of more formal school language, which draws upon the potential for the cognitive development of the learner as CALP.

Transferability of Skills

Transfer occurs when learning in one situation influences the potential for performance in a new situation. If it were not possible to draw upon previous experiences and information, human beings would be limited in the amount or kind of knowledge acquired in a lifetime. Transfer of learning is a significant element in the context of planning reading programs for non-native English speakers. Once students leave the primary grades, they are expected to read and write in almost every school subject. Therefore, the potential for transferability of skills from one system of written language to another should be seriously examined. Transfer takes place when there are elements in the new task similar to those in the task or skill previously acquired. For languages that share the same alphabet and have common features in the visual symbols, there are immediate transfer possibilities. For Asian languages with logographic writing systems, for other non-alphabet systems, or for different alphabetic writing like the Armenian alphabet, transfer is not based on the similarity of elements but on the more general understanding that the visual symbols represent the auditory ones. This transfer is based on the application of principles and generalizations. The sensory-motor requirements of reading and writing involve the transfer of other skills. Students who have learned how to use pencils, pens, rulers, protractors, and other classroom tools do not have to develop fine muscle control or eye-hand coordination a second time. The tracking of the eye and hand in the direction required by the conventions of the writing system may vary (Chinese is read from top to bottom, Hebrew from right to left, Spanish from left to right, and Japanese from top to bottom and then from right to left), but the awareness that there is a directionality and that it is an arbitrary feature of the specific writing system is transferable. There are good reasons to believe that attitudes and habits transfer. Positive feelings about reading in one language are likely to carry over to another. The habits of attention, concentration, persistence and task completion can transfer well to learning the new language.

Transfer of reading abilities from the first language to the second language can be identified in both general and specific terms for pre-reading, decoding, and comprehension skills. During the preparation for reading, students have been encouraged to develop good listening habits. Having learned how to listen for a sequence of events, immediate recall of facts, rhyming elements, discovering relationships, and for other receptive language tasks, the students carry over their response set to the demands of the new, unfamiliar language. Visual-perceptual training transfers as well. When students have become skillful in observing the visual details of one form of written language, this observation of the visual symbol system's significant features is readily available for transfer to another form. If the writing system is one that uses diacritically marked forms, the necessary attention to detail which is given to see differences in specific words as in *río, rió* or *papá, papa* (words whose meanings are significantly altered by the small detail of an accent mark or its placement), will transfer. Figure must be distinguished from ground in any language, and the background of page must be separated from the material written upon it. This visual-perceptual skill developed in one language transfers easily to another.

The visual-motor skills needed to track the eyes and hand in a specific direction to follow the sequence of a language's written patterns, the coordination of eye and hand in writing and spelling those patterns, and the development of strength and motor control are abilities that need to be learned and practiced. The application of motor skills to any reading and writing system may be transferred without change or put to use in new language learning with modifications to accommodate the differences that may exist between the first and second language's writing conventions. For languages that use a left-to-right direction such as English, Vietnamese, Spanish, and Portuguese, no change in eye or hand movement is needed. Farsi, Hebrew, or other languages read from right to left, however, require the student to change directions. Yet the eye and the hand must still move smoothly together. Though preparation for reading and writing is *specific* to the language in the matter of oral vocabulary development, ear training for language sounds, and knowledge of word order, all the sensory-motor skills and visual-perceptual abilities will transfer exactly as they have been learned or with modification that can be readily encouraged.

The act of making a connection between the sounds of a language (speech) and the graphic representation of that language (print, logograph, and ideograph) has been referred to as *decoding*. Developmental programs designed to introduce reading, writing, and spelling often stress the acquisition of techniques and strategies that assist students in making the speech-print associations needed to "crack the code." Using sound-symbol relationships, applying knowledge of word structures, and finding grammatical clues are examples of such skills that are encouraged in initial instruction. These are tools intended to help students recognize in written form what is known by the student in oral context. Thus, students begin to "see" what they have "heard." The extent to which decoding skills transfer from one language to another depends upon the two writing systems. Those using a Roman alphabet have greater potential for transfer according to the doctrine of identical elements. Languages written according to alphabetic principles may have common features that will transfer. Written languages vary; and transfer potential will also vary on the basis of the likenesses *and* the differences to be found among their alphabets, their syllabaries, and/or other arbitrary conventions of their written systems. Awareness of the rule-governed manner by which reading decoding skills are learned, remembered, and practiced will transfer by generalization.

There is little or no effective reading at the decoding level. Until students have made the speech-print connection, they are not reading. Essentially, comprehension of written material requires the exercise of intellectual skills. Students must draw upon specific backgrounds of experience and concepts. They must use memory, reasoning, and creativity as they interpret and judge what has been read. Each comprehension task calls upon students to think. At the early levels, simple, literal comprehension is required; but as the reading material becomes more complex, the reader is expected to exercise interpretive and inferential abilities of a higher order. Reading comprehension demands thinking in *any* language. If students learn in the primary language to recognize a main idea, find supportive details, order a sequence of events, identify major characters, determine the existence of bias, or analyze emotional tone, then these *thinking* skills are abilities that do not ever have to be learned again. There is complete transfer of cognitive function to the new language. For pre-reading, decoding, and comprehension skills, the power and potential of transferability cannot be underestimated.

It is reasonable to infer that the basis for language transfer in reading is found in the construct of CALP, which undergirds the potential for literacy in general and contributes to the ultimate flowering of literacy skills specific to the instructional program. However, it is vital to recognize that only *strong* skills transfer and that the sequence of reading skills in any language may be arranged to make the most of the transfer possiblities between languages. This precept of transfer should give planners of simultaneous reading programs in two languages or programs of premature introduction to the second language literacy pause for thought. Violations of learning principles could easily be responsible for the reading failure presently found among the minority language students.

POTENTIAL FOR L₁ READING SKILL TRANSFER TO L₂

Skill Areas	Language Specific Transfer	Language General Transfer
I. Sensory-Motor Transfer		
A. Visual Skills		
1. Eye-hand coordination		x
2. Fine muscle control		x
3. Visual attention to detail		x
4. Figure-ground awareness		x
5. Visual perception	x	x
6. Visual discrimination	x	x
7. Visual memory	x	x
8. Visual sequencing		x
B. Auditory Skills		
1. Figure-ground awareness		x
2. Auditory perception	x	x
3. Auditory memory	x	x
4. Auditory discrimination	x	x
5. Auditory sequencing		x

Table (continued)

Skill Areas	Language Specific Transfer	Language General Transfer
C. Spatial Skills		
1. Directional organization		x
2. Top-to-bottom orientation	x	x
3. Lateral orientation	x	x
4. Spatial integration		x
II. Transfer of Identical Elements		
A. The Common Features in Writing Systems		
1. Logographs, ideographs	x	
2. Alphabets	x	
3. Sound-symbol associations	x	
4. Capitalization	x	x
5. Punctuation	x	x
6. Lines or other spatial constraints of the writing	x	x
III. Transfer by Principles and Generalizations		
A. Reading as a Process		
1. Understanding speech-print relationships		x
2. Speech-print connections	x	
3. Concepts of words, syllables, sentences, paragraphs		x
4. Comprehension (thinking skills)		
a. Main idea		x
b. Sequence of ideas		x
c. Supportive details		x
d. Inferencing		x
e. Predicting outcomes		x
f. Drawing conclusions		x
g. Recognizing emotions		x
h. Seeing cause and effect		x
i. Distinguishing fact from fiction		x
j. Recognizing propaganda		x
5. Rule-governed aspects of reading	x	x
6. Study skills		x
IV. Transfer of Habits and Attitudes		
A. Non-cognitive Transfer		
1. Attention		x
2. Listening skills		x
3. Concentration		x
4. Persistence		x
5. Task completion		x
B. Self-esteem Transfer		
1. Being literate		x
2. Feeling capable		x
3. Possessing specific competencies		x
4. Achieving		x
5. Believing in one's ability to learn		x

The Nature of Reading

A very sensible definition of reading is given by Johnson and Myklebust (1967) who state that reading is a response to a visual symbol superimposed on auditory language. Beginning readers bring their experiences as encoded and stored to the page of print. They practice making accurate and speedy associations between auditory and visual language symbols. They grow to be efficient, rapid readers until they are scarcely aware of the speech-print relationships. Capable students who are free from any serious learning problems read well, expand their real and imaginary worlds, and become literate. Accomplished readers have engaged in a process taking them through a sequence of activities as follows: (1) see print, (2) transform print into recognizable sounds and arrangements of sounds, (3) relate what has been recognized to experience, (4) make the speech-print connection (the code), and (5) store print and the associations (meaning) for further use. This process moves the reader from the known to the unknown, from a reality represented by sounds, to a new reality represented by symbols. Successful reading depends upon the number and quality of experiences stored; the general level of oral language development; the keenness of sensory-motor skills; the suitability of the instructional program for the reader; and the personal differences in interest, motivation, intelligence, and health. For all persons reading any language, reading is a process of seeing print, hearing speech, and associating whatever it is that has been seen and heard with stored and remembered experiences, called "referents." When the reader sees the word "acrolith," for example, this visual stimulus must be changed into an auditory one. The reader may decide, according to the word recognition strategies he or she uses, to say the word. If the reader doesn't know very much about Greek statues, the meaning of what has been seen and said will be unclear or completely lacking. Reading has not been accomplished until the meaning is attached. Sometimes a reader can use context clues, picture clues, or other techniques that will help gather the meaning from material that may be unfamiliar. If reference to acrolith is within the subject matter content of Greek art, then the reader may be able to reduce the uncertainties in Smith's terms (1971) and gain an understanding of what has been read. The nature of the process itself calls to mind the "Vernacular Advantage Theory" when other conditions of instruction are considered (Modiano, 1968; Engle, 1975). Oral language grows out of specific contacts with a particular environment; these experiences are mediated by the conventions of a specific speech community. Spoken language, as acquired, forms the basis for the specific conventions of the writing system of that same community. The mutuality, the interdependence between spoken and written language can be perceived by the reader. There is little need to be reminded that many readers have difficulty learning to read their own language. Reading is more than a perceptual and a sensory-motor process, it is also a cognitive process. The successful reader must bring a background of concepts and ideas to a page of print. The amount and kind of comprehension the reader takes from that page is in direct proportion to what is brought. The reader must supply the context. Unlike personal exchange in informal situations where meaning can be obtained from the contextual flavor of the situation, the exchange between reader and author may have a context that is known only to the writer. As Cummins (1980) has suggested, while language development of students may be adequate for situations in which the context is supplied informally, such language development may be quite inadequate for successful functioning in the decontextualized demands of formal schooling, particularly in the written language of textbooks. This statement could apply to both language majority and language minority students alike. The important differences for the language minority students is one of distance from the context. They may have had far less exposure to the concepts represented by the vocabulary and may have not had the time to become familiar with the vocabulary and/or the grammatical and syntactical clues needed to predict meanings.

Human speech is graphically represented in a variety of forms that may be alphabetic, syllabic, logographic, or other symbolic indicators of the spoken word. Speech existed long before its graphic representation. Both oral and written forms of language are interdependent and share a mutual relationship. Well-developed speech provides the foundation for skill development in reading and writing. When students learn to read and write, they must organize the visual system of language in such a way as to make it meaningful according to the auditory system. They must make sense of writing by making a connection with the spoken language as represented. Words and their arrangements, which students have learned to describe and explain their experiences, become available to them in a visual form. The act of reading is a receptive one in which students see print, hear speech, and connect them to referents remembered and stored from their personal experiences (Thonis, 1970). Until the essential attachment to a meaningful referent has been accomplished, it cannot be said that students are reading.

In the usual course of human development, normal children learn to understand and to speak the language of the speech community into which they have been born. If the language has a written form, it is generally expected that the children will also learn to read and write that same language. In most parts of the world, this learning of the written forms of language is ordinarily provided during the years of middle childhood. Literacy is a task of the school-age years and is accomplished in a school setting. Thus, the students learn to listen, speak, read, and write the language that makes sense to them in the total environment in which they are living and growing. Reality has been interpreted and labeled by speech; speech is preserved through its representation in writing; and discrepancies that may exist between what is heard or said and what is read or written can be clarified and supplemented by the connections between reality, its oral label, and its written form. All writing systems are imperfect, but their imperfections can be managed and meaning can still come through when the students fill in any gaps in comprehension from their experiences and from their reservoir of oral language.

Students who speak Cantonese, Korean, Punjabi, Spanish, or one of the hundreds of languages other than English and who are learning to read and write in English, often have difficulty in supplying the needed information to obtain meaning. They may have a wealth of data stored, but their memories and concepts are not retrievable in response to English stimuli. The essential connections between speech, print, and referent cannot be formed. Smith (1971) has referred to reading comprehension as an act of "reducing the uncertainties" found in written language. When language minority students are attempting to deal with the uncertainties, they are (or may be) already burdened by the additional unknowns of the new visual forms, the unfamiliar structures, the strange vocabulary items, and the different view of reality. When these students see English print, hear their native speech, and seek meaningful referents drawn from their cultural heritage, they may fail to make connections. At best, their reading skill is stopped at the decoding level or, at worst, the written material may not make any sense to them at all. School districts with large numbers of language minority students only need to examine their own annual testing programs to discover the failure rates of these students.

There has been interest and excitement generated over the programs of reading instruction among select groups who have been introduced to reading by way of the second rather than the first language (Bowen, 1977; Tucker, 1977; Cohen, 1974). These "immersion" programs may take a variety of organizational models. The investigators take issue with the assumption that the speech-print connection is of primary importance and suggest that social-cultural factors may contribute more positively to the literacy skills of language minority students. English-speaking children placed in the Spanish language arts curriculum or

French-speaking children assigned to English classes are two examples of immersion programs. The theorists have been careful to distinguish between immersion programs and submersion ones (see Glossary). Though they both represent a plan of instruction in which the child's home language is not used primarily, the important difference between programs of submersion may be found in the status of the school language, the continued valuing and use of the home language outside of school, the point at which all students begin in the school's language, and the attitudes of the school-community toward learning the language (Cohen and Swain, 1976). It has been suggested that language minority students are often considered school failures because they cannot use the language of the dominant culture effectively while language majority students immersed in a second language are given rewards and approval for each small increment of learning via that second language. This distinction becomes an important one for language minority students who are mixed in reading classes with English speakers. For these students, their submersion practically guarantees reading difficulties and limited achievement.

The Lambert and Tucker research (1972) suggested that English-speaking children immersed in French reading programs in Canada continued to achieve adequately in English reading without receiving instruction in it. Cohen (1975) found that English-speaking students who learned to read Spanish first, achieved grade level competence in English. These experiments and others of a similar type are generally cited as support for placing students from language minorities in English reading programs immediately. Immersed or submersed, the language minority students must keep afloat, learn to swim, or eventually sink. The data from studies on immersion and submersion point up the social and cultural determiners of successful school achievement, the potential for language skill transfer, and effective dimensions of learning. Setting aside for the moment the social and cultural factors, it appears reasonable to suggest that the advantage of dealing with one's experiences, speech, and written language all within the same common framework of the vernacular are undeniable. If the home language is absolutely unacceptable for political or social reasons or if the language has positively no economic value, then the speech-print connections must still be made in the second language. The language minority students from this group should have opportunities for extended readiness to read with rich and varied activities designed to promote oral language sufficient to support the print of English.

Student Background Factors

The language minority student is first a student and must be seen as a maturing, developing person. Students in elementary and secondary schools are normally en route to the expected developmental milestones in physical, social, emotional, and intellectual maturity according to the universal rules of human growth. Sometimes it is necessary to remind teachers and administrators of this ordinary fact when language minority students are under discussion. The descriptor, "language minority" appears to take precedent over the word, "student," as educational plans are considered for them. Language minority students share the same needs as students of any language. Every serious professional in education knows what these commonalities of needs are. When it comes to identifying language and literacy needs, however, there is likely to be little agreement as to what those needs may be. One of the serious drawbacks on planning for minority language students stems from a lack of information about the language background. Often, all of the students are grouped together under one description: bilingual. The nature of the individual student's bilingualism is rarely identified with care and precision. In fact, the label "bilingual" often conceals more about the student than it reveals. Students may be at a serious disadvantage because once having been labeled bilingual, they may then be assumed to fit some pre-determined category and may be viewed as being the same. Thus, their basic needs may be ignored and their language needs may be undifferentiated. The descriptive designation, "bilingual," has been applied to students who come from another country, to students with certain physical characteristics, to students with ethnic surnames, and to students whose parents speak accented English. The criteria for using the term are often vague or misunderstood. To be bilingual suggests that students are capable of using two languages. Further, it is assumed that both languages can be used with relatively equal facility. To describe precisely what is meant by the term "bilingual student," it is necessary to determine how the students can function in both oral and written language. There are sounds, structures, vocabulary, and meaning systems for both dimensions. When students are competent listeners, speakers, readers, and writers in one language, they control eight dimensions as native speakers. When the students add the sounds, structure, vocabulary, and meaning systems of the second language, eight more are added. Thus, bilingual persons are capable of managing 16 separate and mutually supportive facets of both languages (proficient bilingualism). These students are rare, especially in United States' classrooms where monolingual, monoliterate education has inhibited dual language opportunities.

If reading programs are to suit the varying degrees of proficiency in languages that language minority students bring to school, they must be designed on the basis of better information about language minority students and their functioning levels in the several dimensions. Language minority students may listen and understand but not speak, or speak but not read or write, or write and read but not speak. The combinations of possible competencies among the receptive and expressive phases of both oral and written language are many. The decision to assign a student to a reading class in the first language, to immerse the student in a second language reading group, to submerse the student in a particular reading program, or to offer two reading programs simultaneously could be improved by careful, thoughtful assessment of language strengths in all 16 language functions.

The schooling opportunities that language minority students may have enjoyed in another setting may influence their abilities to cope with programs of reading instruction. Young students may not have had formal lessons in reading. They may still be at the pre-reading level of development and may only need to continue along the usual course of reading readiness. A few older students may also be found to be preliterate because they may have come from small towns and villages where they could not have attended school. Both of these groups of students share similar needs in getting ready to read. They need to coordinate eye and hand, refine motor responses, become aware of directionality and spatial factors of the written language, and sharpen their perceptual skills. These prerequisites for skillful reading apply across languages. There are specific background skills needed for different languages that must be addressed in specific ways. At the pre-reading level, it is essential to consider the general factors that promote strong background abilities for literacy and the specific skills that must be nurtured within the context of a specific language. For example, the accuracy and speed with which students note differences in forms of written language is a general ability that promotes attention to fine visual details. This awareness can be applied in a global way to any writing system. But, the distinction of detail between *b* and *d* or *w* and *m* would be only specific to forms of the Roman alphabet and would not necessarily apply to all alphabets.

Language minority students who have already learned to read their own language often amaze the reading teacher in a second language class. Adequate or better skills in the first language and good study habits may combine to help such students ease into the demands of the new writing system. If students are developmentally mature enough to have reached levels of thinking logically and abstractly, then they appear to be much better able to fit well into the new reading program. Such students call to mind the several constructs proposed to explain the apparent success of older students. Lambert (1975) writes of the *additive* effects of learning a second language while retaining the first. Majority language students who are immersed in a second language program have the opportunity to acquire the second language at no cost to the first. Older students already fluent and literate in one language may also enjoy this additive quality. On the other hand, it would appear that students with poorly developed language and literacy skills in the first language who are forced to take on another system prematurely or at the expense of the first may suffer *subtractive* effects. Cummins (1979) has considered these positive and negative influences in his "Threshold Hypothesis," which posits that the level of language competence of language minority students may influence intellectual growth. Cummins (1980) also states that a "Developmental Interdependence Hypothesis," which assumes that second language competence is partially a function of first language competence at the time of exposure to the second language, may account for the modest success of native language and literacy programs in the elementary grades. One obvious effect of such programs would be the time and opportunity provided to acquire concepts and to develop the vocabulary that explains them. Too, practice with more complex syntactical patterns and instruction in word formation and informal grammar improves the understanding of how a language system works and what generalizations about written forms can apply.

Many of the language minority students can be described as functionally illiterate. These are students who appear to have poorly developed language and literacy skills in two languages. They may not ever have learned to read and to write in their native language and may have had little success in learning to read the second one. These students are at a great disadvantage in the classroom because after the first or second grade, most of the school work is carried on in reading and in writing. Lambert (1975) would see these students as suffering from the subtractive effects of their language experiences. In Cummins' terms (1979), they would still be functioning below the first threshold. Language minority students who are failing to learn to read in school can easily be recognized in this group of under-achievers. It would appear that the vital role of first language development in nurturing intellectual growth has been ignored and most of these students have been struggling to organize school content in the second language. Both first and second language organizing fails because neither of them is fully developed. An unfortunate consequence is the loss of self-esteem and the deep sense of failure that may prevent students from becoming successful readers even when compensatory programs are offered. Students are likely to perceive their school problems as their own fault rather than the possible fault of an inappropriate program of reading instruction.

Reading Program Alternatives

Given the resources of funds and personnel, schools appear to have several alternatives from which to select when planning reading instruction for language minority students. The first choice is rooted in "Vernacular Advantage Theory" (Modiano, 1968; Engle, 1975; Skutnabb-Kangas and Toukomaa, 1976; Cummins, 1979). In first language literacy programs there would be continued opportunities to develop the native tongue and to grow in the extension of the home language. Additional concepts, word knowledge, expanded structures, and on-going practice would serve to extend and enhance the first language. Literacy in the native language as a basis for later second language literacy skills would make possible, in the future, a balanced bilingual competent in all facets of both languages. Idiomatic language, metaphor, figurative usage, and other deep insights into the language could be cultivated and enjoyed. The content of reading material would be realistic and relevant to the cultural legacy of the learner. There could be more interest and enthusiasm for reading the history, legends, folklore, and literature of one's own people. The pride and delight among family members who share the same language and ethnic heritage should offer additional motivation to learn to read and write well.

Another choice would be to place students in the second language literacy program immediately. There would be a need to provide extended pre-reading activities to provide the background skills of oral language, vocabulary, sentence patterns, and other skills specific to the language. It would be very important to move cautiously on the speech-print connections; to offer sequential activities of listening, speaking, reading, and writing; and to ensure that students were seeing what they were also hearing. It would be unwise to make unnecessary chore of pronunciation as long as the first language flavor did not interfere with obtaining meaning. Pacing for instruction would be a critical variable. The time allowed for practice and review of material would need to be adjusted to accommodate the various language proficiencies of students in the second language. Complexities of written vocabulary and written structures should not outdistance the oral control of words and word patterns. Unless the language minority students have had private opportunities for literacy in the native language or were already fluent, literate persons, it is doubtful that they would have the chance to develop fully as bilingual, biliterate individuals. The materials drawn principally from the literature of the language majority group would almost likely contain irrelevancies and cultural content that could be completely devoid of meaning for the readers. There would certainly be more books and other media to use in the community. Library shelves usually burst with the literature of the majority language. One difficulty may lie in the fact that for older students with more mature interests, some of the supplementary reading materials may be too advanced; and the reading materials on their levels may be more suitable for younger students with less sophisticated tastes. Language minority students in such programs may develop confidence in themselves if they are successful. Self-esteem comes from being just like the others in the group and able to read the language of the school and the community just like everyone else.

In many programs in the United States, language minority students enrolled in various types of bilingual instruction are in two reading programs—one in their first language and one in English. These simultaneous plans of reading instruction may provide parallel textbooks, alternative days of instruction, or native language reading in the morning and English reading in the afternoon. Some new programs have been designed to offer the two reading systems together in a kind of translation model. The impact of simultaneous reading has not been clearly demonstrated despite the fact that many of the potential sources of confusion could be predicted from a logical if not from an empirical position. In the Redwood City group who received simultaneous reading instruction (Cohen, 1975), there seemed to be poor achievement demonstrated. The results were interpreted as indicative of the retarding effect of simultaneous reading in English and in Spanish. It is especially unfortunate that the evaluations of Title VII programs are insufficient for drawing conclusions (Troike, 1978). Many federally funded programs have placed the students in two reading programs at the same time. One other complicating factor is the language of the classroom, which may be designated as a bilingual class but that is, in reality, a monolingual English-speaking classroom most of the school day. Speech-print connections may suffer from confusion in two simultaneously presented writing systems. Students may be attempting to deal with several unknowns. The opportunities to extend and enhance the native language may be limited if most of the school day is carried out in the second language. The potential for true biliteracy may not be fulfilled when the reading lessons are crowded into everything else that has to be accomplished. One complaint of teachers of simultaneous reading is that there isn't enough time for the practice, review, and repetition needed for overlearning two writing systems, two spelling systems, two punctuation systems, etc. Further, depending on the other language, there is the possibility of language interference. Vocabulary items may get mixed up, not in the clever code-switching of accomplished bilinguals, but in a confusion over which word comes from which language. When the students see the label *reloj* on the clock on the wall in the classroom, do they think it spells "clock?" In simultaneous reading plans, there is a valiant attempt to offer culturally relevant content for both reading activities.

One discrepancy in classrooms of the United States may be found in the abundance of beautiful books for the English reader and the scarcity and/or poor quality of many imported materials in the minority language. Non-print media such as films, filmstrips, study prints, records, and tapes may be hard to find as well as expensive. The interests, values, and motives of students and their families in programs will vary depending on how well-informed they are about the program of bilingual reading and on their own personal goals. Some parents have simply been passive about the enrollment of their children in dual language curricula, hoping fervently for them to become skillful in English. They may enjoy and approve of the native language activities but remain more committed to English language skills. Other parents are filled with emotion and gratitude to school personnel who have valued their children's native language and who have helped them perfect it. Parents often recall with pleasure the wealth of children's literature, the poetry, rhymes, riddles, and fables of their own childhood experiences. Many of these parents are ardent supporters of first language literacy. The response from the community will be different for different social, language, and economic status groups. In the United States, schools providing dual language instruction are doing so generally in response to a legal mandate. Many programs are merely tolerated at a token level to meet the minimum requirements stated by law. When the educational establishment or the community at large is not happy about the legal requirements, it is unlikely that reading programs operating on a simultaneous basis in order to have things both ways can be successful.

The alternatives of initial reading instruction in the native language, in the second language, or simultaneously in both languages are likely to be considered on the basis of social and political factors. Linguistic reasons that support initial reading in the first language are found in the tasks of decoding and comprehending the graphic forms. Decoding skills are developed through the use of methods and materials that demonstrate to the learners how the writing system is organized and how it works. Since most writing systems of the world operate on some kind of alphabet principle, decoding skills provide practice in the acquisition of the alphabet, the names of the letters, the sounds they represent, syllables, words, affixes, and other parts of the written conventions. A knowledge of the system permits beginning readers to crack the code. Across many languages, readers are introduced to graphic representations by this emphasis on small parts of the written language. Once students have developed the awareness that what has been spoken can be represented by some written form, learning the code, whether logographic or alphabetic, is basic to reading success. Decoding skill alone, however, will not create competent readers in any language. Comprehension skills are those that make it possible for written language to make sense to the readers. Once the code has been cracked, the students can understand the author's words. Meanings are not conveyed in letters, syllables, words, or small groups of them. Comprehension is really thinking, and teaching to promote adequate comprehension skills can be far more difficult than teaching to develop the ability to decode. For majority language students who learn to read and write their own language, the establishment of strong levels of comprehension has been a great challenge to reading teachers. For minority language students, the inadequacies of their comprehension skills have been alarming. Reading programs for all students must address the apparent discrepancies between decoding and comprehension skills, but for language minority students the issue is more than a faulty connection from code to meaning.

At the first level of comprehension, the student merely has to understand what the author has said. Then, after the students have made sense of what they have read, they may need to use it in some way. They understand the idea the author is trying to express, but because meaning is not necessarily wrapped up in small segments of written materials, the students may need to read larger passages to determine the main idea or essential message. They may need to search for details that support or substantiate this generalization. They may interpret what they have read in the light of their own experiences. When the students have enough information, they can abstract from the data and consider how the generalizations they have discovered may be used in other contexts. To accomplish this, the students must know how to sort, sift, classify, and organize what they have read. Further, they must connect or relate these discoveries in some order. There may be thousands of words arrayed in a variety of patterns, but they have to organize them into a system so that they can efficiently and economically draw out the relationships, the sequence, and the main ideas. They may then judge the relevance of what they have read. While engaged in all these activities, they have been thinking. They have been using and developing the abilities to comprehend, interpret, reason, generalize, abstract, solve problems, and decide. Given the developmental opportunities to acquire oral language, to add written language, and to use both oral and written skills in thinking, the students have been expanding and refining these abilities in mutually supportive ways. It may be said that speech and print have a symbiotic relationship, one in which the health of one contributes to the health of the other, and that thinking is supported by both.

If the learner has one oral language and learns to read the same language, and subsequently uses that language as an instrument that serves thinking (in ways that are not clearly understood or even agreed upon), then the student develops fairly clear relationships between speech and print and between language and thought. Programs of literacy in the primary language provide rich opportunities for this development. When second or third languages are introduced, thinking skills, abstracting, generalizing, connecting, interpreting, organizing, and judging are already a part of the learner's cognitive abilities. The new demands of the new language and the new written symbol system do not require new thinking strategies. The words and their arrangements into structural patterns will require some specific teaching, but there will be no need to begin over again in developing thinking skills. The words are different, but the melody is the same.

How do considerations of these speech, print, and thought relationships apply to students in classrooms of the United States? Although it is always hazardous to divide human beings, especially young human beings, into groups, for the sake of discussion, it is necessary to describe students in broad categories. First, there are monolingual English speakers who listen, comprehend, speak, read, write, and spell in English. Some of these students are highly successful, some moderately so, and some fail in their efforts to become competent, literate persons capable of thinking. A second group may be students for whom English is not the home language but whose primary language is used among large numbers of their ethnic background in a given community, the educational program offering them first language literacy. The Spanish, Chinese, Portuguese, Filipinos, Koreans, and Vietnamese are examples of this group of students, many of whom are being taught in programs of dual language and dual literacy—English and the native language. A third group of students may be described as speakers of other languages whose home language may be difficult to offer in an educational setting in the United States. Children from homes where Cambodian, Laotian, Samoan, or Punjabi is spoken usually find themselves in classrooms where there are few or no resources for the use of their native language as a basis for first language literacy. For these students, reading in English may become a difficult task and a stumbling block to thinking. The teacher must build a broad base of oral English, a foundation firm enough to support the English writing system. The richer and fuller the experiences that students have labeled in English, the more abundant and supportive are their available resources for thinking. A fourth group of students may be described as those who have some English and some other language, neither of which has been developed fully. These students may have bits and pieces of both; they may have gone back and forth between the two. They may even have a little of both writing systems. These are frequently the students who are in grave trouble because of their language confusion and their despair of ever understanding the mysteries of the written forms. Needless to add, such poorly developed skills do not serve thinking very well.

The Methods

Reading methods for language minority students are often debated from the viewpoint of whether the code or the meaning approach is the better. The synthetic method in which the letters, sounds, syllables, and smaller segments of the written language are introduced may lend itself well to certain languages that offer reasonably dependable speech-print correspondence. The analytic methods in which whole words or utterances are presented may stress meaning at every level. How the parts of the writing system go together are not considered of great importance. Making sense of the written material and comprehending the ideas and events are the important goals of the reading instruction. For languages with many irregularities in the speech-print correspondence, like French or English, the analytic approach has worked well for some students. Eclectic methods offer the opportunities both to learn the code and to obtain meaning. Regardless of the method, to read is to comprehend and to comprehend is to think.

In the broadest sense, all methods can be grouped into three major categories: (1) synthetic approaches, (2) analytic approaches, or (3) approaches that combine both the synthetic and analytic. Synthetic methods stress part-whole relationships and give emphasis to building meaningful words or sentences as letters, sounds, and/or syllables are mastered. There is a heavy responsibility to learn how to "crack the code." Analytic methods focus on whole words and meaningful sentences, which can be examined further for their elements. A synthetic-analytic method may combine features that offer both the *code* and the *meaning* emphasis.

Synthetic Approaches. Several of the traditional reading methods used in learning to read those languages based upon an alphabetic writing principle are synthetic. For example, the onomatopoeic method is one in which the pupils learn to make a single sound association for each visual symbol in order to remember the speech-print relationship that is represented. Each time the pupils see a symbol, they are to associate the letter with a familiar sound from the environment. For example, when learning the *u,* children are told to recall the sound of a train whistle; or when learning the *t,* they are reminded of the ticking of a clock. As they build a repertoire of such associations, they gradually accumulate enough of them to read at least at the level of decoding. The onomatopoeic method is frequently a delight to young learners. It *is* fun and it can be paced according to the rate at which pupils are making, storing, and retrieving connections between sounds and symbols. However, it can be a very artificial approach, one resulting in lessons that are very contrived and that contain stilted, unnatural language. It places such a strong emphasis on the recall of discrete elements that the *code* may emerge to detract from the *meaning.*

Another synthetic method is the alphabetic method. The pupil learns all the *names* of the letters of the alphabet. Unlike the onomatopoeic method, no attention is given to the sounds represented by the letters. The learner uses his/her knowledge of letter names to unlock words by spelling them, for example, in English *em a em a* (mama); *em a tee* (mat); or *eme ah eme ah* (mama); *ce ah ese ah (casa) in* Spanish. The method is easy to initiate and convenient for teachers, but it can be cumbersome and limiting. The pupils are blending *letters* not *sounds,* and they may become confused when they are unable to unlock words that have been obscured by their spellings. Because the *whole* of anything is more than the sum of its parts, attention to small elements of written language may tend to create readers who fail to grasp the larger, more meaningful units.

The phonic method has many enthusiastic supporters. A phonic method is one in which the sound system of the language is primary. Pupils must hear speech sounds (the phonemes) and make accurate and rapid associations with the written symbols (the graphemes) representing them. Once they have the speech-print connections mastered, they are then able to decode, that is, they can transform the written symbols back into the spoken ones. The phonic method has been very popular in Spanish because there is a good *fit* between speech and print. The written language is a fairly consistent and predictable representation of speech. Thus, with *few* exceptions (as contrasted with the many discrepancies existing between speech and print in English, French, and several other languages), the sound-symbol associations can be learned with relative ease by most pupils. There are, of course, the few irregularities, the sound of *s* represented by the symbols *s, z, c,* followed by *i* or *e;* the symbols *y*, and *ll* representing the same sound; the changing sounds represented by *c* or *g* when followed by *i* or *e* in contrast with the sounds represented by the same *c* or *g* followed by *a, o,* or *u;* the silent *h* in *hombre,* and the changing of the silence when the *h* is found in combination with *ie* or *ue* as in *hielo* or *hueso,* etc. There is also a very elaborate diphthong system and a system of diacritical marks to be learned. Fortunately for the reader of Spanish, both these tasks are made easier by a very simple, unchanging set of rules. For these and other reasons, teachers find many advantages in *el método fónico,* particularly at the very beginning. The speech-symbol relationships may be presented by means of picture-symbols, which requires the learners to make an association with a picture, usually one representing an object in their world. The pictured object's name begins with the sound to be represented by the letter. The sound-symbol relationships may also be taught directly by presenting the letter name and the sound represented by the letter together with illustrations of the sounds in words familiar to the children. For example, the name of the letter *m (eme)* is taught as representing the sound *mm* while the child listens for this sound in words such as *mamá, miel, muñeca, mariposa,* etc. At first, just *beginning* sounds are given attention but later, pupils may be asked to listen for and hear sounds in other positions within words. There are few *ending* sounds to learn because in Spanish there are only 11 possibilities, and then pupils can be encouraged to recognize sounds and their written symbols in *medial* positions. *El método fónico,* in its several variations, lends itself to a reasonable sequence with short units of speech-print understandings to be acquired and practiced as the program progresses. It can become boring and seem unrelated to the *total* act of reading unless the teacher adds the element of interest with tongue twisters *(trabalenguas),* rhymes *(rimas),* poems *(poesía),* and other language activities. Further, the method does focus on parts of words and may result in pupils learning to decode at the expense of gaining meaning. It is wise to remember that phonic skills in many languages may be great for unlocking unfamiliar words but, by themselves, contribute little to the comprehension of those words.

The syllabic method is another very traditional and time-honored method that depends heavily on the child's auditory memory. For example, in Spanish, pupils learn the written syllables in patterns of consonant-vowel such as *ma, me, mi, mo, mu,* and vowel-consonant, *am, em, im, om, um.* They are then taught to put syllables together to create words, *mamá, memo, amo, Mimi,* etc. Soon, syllables and words are strung together to create sentences, *Amo a mi mamá* and *Mi mamá me ama a mí. El método silábico* has some of the advantages of other part-whole approaches in that small units of speech-print relationships can be offered to pupils as they are able to internalize and use them. *Las silabas* can be organized and sequenced carefully to permit pupils to begin using them immediately in words and in sentences that provide meaning. The opportunity to apply the skills directly to the act of reading allows learners to feel that they are not merely acquiring some isolated information like letter names and letter sounds, which may often appear only peripherally related to *real reading*. Of this method it must be said, however, that it falls heir to the same criticism as other approaches that emphasize small units of speech sounds and their written representations in symbols.

Analytic Approaches. Among the analytic ways of teaching reading, the language experience approach has been used with some degree of success. The pupils are encouraged to respond to events in their experience by recalling what they have thought about and can put into words. The teacher or teacher aide then writes what has been said, reads it back, asks for several repetitions of it until the pupils, too, can read what has been written. Since the material comes from a meaningful experience in the pupils' own world, there is no question of comprehension. The pupils see the relationships between thinking, speaking, reading, and writing. They next learn the writing system and can create their own accounts of personal experiences. The teacher is responsible for maintaining a rich and interesting classroom environment that will elicit language and generate experiences about which talking, writing, and reading can be accomplished. For pupils from any language, the language experience approach can be a delight. They may draw upon culturally relevant and familiar topics that are near and dear to them. They are assimilating written language in whole phrases or sentences that make instant sense because they are their very own thoughts. The teacher enjoys the pupils' interest and motivation. However, this approach demands much of both teacher and learners. The teacher must manage an enormous amount of material, different for each child, since each pupil's language and experiences are unique. There is the ongoing requirement to change and to create new stimuli for more complex language and its written representation. In order to keep track of pupil progress, there is the considerable burden of recordkeeping so that the teacher will be able to follow individual development in the various reading skills. There is little or no control of vocabulary so that practice needed for mastery may not occur and words learned today may be forgotten tomorrow. The success or failure of such a reading approach depends in large measure upon many other classroom variables, one of which being how the teacher uses stories the pupils have produced.

The global method is one in which whole words and entire sentences are produced visually and the pupils are told what they are. They then memorize the words without ever taking them apart to look at their smaller elements. It is a *look-say* approach that stresses meanings and ignores the writing system as a code. Expressions such as *Hoy es lunes, Today is Monday; Hace sol;* or customary classroom amenities as *Buenos días, niños; Sienténse, niños; Good morning, children* are taught in their entirety. Theorists who support this method argue that dividing the words into syllables and learning the letters and sounds may create absurdities and destroy meaning, the heart of the reading process. The global method has its merits. It offers reading activities pupils can readily understand *if the written material is prepared by the teacher at a level commensurate with pupils' experience*. It places a great burden on memory, however, and has been said to offer few or no opportunities to acquire basic awareness of how the writing system works. Expansion of the reading vocabulary and development of specific reading skills may not take place unless the teacher goes further with supplementary activities designed for specific skill practice.

The generative word method operates much as the global method. Whole words and complete sentences are presented, illustrated, and pronounced by the pupils. After they have memorized the material and can read it, they *then* are taught how to analyze sentences and words into their component elements. Thus, they go from a meaning emphasis to the code and analyze how the code has been put together to create the meanings for them. They may discover syllables, sounds, letters, punctuation marks, and capitalization. When pupils have finished the analysis, they have a good grasp of both the *code* and the *meaning*. It has been said that one danger is the pitfall of passivity in the pupils. The teacher must do most of the analyzing; and once the pupils *know* what the written language represents, there is not much motivation for them to dig back into the *parts* that have created a meaningful *whole* for them already.

Eclecticism. The eclectic method is one that combines successful elements of both synthetic and analytic approaches in an attempt to offer pupils an effective reading program. It may include the presentation of whole sentences, identification of speech-print relationships by phonics, *look-say* practice with flash cards, use of the learner's own language, use of pictures for clues, and a variety of other features drawn from several methods.

It is prudent for teachers to consider *first* the pupil who is to be served by the reading approach and to recognize that no *one* method has a monopoly on success in the classroom. There are pupils with great visual memories, pupils with well-developed oral language, and pupils with good tactile-kinesthetic skills. There are *also* pupils who are weak in one or more of these areas. Add to this the fact that some pupils have long attention spans and some do not; some can persist in the completion of a task and some cannot; some are able to take direction and follow instructions and some are not. Yet all pupils have *something* the teacher may draw upon to ensure that they find a measure of success in learning to read.

Which of the methods are applicable to the teaching of both English and native language reading? Any method wisely used by a careful, knowledgeable teacher can be applied *if* it is suitable for the background and unique needs of pupils (Thonis, 1976). If pupils' auditory integrities are weak, a method that demands hearing and discriminating among fine speech differences (as required by the phonic method) would be a poor choice. If pupils have phenomenal visual strengths, a method that taps this ability to remember visually presented materials and arrange them in proper sequence (as the global method demands) may be an excellent alternative. Pupils with impressive command of oral language and rich stores of experiences may find an introduction to print that uses their language and experience an exciting encounter. It is the teacher who must select the best methods to make the most of the reading opportunities. For language minority pupils, the language experience approach could be very effective in the teaching of *both* English and native language reading. A phonics method, one demanding the pupil to hear sounds and speech patterns, could be most productive for native language reading and a disaster for English reading. Pupils could find it difficult if not impossible to hear accurately and to discriminate among the sounds of English. A method using whole words and sentences taken solely from an English-speaking cultural setting may be totally devoid of sensibility or interest for language minority pupils. Thus, the choice of methods conceivably could be different for the *two* reading classes. It would be a grave error to assume that the *same* methods would necessarily apply to the teaching of both. It is essential to determine the method of the basis of first- and second-language readiness to read *each specific language* and the levels of language development in both native language and in English.

Transition Period. What about the transition period during which the pupil is led from first- and second-language literacy in English? Reading teachers should develop criteria for placing their language minority students in the reading classes in English. Among these criteria are such considerations as the pupils' successful accomplishments in the native language reading class, their proficiency in oral English, their specific ear-training for the English sound system, and their expressed interest in discovering the content to be unlocked in English print. The most important consideration in these criteria is time. Pupils must be given sufficient time to establish strong literacy skills in their first language.

Once the decision is made that the pupils have met the standards set and that they could benefit from instruction in reading English, there are some additional factors to consider. The first concern is with the reading skills, which pupils will be able to transfer immediately from native language reading to English reading. The greatest transfer benefit, however, is the confidence of an already literate learner who has successfully managed the rigors of print and will face the second writing system with self-assurance. The second consideration in the recognition of potential phonological, lexical, or structural sources of interference from the writing system that need to be anticipated and minimized. The English reading teacher must watch for any problems and attempt to prevent them. A third concern is to provide knowledge and opportunities to practice new skills specific to English reading. Word order patterns, punctuation rules, multi-semantic vocabulary items, and other features unique to written English must be learned in addition to those elements that have transfer possibilities. Thus, transition to English demands *at least* the following: (1) definitive criteria for assessing pupils' readiness to engage in reading English, (2) recognition of areas that do not have to be taught again, (3) clear understanding of skills that may transfer immediately, (4) keen sensitivity to interference problems and the expertise to deal effectively to minimize them, and (5) considerable competence in the contrastive sounds and structural systems of both the native language and English.

Good choices for the transitional stage might be the language experience approach supported by a cautious program of phonic skills based on sounds pupils can *hear* and *say*. Another method might be a *linguistic* program, which presents short written patterns on the basis of a regular sound-symbol correspondence *(man - Dan - ran - fan,* etc.) and support this somewhat sterile, artificial written language by rich oral English in poems, storytelling, choral speaking, and dramatizations. Still another might be a carefully paced basal reader approach augmented by pictures, news events, and descriptions of life in the language minority community as written in English. In this manner, the content of the basal stories could be enlivened by content of cultural relevance to learners. There are many combinations of methods that could well support the second language literacy plan in English. Teachers should be encouraged to sift among the many methods for the winning combination for their own pupils.

Management Systems. What is the role of management systems in a bilingual reading program? It is always desirable to have *some* means of charting pupils' progress in reading. If pupils are learning to read in one language, *it is important;* if they are learning to read in *two* languages, *it is absolutely essential.* Yet, the teacher must guard against the management system taking over the program. The management system is a bookkeeping system only; it is not the reading program. To be useful, the system should be short and simple. It should be easy to use and convenient for the teacher who will use it. The system should contain some built-in flexibility to accommodate differential levels of pupils and the transiency rates in areas where pupils experience a high rate of school transfer. A management system should not be too costly, not only in terms of the school's budget, but it must also not extract a high price in terms of the teacher's time, tears, and frustration. The system should be selected on the basis of its consistency with the established program within the district. If some provision for the pupils' checking their own progress can be build into the system, it provides greater freedom from the paper chase that so often burdens teachers and teacher aides. Wise experienced teachers have always had a management system of some kind. The system should work for the reading program and be supportive of it. Teachers and administrators must be cautious that the management system does not work against the program and does not become an end in itself.

What is the importance of assessment? Assessment can be very important and can contribute greatly to the success of a program of reading in two languages. The major problem lies in the identification of appropriate ways to assess the gains pupils are making and to redirect one's efforts if gains are in evidence. Assessment may involve the administration of standardized tests, the observation of pupils, the application of informal measures, and other assessment techniques. It is wise to remember that assessment is an appraisal of the program; *it is not the program.* Therefore, assessment should be economical of both teacher and pupil time. The *use* of information obtained through assessment is of much greater value. As teachers appraise the progress of pupils, they may change objectives, edit materials, or alter timelines to improve pupils' chances for success. Assessment should be the servant not the master of the reading program.

The Teacher. The most important element in an instructional plan for minority students who are learning in a classroom designed for the language majority students is the teacher. It is always a competent and caring teacher who makes the method and materials work. For language minority students, the teacher ideally should know and appreciate the language and culture of the students. The teacher should be skillful in assessing language, development, and achievement levels. The teacher needs to be flexible and creative in making adjustments to the plan of reading instruction to accommodate a variety of levels in language achievement. The teacher needs to be well-organized and well-informed about the availability of materials, personnel, and other resources to supplement classroom opportunities. The teacher should be strong in the conviction that language minority students are capable of learning to read and write at the same level of excellence as their majority language peers. The teacher needs to continue to search for improved methods of assessment and instruction as new research points the direction toward better reading programs for language minority students. The teacher must be willing to take the time necessary to bring these students along.

All instruction for all children should be intended to increase self-confidence and self-esteem. The school is only one source of nurturance of ego strengths; but it is a very powerful one for developing, maturing students. When the reading program alternatives are considered in relation to this sense of self-worth, it may be useful to consider first the status of the minority language in the school and outside of it. When the value of minority language is rejected by the community, this message may diminish students' sense of self. There are certainly some social conditions over which the school has little or no control, and the societal rejection of a minority group and their language may be one of them. Within the school itself, however, the importance of the mother tongue in the enhancement of intellectual growth; the relevance of the speech-print connection in the improvement of literacy skills; and the role of first language development in the extension of second language competency can be communicated to everyone who works with language minority students. School-community contacts should be used to explain and describe the needs of language minority students from the framework of development and learning theories not from a social, political viewpoint. A climate of acceptance at school may serve the students well in supporting their self-esteem and in increasing their confidence in their abilities to succeed in language and literacy accomplishment.

The Materials. When majority language students are learning to read, one of the joyous opportunities they have is their practice outside the classroom. They can take their readers home or go to the libraries with their parents or family members. They are surrounded by signs, advertisements, newspapers, menus, and numerous written reminders that reading and writing are valued. Out of school practice reinforces the skills being developed in their daily lessons and results in improved learning. For language minority students, however, the extra practice depends on several conditions. Many language minority children learning to read the vernacular have parents who do not read. There are few library books on the shelves in the school and community libraries to challenge and delight them. The majority language surrounds them when they leave the classroom. Newspapers, magazines, restaurant lists, notices, and other written material are offered in the language of the majority. Or, if language minority students are attempting to read in the second language, they may find it very difficult to handle the concept loading and speech-print connections of the uncontrolled media beyond the classroom. If they wish to share their second language literacy skills with their family, it may turn out that parents do not read the language. These are social and cultural factors discussed by Bowen (1977) and Tucker (1977) who feel that social and cultural considerations are more important than linguistic ones in deciding which literacy program is best for language minorities. The school is an institution created by society and is expected to reflect the values of that society. The expectations of the school and the community certainly must be weighed.

An important issue is the selection of reading materials for language minority students. There are the dual concerns for the suitability of the materials and their availability. If the reading decision results in the teaching of language minority students to read in their native language, it may be very disappointing for the students to find few or no books to read. When majority language students learn to read, they are likely to find the delight and wonder of stories, records, tapes, and other media for practice and for pleasure. Minority language students ordinarily do not find such treasures in school and community libraries of the United States. Like most skills, the skills of literacy are of little value if they are not used. If these students are to enjoy their hard-won skills, the school must consider seriously the addition of native language books and other materials to supplement the classroom instruction and to extend opportunities for growth in reading and thinking skills.

An appraisal of the suitability of materials is often a difficult task because there are so many elements involved in their selection. Minimally, teachers should take into account appearance, illustrations, authenticity of language, representative nature of the content, relevance to the curriculum, and cost. Materials should be attractive; the print should be an appropriate size; the quality of paper and binding should be adequate for the kind of use anticipated; vocabulary, structure, sentence length, and concept load should be suitable; and the political or religious content should be acceptable to the community. It is especially important that the materials are not hastily patched together translations of English. The cultural content should be interesting and relevant to the language minority students. The international literature of childhood and adolescence is stocked with charming stories that enchant students everywhere. Many classics from English have been lovingly translated into other languages with great care and with attention to idiomatic expressions, figurative language, vocabulary, and cultural detail. The concepts and values drawn from other cultural settings should be free from stereotyping. The views of various ways of living should be presented objectively. Reading materials should emphasize the commonalities among various groups as well as their differences. Reading materials carefully chosen on the basis of the language needs and developmental levels of minority students contribute greatly to learning success.

The Parents. It is noteworthy that successful reading programs, regardless of approach or language sequence, generally include strong support for reading at home. The literature describes the importance of the value given reading, the reading interests of parents, the availability of reading material, and the many other family variables that may contribute or detract from pupils' learning to read. The traditional recommendations offered have been invitations to parents to volunteer in classrooms; serve on school committees; read to their children at home; take them on visits to museums and places of historic interest; and other such suggestions requiring time, transportation, materials, money, and a knowledge of community resources that many minority language families lack. School personnel also have been fairly consistent in their recommendations that language minority families use the majority language in the home. Parents who do attempt to follow this suggestion are likely to be providing poor language models and restricted language practice in the majority language while at the same time denying their children the richness and variety of their native language competence. It would appear that educators need to be more aware of the practical realities of language minority families and more knowledgeable about the impact of language on literacy before making suggestions that may not be in their students' best interests.

It is highly consistent with the research to encourage parents to continue using the native language at home. They should be urged to speak with and listen to their children. Both listening and speaking vocabularies can be increased and the background of concepts extended. Language development is part of total development. Children's home experiences can offer vital opportunities for learning about the family's history and heritage. The songs, dances, proverbs, poetry, recipes, games, and the hundreds of other remembrances from the childhoods of parents and grandparents offer not only a sense of self but also a wealth of language skills. Legarreta-Marcaida (1981) has an exciting and practical list of suggested activities that enhance the parents' contribution to their children's reading potential.

In encouraging parents to continue using the home language, educators must take time to explain clearly their reasons for this recommendation. Often, parents do not appreciate the educational value of the home language in an English-speaking society. They need to be reassured that English language competence is a major instructional goal. They also need to be told that native language proficiency contributes to these second language skills. The school has a significant responsibility to facilitate understanding of the rationale, which supports the sequence of language and literacy instruction.

The Best of Biliteracy

Cummins (1980) has stated that cognitive academic language potential is strongly related to reading and writing skills. This potential permits readers to process written language and manipulate the content in reasoning and in dealing with abstractions. It is this ability that promotes effective reading comprehension skills. The question of the most appropriate reading program alternatives for the minority language student can then be considered from the multiple viewpoint of: (1) which language promotes cognitive development; (2) which writing system makes the best connection with language and cognition; (3) which reading program will be supported by social, political, and cultural factors; and (4) which alternative is best suited to the minority student's stage of development. There are doubtless other variables to consider in reviewing the many complexities of literacy and biliteracy in a country where the expected outcomes of the program have been the creation of monolingual and monoliterate students. This goal has been in place for a long period of educational history in the United States.

The case for native language reading instruction for language minority students is strong. The rationale can be defended on logical grounds and empirical evidence. The perceptual, sensory-motor, and cognitive processes learned and practiced in any language have tremendous potential for transfer of developmental and learning principles are not violated. Once language minority students have learned to read well and have understood the strategies for obtaining meaning from print, these abilities provide a solid foundation for literacy skills in the second language. The essential characteristic of first language skills available for supporting the addition of the second language is strength. Only strong learnings transfer. Hasty, premature introduction to the second writing system may result in two weak sets of skills, neither of which serves well enough to be the carrier of content in school subjects.

Language minority students need access to content areas by way of the language and literacy, which makes sense to them. Mathematics, social science, physical science, and other school subjects can be acquired and clarified in the stronger language and once fully understood, can be labeled in the second language. Reading instruction is not an end in itself. The reason that the years of middle childhood are usually emphasized as the period for acquiring reading and writing skills may be found in the timetable of human development. These are the years for acquiring the basic instruments for lifelong learning. The growing complexities of subject matter after the fifth grade matches the students' increased abilities to manage abstractions and formal logic. Reasoning abilities, well-supported by language and literacy, allow students to expand their understanding of the world and the people in it. If students are not given the opportunity to learn and fully develop their native language, the subject areas must be taught at a slower pace and with as much non-verbal representation as possible. Even with this effort, language minority students may not be able to keep up with their language majority classmates. High achievement is possible when students are given textbooks for content areas in their stronger language and at the suitable level for their age and grade placement. If the students cannot read second language texts, alternative methods of presenting concepts must be identified.

There is no argument among language researchers, developmental psychologists, and reading theorists that written language is strongly related to some aspects of oral language. There is also agreement that language and literacy skills are mutually supportive and essential to cognitive growth. In the best possible conditions for learning, students would all read first the language, which has made their world a meaningful place. They could come from the language of their families to the language of instruction with confidence and ease. With the addition of literacy, students could advance through the curriculum to the extent that good instruction and intellectual potential would permit. Language majority students do this and some are very successful; others are not. Yet, the difficulties when they do arise are not compounded by language differences as they are for minority students. With the growing numbers of these students in classrooms of the United States, there is a serious need to re-examine reading instruction alternatives for them. It is only reasonable to expect that all communities cannot offer the advantages of vernacular reading for all language minority students. It is also very reasonable to consider initial and continuing native language reading instruction in communities where large numbers of the same language groups are found.

Regarding the differences existing between immersion and submersion programs, it may be useful to attempt to change some of the negative influences through a better exchange of information. The language majority group often fails to understand that the end in view is also excellence in English. There must be a continued effort to clarify the speech-print connection in literacy and to emphasize the important role that language and literacy skills play in the development of intelligence. A central purpose of the school is to teach students to think. Thinking includes, among other entities, problem solving, evaluating, creating, and reasoning. Well-developed speech and strong reading skills are instruments that nurture thinking. For language minority students, there is the rich potential for speaking, reading, writing, and thinking in two languages.

Transferability of first language skills, both oral and written, is important and possible. The potential for transfer of sensory-motor skills, identical elements, principles, patterns, and attitude must be recognized and promoted depending upon the languages involved. There should be a sequence of language and literacy skills that searches out transfer possibilities and watches carefully for potential interference. Exit criteria are *not* applied, as the central issue to consider is the *addition* of more formal second language instruction and the introduction of the written English forms. There must be the expectation that when English language skills are sufficiently strong they, too, will carry content in the subject areas. Self-esteem is promoted not only through the accomplishment of English but also by the advancement of native language abilities. The school personnel, rather than recommending use of English in the home, continues to encourage use of the native language in family activities, which enlarge the students' view of their environment and improve their background of information. The program is one based on the *common underlying proficiency model,* which recognizes the value of stimulating general language growth by way of the native language channel. The common underlying proficiency model also makes sense in terms of stressing the use of the stronger language for instructional purposes. There is the logical assumption that first language strength contributes to second language acquisition and that second language achievement is not diminished by the development of the first language. Rather, excellence in the native language improves the chances of better second language functioning. It is reasonable to expect that students who talk well, read easily, think effectively in their own first language, and have developmentally reached the stage of abstract thinking will *also* talk well, read easily, and think effectively in the second language.

REFERENCES

Bowen, J. Donald. "Linguistic Perspectives on Bilingual Education," *Frontiers of Bilingual Education,* eds., Bernard Spolsky, and Robert L. Cooper. Rowley, Massachusetts: Newbury House, 1977, pp. 106-118.

Cohen, Andrew D. *A Sociolinguistic Approach to Bilingual Education: Experiments in the American Southwest.* Rowley, Massachusetts: Newbury House, 1975.

____. "The Culver City Spanish Immersion Program: The First Two Years," *The Modern Language Journal,* LVIII, No. 3 (March, 1974), 95-103.

____, and Merrill Swain. "Bilingual Education: The 'Immersion' Model in the North American Context," *TESOL Quarterly,* X, No. 1 (March, 1976), 45-53.

Cummins, James. "The Construct of Language Proficiency in Bilingual Education." Paper presented at the Georgetown Roundtable of Language and Linguistics, Georgetown University, March, 1980.

____. "Linguistic Interdependence and the Educational Development of Bilingual Children," *Bilingual Education Paper Series.* Vol. 3 No. 2. Los Angeles, California: National Dissemination and Assessment Center, California State University, Los Angeles, September, 1979.

Engle, Patricia Lee. *The Use of Vernacular Languages in Education: Language Medium in Early School Years for Minority Groups.* Papers in Applied Linguistics, Bilingual Education Series, No. 3. Arlington, Virginia: Center for Applied Linguistics, 1975.

Furth, Hans G. *Thinking Without Language: Psychological Implications of Deafness.* New York: The Free Press, 1966.

Johnson, Doris J., and Helmer R. Myklebust. *Learning Disabilities: Educational Principles and Practices.* New York: Grune and Stratton, 1967.

Lambert, Wallace E. "Culture and Language as Factors in Learning and Education," Education of Immigrant Students, eds., A. Wolfgang. Toronto, Ontario, Canada: Ontario Institute for Studies in Education, 1975.

____, and G. Richard Tucker. *Bilingual Education of Children: The St. Lambert Experiment.* Rowley, Massachusetts: Newbury House Publishers, 1972.

Legarreta-Marcaida, Dorothy. "Effective Use of the Primary Language in the Classroom," *Schooling and Language Minority Students: A Theoretical Framework.* Los Angeles, California: Evaluation, Dissemination and Assessment Center, California State University, Los Angeles, 1981.

Modiano, Nancy. "National or Mother Tongue in Beginning Reading: A Comparative Study," *Research in theTeaching of English,* II, No. 1 (Spring, 1968), 32-43.

Shuy, Roger W. "Problems in Assessing Language Ability in Bilingual Education Programs." 1976. (Mimeographed.)

Skutnabb-Kangas, Tove, and Pertti Toukomaa. *Teaching Migrant Children's Mother Tongue and Learning the Language of the Host Country in the Context of the Socio-Cultural Situation of the Migrant Family.* Helsinki: The Finnish National Commission for UNESCO, 1976.

Smith, Frank. *Understanding Reading: A Psycholinguistic Analysis of Reading and Learning to Read.* New York: Holt, Rinehart and Winston, 1971.

Thonis, Eleanor W. *Teaching Reading to Non-English Speakers.* New York: Collier Macmillan International, 1970.

Troike, Rudolph C. "Research Evidence for the Effectiveness of Bilingual Education," *Bilingual Education Paper Series.* Vol. 2, No. 5. Los Angeles, California: National Dissemination and Assessment Center, California State University, Los Angeles, December, 1978.

Tucker, G. Richard. "The Linguistic Perspective," *Bilingual Education: Current Perspectives.* Vol. 2. Arlington, Virginia: Center for Applied Linguistics, 1977.

APPENDIX

BILINGUAL EDUCATION PROGRAM QUALITY REVIEW INSTRUMENT, KINDERGARTEN THROUGH GRADE SIX

1981-82

BASIC FORM

CONTENTS

Part One: Introduction

Background

For the past several years, the Office of Bilingual Bicultural Education has undertaken a major project to assist school districts in planning, implementing, and evaluating programs for language minority students at the elementary school level, kindergarten through grade six. This effort has focused on bridging the gap between current research and theory and promising program practices. The Bilingual Education Program Quality Review Instrument, Grades K-6 (Bilingual PQRI/K-6) and other publications represent the Office of Bilingual Bicultural Education's best efforts to provide timely technical assistance based on the most recent research studies in the field of bilingual education.

The Bilingual PQRI/K-6 serves four major purposes. First, it is a guide to be used by school district personnel in designing and improving bilingual education programs. Second, when used as an on-site review instrument, the Bilingual PQRI/K-6 furnishes schools with important formative evaluation input regarding their programs for language minority students. Third, the instrument is a data collection device that assists the Office of Bilingual Bicultural Education in identifying current practices and promising developments in bilingual education programs at the project, school, and classroom levels. Finally, the Bilingual PQRI/K-6 is a vehicle by which the Office of Bilingual Bicultural Education can promote research-based standards for the operation of bilingual education programs.

The items of quality contained in the Bilingual PQRI/K-6 are based on major principles concerning educational programs for limited- and non-English proficient students. The principles were developed by Office of Bilingual Bicultural Education personnel after a careful and thorough review of the literature on educational practices for language minority students; and they represent a synthesis of the most recent, well-controlled research and evaluation studies. The items of quality included in the Bilingual PQRI/K-6 correspond to a set of state standards for bilingual education programs.

Development of the Bilingual PQRI/K-6

In 1977, staff members in the Office of Bilingual Bicultural Education developed the original version of the Bilingual PQRI/K-6. Assisted by two private evaluation firms, the staff field-tested the instrument in more than 40 schools operating state and federally funded programs. Additionally, the instrument was critiqued at a field input session attended by more than 30 classroom teachers, resource specialists, and program directors.

In 1978, only minor revisions were made in the instrument. Nevertheless, initial steps were taken to ensure that the items of quality included in the Bilingual PQRI/K-6 were based on research studies and program evaluations. Earlier, many of the items in the instrument were based solely on legal requirements or the suggestions of bilingual educators and other program specialists. In June, 1978, a special symposium on the Bilingual PQRI/K-6 was held in Asilomar, California. The purpose of the symposium was to discuss current research and evaluation findings regarding primary language development in bilingual cross-cultural programs. The results of the symposium provided the stimulus for future revisions of the Bilingual PQRI/K-6. The following specialists participated in the Asilomar Symposium:

Rosa Kestelman
East Los Angeles City College

Susana Maiztegui
Stockton City Unified School District

M. Pilar de Olave
University of San Francisco

Rosaura Sanchez
California State University, San Diego

In 1979, the Bilingual PQRI/K-6 underwent a major review. The Office of Bilingual Bicultural Education contracted a group of technical experts to assist in making modifications and expanding the scope of the instrument. The following researchers and specialists participated in intensive work sessions:

Alma Flor Ada
University of San Francisco

Eduardo Hernandez-Chavez
Instituto de Lengua y Cultura
Concord, California

Dennis Parker
Corona-Norco Unified School District

Jacquelyn Schachter
University of Southern California

Eleanor Thonis
Wheatland Elementary School District

Additionally, a draft of the instrument was sent to recognized researchers in bilingual education and linguistics. Written critiques were received from the following:

Theodore Andersson
University of Texas, Austin

Alfredo Castañeda
Stanford University

James Cummins
Ontario Institute for Studies in Education

Tracy C. Gray
Center for Applied Linguistics
Arlington, Virginia

John J. Gumperz
University of California, Berkeley

Christina Bratt Paulston
University of Pittsburgh

Since 1980, relatively few revisions have been made to the Bilingual PQRI/K-6. However, the instrument is now supported by a series of articles focusing on language development and language acquisition in bilingual settings. **Schooling and Language Minority Students: A Theoretical Framework** has been developed by the Office of Bilingual Bicultural Education as a means of providing to school districts a theoretical rationale for the design and implementation of instructional programs for language minority children. The standards of implementation promoted by the Bilingual PQRI/K-6 are, as accurately as possible, based on the empirical evidence presented in the above-mentioned collection of papers.

Each year, teachers, resource specialists, and school administrators are given an opportunity to provide input regarding the Bilingual PQRI/K-6 and the review process. Field input meetings have been held in northern and southern California in addition to special feedback sessions with reviewers. Also, staff members, parents, and community members associated with the schools reviewed are given opportunities to react to the instrument and the review process. In 1980, approximately 200 evaluation forms were received from 24 schools. Reports were received from classroom teachers (87), administrators (28), instructional aides (53), resource teachers (19), parents/community members (3), and others (7). Some of the results from this survey are displayed below:

Question	Response		
	Yes	No	Don't Know
Has your program used the Bilingual PQRI/K-6 as a resource document?	149	27	21
Have you personally used the Bilingual PQRI/K-6 in planning for program improvement?	139	46	12
Will you include the findings from the Bilingual PQRI/K-6 in planning for program improvement?	174	5	18
From a technical point of view, was the review conducted properly?	158	11	24
From a human relations point of view, was the review conducted properly?	154	28	11
Did the reviewers communicate well both in English and the primary language of the limited English-proficient students?	150	11	32
Were both the purpose and process of the review visit completely and clearly explained by the reviewers?	168	21	4
Can you suggest any ways in which the review process could be improved?	100	76	17

In summary, it is clear that the Bilingual PQRI/K-6 has made an important contribution in assisting bilingual program teachers, aides, and administrators in designing, implementing, and modifying programs for language minority students.

Current Utilization of the Bilingual PQRI/K-6

The use of the Bilingual PQRI/K-6 allows for consistent and objective reviews of elementary school bilingual education programs. The instrument matches school level services with the California standards for bilingual education. The instrument is intended to be used by reviewers who are experienced bilingual educators and who are bilingual and biliterate in the minority language of the program being reviewed.

The Bilingual PQRI/K-6 is used by the Office of Bilingual Bicultural Education to conduct reviews of bilingual programs funded under the provisions of ESEA, Title VII. For this purpose the instrument has been recognized by the Office of Bilingual Education and Minority Language Affairs of the United States Education Department. In addition, the California State Department of Education promotes the standards in the Bilingual PQRI/K-6 as sound educational practices to be used with language minority students in bilingual programs required by state law.

Administration

Typically, the Bilingual PQRI/K-6 is used by a team of trained reviewers at a single school site. During a two to three day visit, the reviewers evaluate bilingual program services for students from one specific minority language group. Not more than seven classrooms are reviewed during any one visit. Reviewers are trained by personnel in the Office of Bilingual Bicultural Education and conduct reviews in accordance with the directions found in the current edition of the **Reviewers Manual—Bilingual PQRI/K-6.**

Presently, the "basic form" of the Bilingual PQRI/K-6 contains 19 items of program quality. Each item includes one or more criterion statements. The ratings are based on information collected by: (1) interviewing school site staff, (2) observing classroom activities, and (3) examining student records. A rating reflects the number of observations in which the reviewers determine that the criterion is met as compared to the total number of observations made by the reviewers.

The following is a sample rating:

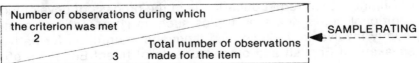

For instance, if a reviewer rated a particular criterion statement ⅔, this would mean that out of three total observations made, the criterion was met in two of the observations.

A set of operational definitions is included in Part Three of this document. The definitions are intended to provide readers with a greater common understanding of the bilingual education terminology used in the Bilingual PQRI/K-6. The operational definitions also assist reviewers in making more accurate determinations when rating individual criterion statements.

If a bilingual program selects an approach or methodology that is different from that stated in an item or corresponding criterion statement, the program may still receive credit for meeting the criterion provided that a level of equal effectiveness can be demonstrated. To demonstrate such effectiveness, the program must furnish the following evidence: (1) a written description of the approach or methodology selected, and (2) findings of a research or evaluation report which supports the use of the alternative.

Design

The Bilingual PQRI/K-6 consists of four parts:

Part One: Introduction
Part Two: Bilingual Program Profile
Part Three: Operational Definitions
Part Four: Items of Program Quality

Part Four is further divided into five components:

Component 1:   Primary Language Development
Component 2:   Second-Language Acquisition
Component 3:   Classroom Management
Component 4:   Staffing and Staff Development
Component 5:   Family Services

Each component consists of a series of items and corresponding criterion statements.

In some instances, school officials request review of an instructional or support component not included above. The Office of Bilingual Bicultural Education is in the process of developing additional components on topics such as (1) parent and community involvement, (2) second language instruction for native speakers of English and other students of fluent English proficiency, and (3) multicultural education. Upon request, one or more of these supplementary components will be used in addition to the "basic form" of the Bilingual PQRI/K-6.

Theoretical Framework

The following major principles, related principles, and standards of implementation constitute a theoretical framework for the design and implementation of bilingual education programs.

The Goal of Bilingual Education Programs

The goal of bilingual education programs is to allow all participating students to develop the highest degree possible of language, academic, and social skills necessary to participate fully in all aspects of life.

Major Principles of Bilingual Education Programs

Supported by a substantial amount of empirical evidence, the four major principles upon which bilingual education programs should be based are as follows:

1. In order to gain the maximum academic benefits from schooling, language minority students must develop high levels of language proficiency in both English and the primary language (Cummins, 1979b, 1981; Development Associates, 1980; Duncan and DeAvila, 1979; Kessler and Quinn, 1980; Lambert, 1978; Lapkin **et al**., 1979; Legarreta-Marcaida, 1981; Okoh, 1979; Rosier and Holm, 1980; Swain, 1979; Skutnabb-Kangas and Toukomaa, 1976).

2. Language proficiency consists of at least two dimensions: Basic Interpersonal Communicative Skills (BICS) and Cognitive/Academic Language Proficiency (CALP). Basic Interpersonal Communicative Skills refer to the universal aspects of language proficiency that are normally acquired by all native speakers of a language. Cognitive/Academic Language Proficiency refers to language skills that are associated with literacy and cognitive development and that are learned, usually through formal instruction (Caramazza and Brones, 1980; Cummins, 1980; 1981; Dulay and Burt, 1978; Genesee, 1979; Hammill and McNutt, 1980).

3. For language minority students the development of high levels of Cognitive/Academic Language Proficiency in the primary language forms the basis for similar proficiency in the second language, allows normal academic progress, assists in the acquisition of the second language by in-

creasing the range of "comprehensible input," and promotes positive adjustment of both minority and majority
cultures (Cummins, 1979a, 1979b, 1980, 1981; Cziko, 1978;
Development Associates, 1980; Downing, 1978; Hanson,
1979; Kaminsky, 1977; Lasonen, 1980; Skutnabb-Kangas,
1979, Taft and Bodi, 1980; Tucker, 1975).

4. When given sufficient access to "comprehensible second
   language input" and positive motivation to learn English,
   language minority students acquire Basic Interpersonal
   Communicative Skills in English (Dulay and Burt, 1973,
   1976; Krashen, 1976, 1978, 1981; Legarreta, 1979; Saville-
   Troike, 1978; Terrell, 1977; Wagner-Gough and Hatch, 1975).

Related Principles of Bilingual Education Programs

The following are related principles concerning bilingual
education programs:

1. By the age of five or six, all children except those with
   special learning disabilities have acquired Basic Interpersonal Communicative Skills in a variety of the home
   language (Cazden, 1972; Cummins, 1980; Gaarder, 1979).
2. Sociolinguistic factors inside and outside the school influence the language attitudes of both students and
   teachers. Even though factors exist outside the school, they
   may be influenced by the school (Garcia, 1979; Laosa, 1975;
   Lapkin **et al.**, 1979; Schumann, 1976, 1978).
3. The amount and quality of primary language use in the
   home is positively associated with student readiness for
   the academic demands of schooling and continued
   primary language development in the school (Cholewinski
   and Holliday, 1979; Cooley, 1979; Cummins, 1979a, 1981;
   Laosa, 1975; Ramirez and Politzer, 1975; Shafer, 1978;
   Wells, 1979).
4. The ability of teachers to speak the primary language of
   minority language students is positively related to both
   primary language development and second-language acquisition (Merino **et al.**, 1979; Peñaloza-Stromquist, 1980;
   Ramirez, 1978).
5. The language proficiencies of language minority students
   in English and the primary language vary in accordance
   with a number of factors, such as societal domain,
   language variety, speech situation, relationship between
   speakers, and cognitive demands of the task (Edleman,

1969; Fishman, 1971; Hernandez-Chavez **et al.**, 1978; Labov, 1970).

6. In the acquisition of second language, Basic Interpersonal Communicative Skills, affective factors are more important than biological maturity, age, or language aptitude (Chastain, 1975; Krashen, 1973; Schumann, 1975, 1978; Seliger, 1977; Terrell, 1977).

7. Teachers' knowledge of second-language acquisition and first-language development processes is positively related to English language acquisition and first-language development by language minority students (Peñaloza-Stromquist, 1980; Ramirez, 1978; Ramirez and Stromquist, 1979; Rodriguez, 1980).

8. Second-language acquirers have an innate ability to process "comprehensible language input," to internalize language rules, and to apply those rules to produce an infinite number of appropriate and acceptable utterances (Diller, 1978; Dulay and Burt, 1973; Krashen, 1978, 1981).

9. In a natural communication situation, language minority students will acquire English grammatical structures in a predictable order. However, complete mastery of a specific structure is not a prerequisite for the acquisition of later-learned structures, since speech errors are developmental and a natural part of second-language acquisition (Bailey **et al.**, 1974; Dulay and Burt, 1974; Krashen, 1981; Selinker, 1972; Selinker **et al.**, 1975).

10. Programs with informed and involved parents and community members are more likely to reflect community desires and are therefore more likely to achieve programmatic goals (Fantini, 1970; Gordon, 1978; Levin, 1970; Schimmel and Fischer, 1977; Stearns **et al.**, 1973).

Standards of Implementation for Bilingual Education Programs

The following standards of implementation pertain to bilingual education programs. These standards form the basis for the items included in the Bilingual PQRI/K-6:

1. Language minority students receive instruction in and through the primary language on a consistent basis throughout kindergarten to grade six (Cummins, 1980, 1981; Evaluation Associates, 1978; Legarreta, 1979; Rosier and Farella, 1976; Rosier and Holm, 1980; Skutnabb-Kangas, 1979).

2. On an average, the primary language is used approximately 50 percent of the time (Cummins, 1980, 1981; Evaluation Associates, 1978; Krashen, 1981; Legarreta, 1979; Legarreta-Marcaida, 1981; Rosier and Farella, 1976; Rosier and Holm, 1980; Skutnabb-Kangas, 1979).

3. Language minority students receive formal reading instruction in the primary language. Criteria are established and followed for the introduction of formal English language reading instruction (Cholewinski and Holliday, 1979; Chu-Chang, 1981; Cooley, 1979; Cummins, 1980; Cziko, 1978; Dank and McEachern, 1979; Downing, 1978; Fischer and Cabello, 1978; Genesee, 1979; Legarreta, 1979; Mägiste, 1979; Modiano, 1974; Rosier, 1977; Thonis, 1976, 1980, 1981; Tucker, 1975).

4. Sufficient primary language reading materials are available for language minority students at all grade levels to conduct subject-matter classes and promote reading for both function and pleasure (Rosier and Holm, 1980; Santiago and de Guzman, 1977; Thonis, 1976, 1980, 1981).

5. Sufficient bilingual teachers are available to instruct language minority students. Such teachers have native or near native proficiency in the primary language, possess the appropriate adult-to-child and adult-to-adult registers, and are sensitive to and accepting of varieties of the minority language (Adams and Frith, 1979; Legarreta-Marcaida, 1981; Merino **et al.** 1979; Peñaloza-Stromquist, 1980; Rosier and Holm, 1980).

6. Teachers are knowledgeable of the primary language development process (Peñaloza-Stromquist, 1980; Ramirez, 1978; Ramirez and Stromquist, 1979; Thonis, 1976, 1981).

7. In instructional settings, the teaching staff avoids creating situations that promote language mixing (Dulay and Burt, 1978; Legarreta, 1979; Legarreta-Marcaida, 1981).

8. Second-language acquirers are provided with sufficient exposure to "comprehensible second-language input" (Krashen, 1976, 1978, 1981; Terrell, 1977, 1981).

9. "Comprehensible second-language input" opportunities focus on communicative content rather than on language forms (Dulay and Burt, 1976; Krashen, 1976, 1978, 1981; Terrell, 1977, 1981).

10. "Comprehensible second-language input" opportunities are created, in part, by the use of concrete contextual referents (Asher, 1977; Dulay and Burt, 1973, 1976; Krashen, 1978, 1981).

11. During "comprehensible second-language input" opportunities, students are grouped in a manner that ensures that the input is comprehensible to all participants (Dulay and Burt, 1973, 1976; Krashen, 1978, 1981; Terrell, 1977, 1981).

12. Especially in the initial stages of second-language acquisition, the teaching staff allows students to respond in L_1, L_2, or a combination of both (Cohen and Swain, 1976; Schumann, 1975, 1978; Terrell, 1977, 1981).

13. During "comprehensible second-language input" opportunities, the teaching staff seldom corrects the language form errors of L_2 acquirers (Dulay and Burt, 1976; Krashen, 1981; Terrell, 1977, 1981).

14. Teachers are knowledgeable of the second-language acquisition process (Ramirez and Stromquist, 1979; Rodriguez, 1980).

15. School personnel use a variety of information sources relating to student language proficiency, use, and attitude when diagnosing students' needs and determining their placement (Cummins, 1980, 1981; Rosansky, 1979).

16. Staff members are given language, methodology, and cultural training to develop the skills necessary to implement instructional programs for language minority students (Ramirez and Stromquist, 1979; Rodriguez, 1980).

17. Parents and community are given sufficient, accurate information regarding instructional programs for language minority students (Fantini, 1970; Gordon, 1978; Levin, 1970; Schimmel and Fischer, 1977; Stearns **et al.**, 1973).

18. The teaching staff encourages language minority parents to use L_1 in the home with their children, especially in activities such as poems, songs, storytelling, and reading. The purpose of such activities is to provide an appropriate context for quality interaction between parents and their children, interaction in which there is "negotiation of meaning" (Cholewinski and Holliday, 1979; Cooley, 1979; Cummins, 1979a, 1981; Wells, 1979).

19. Opportunities are provided for language minority parents and community to participate on the school advisory com-

mittee and to suggest improvements in the school program (Fantini, 1970; Gordon, 1978; Levin, 1970; Schimmel and Fischer, 1977; Stearns **et al.**, 1973).

20. Evaluation procedures provide decision makers with the information they need to validate or modify instructional activities (Alkin **et al.**, 1979; Patton, 1978).

Position

The adherence to the above principles and the application of the above standards of implementation will greatly improve second-language acquisition and general cognitive/academic achievement of language minority students. For most language minority students, this means significantly improved school programs and greater potential to realize vocational and higher education goals.

Additional Information

For further information on the Bilingual PQRI/K-6 and the school review process, contact the Office of Bilingual Bicultural Education, California State Department of Education, 721 Capitol Mall, Sacramento, CA 95814, (916) 445-2872.

REFERENCES

Adams, M., and J. Frith, eds. **Testing Kit: French and Spanish.** Washington, D.C.: United States Department of State, Foreign Service Institute, 1979.

Alkin, Marvin C., Richard Daillak, and Peter White. **Using Evaluations: Does Evaluation Make a Difference?** Beverly Hills, California: Sage Publications, 1979.

Asher, James J. **Learning Another Language Through Actions: The Complete Teacher's Guidebook.** San Jose, California: Pajaro Press, Inc., 1977.

Bailey, Natalie, Carolyn Madden, and Stephen D. Krashen. "Is There a 'Natural Sequence' in Adult Second Language Learning?" **Language Learning,** XXIV, No. 2 (December, 1974), 235-243.

Caramazza, Alfonso, and Isabel Brones. "Semantic Classification by Bilinguals," **Canadian Journal of Psychology,** XXXIV, No. 1 (March, 1980), 77-81.

Cazden, Courtney B. **Child Language and Education.** New York: Holt, Rinehart and Winston, Inc., 1972.

Chastain, Kenneth. "Affective and Ability Factors in Second-Language Acquisition," **Language Learning,** XXV, No. 1 (June, 1975), 153-161.

Cholewinski, Mitzi, and Sue Holliday. "Learning to Read: What's Right at Home Is Right at School," **Language Arts,** LVI, No. 6 (September, 1979), 671-680.

Chu-Chang, Mae. "The Dependency Relation Between Oral Language and Reading in Bilingual Education," **Journal of Education,** CLXIII (1981), 30-57.

Cohen, Andrew D., and Merrill Swain. "Bilingual Education: The Immersion Model in the North American Context," **English as a Second Language in Bilingual Education,** eds., James E. Alatis, and K. Twaddell. Washington, D.C.: Teachers of English to Speakers of Other Languages, 1976.

Cooley, H. "Multiple Measures of Second Language Acquisition Among Hispanic Children in a Bilingual Program." Unpublished PhD dissertation, University of Wisconsin, 1979.

Cummins, James. "The Exit and Entry Fallacy in Bilingual Education," **NABE Journal,** IV (1980), 25-60.

____. **A Guide to Bilingualism and Minority Language Children.** Toronto, Ontario, Canada: Modern Language Centre, Ontario Institute for Studies in Education, 1979a. (Mimeographed.)

____. "Linguistic Interdependence and the Educational Development of Bilingual Children," **Bilingual Education Paper Series.** Vol. 3 No. 2. Los Angeles, California: National Dissemination and Assessment Center, California State University, Los Angeles, September, 1979b.

____. "The Role of Primary Language Development in Promoting Educational Success for Language Minority Students," **Schooling and Language Minority Students: A Theoretical Framework.** Los Angeles, California: Evaluation, Dissemination and Assessment Center, California State University, Los Angeles, 1981.

Cziko, G. **The Effects of Language Sequencing on the Development of Bilingual Reading Skills.** Montreal, Canada: McGill University, 1978.

Dank, M., and W. McEachern. "A Psycholinguistic Description Comparing the Native Language Oral Reading Behavior of French Immersion Students with Traditional English Language Students," **The Canadian Modern Language Review,** No. 35 (March, 1979).

Development Associates. **Evaluation of California's Educational Services to Limited- and Non-English Speaking Students.** Final Report. San Francisco, California: Development Associates, 1980.

Diller, Karl Conrad. **The Language Teaching Controversy.** Rowley, Massachusetts: Newbury House Publishers, 1978.

Downing, John. "Strategies of Bilingual Teaching," **International Review of Education,** XXIV, No. 3 (1978), 329-346.

Dulay, Heidi C., and Marina K. Burt. "Creative Construction in Second Language Learning and Teaching," **Language Learning,** Special Issue No. 4 (January, 1976).

____, and ____. "From Research to Method in Bilingual Education," **International Dimensions of Bilingual Education,** ed., James E. Alatis. Washington, D.C.: Georgetown University Press, 1978.

____, and ____. Natural Sequences in Child Second Language Acquisition," **Language Learning,** XXIV, No. 1 (June, 1974), 37-53.

____, and ____. "Should We Teach Children Syntax?" **Language Learning,** XXIII, No. 2 (December, 1973), 245-258.

Duncan, Sharon E., and Edward A. DeAvila. "Bilingualism and Cognition: Some Recent Findings," **NABE Journal,** IV (Fall, 1979), 15-50.

Edleman, Martin. "The Contextualization of Schoolchildren's Bilingualism," **Modern Language Journal,** LIII, No. 3 (March, 1969), 179-182.

Evaluation Associates. **Nestor School Bilingual Education Program Evaluation.** Research report, San Diego, California, 1978.

Fantini, Mario D. "Community Control and Quality Education in Urban School Systems," **Community Control of Schools,** ed., Henry M. Levin. Washington, D.C: Brookings Institute, 1970.

Fischer, K. B., and B. Cabello. "Predicting Student Success Following Transition from Bilingual Programs." Paper presented at the Annual Meeting of the

American Educational Research Association, Toronto, Canada, March, 1978.

Fishman, Joshua A. **Sociolinguistics: A Brief Introduction.** Rowley, Massachusetts: Newbury House Publishers, 1971.

Gaarder, A. Bruce. "The Golden Rules of Second Language Acquisition by Young Children," **TESOL Newsletter,** XIII (August, 1979).

Garcia, E. "Bilingualism and Schooling Environments," **NABE Journal,** IV (Fall, 1979).

Genesee, Fred. "Acquisition of Reading Skills in Immersion Programs," **Foreign Language Annals,** XII, No. 1 (February, 1979), 71-77.

Gordon, I. **Parent and Community Involvement in Compensatory Education.** Urbana, Illinois: University of Illinois, 1978.

Hammill, Donald D., and Gaye McNutt. "Language Abilities and Reading: A Review of the Literature on Their Relationship," **The Elementary School Journal,** LXXX, No. 5 (May, 1980), 269-277.

Hanson, Göte. "The Position of the Second Generation of Finnish Immigrants in Sweden: The Importance of Education in the Home Language to the Welfare of Second Generation Immigrants." Paper presented at a symposium on the position of the second generation of Yugoslav immigrants in Sweden, Split, Yugoslavia, October, 1979.

Hernandez-Chavez, Eduardo, Marina K. Burt, and Heidi C. Dulay. "Language Dominance and Proficiency Testing: Some General Considerations," **NABE Journal,** III (Fall, 1978), 41-54.

Kaminsky, S. "Predicting Oral Language Sequences and Acquisition: A Study of First Grade Bilingual Children," Paper presented at the Annual Meeting of the American Education Research Association, New York, 1977.

Kessler, Carolyn, and Mary Ellen Quinn. "Bilingualism and Science Problem-Solving Ability," **Bilingual Education Paper Series.** Vol, 4 No. 1. Los Angeles, California: National Dissemination and Assessment Center, California State University, Los Angeles, August, 1980.

Krashen, Stephen D. "Bilingual Education and Second Language Acquisition Theory," **Schooling and Language Minority Students: A Theoretical Framework.** Los Angeles, California: Evaluation, Dissemination and Assessment Center, California State University, Los Angeles, 1981.

_____. "Formal and Informal Linguistic Environments in Language Acquisition and Language Learning," **TESOL Quarterly,** X, No. 2 (June, 1976), 157-168.

_____. "Lateralization, Language Learning, and the Critical Period: Some New Evidence," **Language Learning,** XXIII, No. 1 (June, 1973), 63-74.

_____. "The Monitor Model for Second Language Acquisition," **Second Language Acquisition & Foreign Language Teaching,** ed., Rosario C. Gringas. Arlington, Virginia: Center for Applied Linguistics, 1978, pp. 1-26.

Labov, William. "The Logic of Nonstandard English," **Report of the Twentieth Annual Round Table Meeting on Linguistics and Language Studies,** ed., James E. Alatis. Washington, D.C.: Georgetown University Press, 1970, pp. 1-43.

Lambert, Wallace E. "Some Cognitive and Sociocultural Consequences of Being Bilingual," **International Dimensions of Bilingual Education,** ed., James E. Alatis. Washington, D.C.: Georgetown University Press, 1978.

Laosa, Luis M. "Bilingualism in Three United States Hispanic Groups: Contextual Use of Language by Children and Adults in Their Families," **Journal of Educational Psychology,** LXVII, No. 5 (October, 1975), 617-627.

Lapkin, Sharon, Christine M. Andrew, Brigit Harley, and Jill Kamid. **The Immersion Centre and the Dual-Track School. A Study of the Relationship Between School**

Environment and Achievement in a French Immersion Program. Ontario, Canada: Ontario Institute for Studies in Education, 1979.

Lasonen, K. "Linguistic Development and School Achievement Among Finnish Children in Mother-Tongue Medium Classes in Sweden," **Scientia Paedagogica Experimentalis,** XVII (1980).

Legarreta, Dorothy. "The Effects of Program Models on Language Acquisition by Spanish Speaking Children," **TESOL Quarterly,** XIII, No. 4 (December, 1979), 521-534.

Legarreta-Marcaida, Dorothy. "Effective Use of the Primary Language in the Classroom," **Schooling and Language Minority Students: A Theoretical Framework.** Los Angeles, California: Evaluation, Dissemination and Assessment Center, California State University, Los Angeles, 1981.

Levin, Henry M. **Community Control of Schools.** Washington, D.C.: Brookings Institute, 1970.

Magiste, Edith. "The Competing Language Systems of the Multilingual: A Developmental Study of Decoding and Encoding Processes," **Journal of Verbal Learning and Verbal Behavior,** XVIII, No. 1 (February, 1979), pp. 79-89.

Merino, Barbara, Robert L. Politzer, and Arnulfo G. Ramirez. "The Relationship of Teachers' Spanish Proficiency to Pupils' Achievement," **NABE Journal,** III (Winter, 1979).

Modiano, Nancy. "The Most Effective Language of Instruction for Beginning Reading," **Teaching the Bilingual,** ed., Frank Pialorsi. Tucson, Arizona: University of Arizona, 1974.

Okoh, Nduka. "Bilingualism and Divergent Thinking Among Nigerian and Welsh School Children," **Journal of Social Psychology,** CX (April, 1979), 163-170.

Patton, Michael Quinn. **Utilization-Focused Evaluation.** Beverly Hills, California: Sage Publications, 1978.

Peñaloza-Stromquist, Nelly. "Teaching Effectiveness and Student Achievement in Reading in Spanish," **The Bilingual Review/La Revista Bilingüe,** VII, No. 2 (May-August, 1980), 95-104.

Ramirez, Arnulfo G. **Teaching Reading in Spanish: A Study of Teacher Effectiveness.** Stanford, California: Center for Educational Research, Stanford University, 1978.

____, and Nelly P. Stromquist. "ESL Methodology and Student Language Learning in Bilingual Elementary Schools," **TESOL Quarterly,** XIII, No. 2 (June, 1979), 145-158.

____, and Robert L. Politzer. "The Acquisition of English and the Maintenance of Spanish in a Bilingual Education Program," **TESOL Quarterly,** IX, No. 2 (June, 1975), 113-124.

Rodriguez, Ana Maria. "Empirically Defining Competencies for Effective Bilingual Teachers: A Preliminary Study," **Bilingual Education Paper Series.** Vol. 3 No. 12. Los Angeles, California: National Dissemination and Assessment Center, California State University, Los Angeles, July, 1980.

Rosansky, Ellen. "A Review of the Bilingual Syntax Measure," **Papers in Applied Linguistics,** ed., Bernard Spolsky. No. 1. Washington, D.C.: Center for Applied Linguistics, 1979.

Rosier, Paul. "A Comparative Study of Two Approaches of Introducing Initial Reading to Navajo Children: The Direct Method and the Native Language Method." Unpublished PhD dissertation, Northern Arizona University, Flagstaff, Arizona, 1977.

____, and Merilyn Farella. "Bilingual Education at Rock Point—Some Early Results," **TESOL Quarterly,** X, No. 4 (December, 1976), 379-388.

____, and W. Holm. "The Rock Point Experience: A Longitudinal Study of a Navajo School (Saad Naaki Bee Na'nitin)," **Bilingual Education Series.** No. 8. Arlington, Virginia: Center for Applied Linguistics, 1980.

Santiago, M., and E. de Guzman. **A Child's Step Forward in Reading: The Effect of Language of Materials and Other Factors on Reading Comprehension Among Grade Four Pupils.** Research Series. Philippine Normal College, 1977.

Saville-Troike, Muriel. "Implications of Research on Adult Second-Language Acquisition for Teaching Foreign Languages to Children," **Second Language Acquisition & Foreign Language Teaching,** ed. Rosario C. Gringas. Arlington, Virginia: Center for Applied Linguistics, 1978, pp. 68-77.

Schimmel, David, and Louis Fischer. **The Rights of Parents in the Education of Their Children.** Columbia, Maryland: National Committee for Citizens in Education, 1977.

Schumann, John H. "The Acculturation Model for Second-Language Acquisition," **Second Language Acquisition & Foreign Language Teaching,** ed., Rosario C. Gringas. Arlington, Virginia: Center for Applied Linguistics, 1978, pp. 27-50.

____. "Affective Factors and the Problem of Age in Second Language Acquisition," **Language Learning,** XXV, No. 2 (December, 1975), 209-235.

____. "Social Distance as a Factor in Second Language Acquisition," **Language Learning,** XXVI, No. 1 (June, 1976), 135-143.

Seliger, Herbert W. "Does Practice Make Perfect? A Study of Interaction Patterns and L_2 Competence," **Language Learning,** XXVII, No. 2 (December, 1977), 263-278.

Selinker, Larry. "Interlanguage," **International Review of Applied Linguistics,** III, No. 10 (August, 1972), 209-231.

____, Merrill Swain, and Guy Dumas. "The Inter-Language Hypothesis Extended to Children," **Language Learning,** XXV, No. 1 (June, 1975), 139-152.

Shafer, R. "Home Learned Language Functions: How They Assist Beginning Reading." Paper presented at the Ninth World Congress on Sociology, Uppsala, Sweden, August, 1978.

Skutnabb-Kangas, Tove. **Language in the Process of Cultural Assimilation and Structural Incorporation of Linguistic Minorities.** Rosslyn, Virginia: National Clearinghouse for Bilingual Education, 1979.

____, and Pertti Toukomaa. **Teaching Migrant Children's Mother Tongue and Learning the Language of the Host Country in the Context of the Socio-Cultural Situation of the Migrant Family.** Helsinki, Finland: The Finnish National Commission for UNESCO, 1976.

Stearns, M. **et al. Parent Involvement in Compensatory Education Programs: Definitions and Findings.** Stanford, California: Stanford Research Institute, March, 1973. (Mimeographed.)

Swain, Merrill. "Bilingual Education: Research and Its Implications," **On TESOL 1979: The Learner in Focus,** eds., C. Yorio, K. Perkins, and J. Schachter. Washington, D.C.: Teachers of English to Speakers of Other Languages, 1979.

Taft, Ronald, and Marianne Bodi. "A Study of Language Competence and First Language Maintenance in Bilingual Children," **International Review of Applied Psychology,** XXIX, No. 1-2 (January, 1980), 173-182.

Terrell, Tracy D. "The Natural Approach in Bilingual Education," **Schooling and Language Minority Students: A Theoretical Framework.** Los Angeles, California: Evaluation, Dissemination and Assessment Center, California State University, Los Angeles, 1981.

____. "A Natural Approach to Second Language Acquisition and Learning," **The Modern Language Journal,** LXI, No. 7 (November, 1977), 325-337.

Thonis, Eleanor W. **Literacy for America's Spanish-Speaking Children.** Newark, Delaware: International Reading Association, 1976.

____. "Reading Instruction for Language Minority Students," **Schooling and Language Minority Students: A Theoretical Framework.** Los Angeles, California: Evaluation, Dissemination and Assessment Center, California State University, Los Angeles, 1981.

____. "Speech, Print, and Thought in Bilingual Bicultural Education." Paper prepared for the Office of Bilingual Bicultural Education, California State Department of Education, Sacramento, California, 1980.

Tucker, G. Richard. "The Development of Reading Skills Within a Bilingual Education Program," **Language and Reading,** eds., Sandra S. Smiley, and John C. Towner. Sixth Western Symposium on Learning. Bellingham, Washington: Western Washington State College, 1975, pp. 49-60.

Wagner-Gough, Judy, and Evelyn Hatch. "The Importance of Input Data in Second Language Acquisition Studies," **Language Learning,** XXV, No. 2 (December, 1975), 297-308.

Wells, Gordon. "Describing Children's Linguistic Development at Home and at School," **British Educational Research Journal,** V (1979), 75-89.

Part Two: Bilingual Program Profile

School _____ District _____

CDS code number ___/___ Minority language _____

Reviewer (1) _____ / Reviewer (2) _____ Date of Review _____

Classroom grade level description	Number of LEP students	Number of other students	Funding sources	Teacher credential status	Instructional aides (description/average total hours daily)	Instructional aide description	Minority Language Proficiency*

Legend

Funding sources

1. EIA/LES-NES
2. EIA/SCE
3. Title VII
4. Title I
5. Migrant Education
6. SIP
7. Other_____

Teacher credential status

a. Bilingual cross-cultural specialist credential
b. Standard credential with bilingual emphasis
c. Emergency credential
d. Certificate of competence
e. Waiver
f. None of the above

Minority Language Proficiency*

x. None
y. Unassessed
z. Assessed

* per operational definition No. 10 (see next section)

Part Three: Operational Definitions

The operational definitions listed below are provided to ensure a common understanding of bilingual education terminology used in the Bilingual PQRI/K-6. When these terms are used in the items and criterion statements, they are italicized to alert the reader that a special term has been encountered.

1. **Basic Interpersonal Communicative Skills:** a construct developed to refer to the basic communicative fluency achieved by all normal native speakers of a language. Basic Interpersonal Communicative Skills are not strongly related to academic performance in formal schooling contexts. Language proficiency assessment instruments, which are based on samples of "natural speech," are essentially measures of one's Basic Interpersonal Communicative Skills.

2. **Bilingual credential:** one of the following credentials or certificates: (a) bilingual cross-cultural specialist, (b) standard credential with bilingual emphasis, (c) emergency credential, and (d) certificate of competency.

3. **Bilingual program orientation document:** a written statement that describes the intent and content of the bilingual education program. Information is included on at least the following topics:
   a. Services for different types of students (e. g., LEP, NEP, and native English speakers)
   b. Probable student and program outcomes
   c. Student identification and placement procedures
   d. Curriculum and instructional services
   e. Staffing arrangements
   f. Parent and community involvement opportunities

4. **Cognitive/Academic Language Proficiency:** a construct developed to refer to aspects of language proficiency strongly associated with literacy and cognitive development. Cognitive/Academic Language Proficiency is strongly related to academic performance in formal schooling contexts. Standardized achievement tests are an example of a measure used to determine one's Cognitive/Academic Language Proficiency.

5. **Communicative-based ESL:** a second language instructional approach in which the goals, teaching methods and

techniques, and assessments of student progress are all based on behavioral objectives defined in terms of abilities to communicate messages in the target language. In communicative-based ESL, the focus is on language function and use and not on language form and usage. Examples of communicative-based ESL instructional approaches include Suggestopedia, Natural Approach, Community Language Learning, and Total Physical Response.

6. **Comprehensible second-language input:** a construct developed to describe understandable and meaningful language directed at L_2 acquirers under optimal conditions. Comprehensible L_2 input is characterized as language the L_2 acquirer already knows (i) plus a range of new language (i + 1), which is made comprehensible in formal schooling contexts by the use of certain planned strategies. These strategies include but are not limited to: (a) focus on communicative content rather than language forms; (b) frequent use of concrete contextual referents; (c) lack of restrictions on L_1 use by L_2 acquirers, especially in the initial stages; (d) careful grouping practices; (e) minimal overt language form correction by teaching staff; and (f) provision of motivational situations.

7. **Continuum of skills—primary language literacy, grades K-6:** a list of developmental skills consisting of two parts:

   a. A list of at least 10 specific reading skills in each of the following topic areas: (1) reading readiness; (2) decoding; (3) literal and inferential comprehension; (4) literary skills such as critical reading, aesthetic appreciation, and reading flexibility; and (5) study skills.

   b. A list of at least 10 specific writing skills in each of the following topic areas: (1) handwriting, (2) spelling, (3) mechanics, and (4) discourse.

8. **Continuum of skills—primary oral language development, grades K-6:** a list of developmental skills consisting of at least 10 specific skills in each of the following topic areas; (a) vocabulary, (b) grammar, and (c) language use/language functions.

9. **Criteria for the introduction of formal English language reading instruction:** a written statement containing specific criteria for the introduction of formal reading instruction in English to LEP students. One criterion must

specify a minimal level of oral English language proficiency. A second criterion must indicate attainment of specified primary language reading skills in at least the following topic areas: (a) reading readiness, (b) decoding, (c) literal and inferential comprehension, (d) literary skills, and (e) study skills.

10. **Criteria for minority language proficiency—teacher aides:** a written document indicating assessment criteria and assessment of each bilingual cross-cultural teacher aide. It specifies a minimal proficiency in each of the following areas of the minority language: (a) pronunciation, (b) grammar, (c) vocabulary, (d) fluency, (e) comprehension, and (f) literacy. The minimal qualifying proficiency is equivalent to a Foreign Service Institute score of S/R-3 + .

11. **Formative evaluation report:** a report summarizing the findings of evaluation efforts carried out to improve a program in progress. The report contains recommendations for program modification and addresses at least three of the following topics:

    a .The extent to which the goal of staffing the program with bilingual personnel is being met,

    b. The extent to which instructional activities are occurring as planned,

    c. The extent to which language use in the classrooms matches the program plan,

    d. The extent to which students in the program are meeting instructional objectives,

    e. The extent to which family services are being provided as planned,

    f. The extent to which project funds are being spent as planned,

    g. The extent to which information regarding the intent and content of the bilingual program has been disseminated to all parents, and

    h. The extent to which staff development activities are occurring as planned.

12. **Grammar-based ESL:** a second language instructional approach in which the goals, teaching methods and techniques, and assessments of student progress are all based on behavioral objectives defined in terms of abilities to

produce grammatically correct utterances in the target language. In grammar-based ESL, the focus is on language form and usage and not on language function and use. Examples of grammar-based ESL instructional approaches include Grammar-Translation, Audiolingualism, and Cognitive Codes.

13. **Immersion classes:** subject-matter class periods delivered in L_2 in which teachers: (a) group L_2 acquirers together, (b) speak in a native speaker-to-second language acquirer register similar to "motherese" or "foreigner talk," and (c) provide L_2 acquirers with substantial amounts of "comprehensible second language input."

14. **Individual student language profile:** a written record, readily accessible to classroom teachers, that contains information on at least four of the following topics:
   a. Home language use,
   b. School language use,
   c. Student and parent attitudes toward the home language, culture, and bilingual education,
   d. Language test results in both L_1 and L_2 (Bilingual Interpersonal Communicative Skills and Cognitive/Academic Language Proficiency measures),
   e. Results of interviews by bilingual education specialists, and
   f. Classroom teacher observations.

15. **Planned instruction:** at least three organized lessons totaling at least 100 minutes of instruction each week. Students receiving planned instruction in or through the minority language have a textbook or equivalent material in that language for each specific subject area.

Part Four: Items of Program Quality

Component 1: Primary Language Development

1. The program has a continuum of skills for primary oral language and literacy development.

   a. Teachers can show a **continuum of skills—primary oral language development, grades K-6.**

   K-6

   b. Teachers can show a **continuum of skills—primary language literacy, grades K-6.**

   K-6

Comments: _____

_____

_____

2. Primary oral language and primary language literacy instruction are conducted on a regular basis.

    K-6

    a. Teachers can show a schedule or lesson plan indicating that designated students receive **planned instruction** in primary oral language.

    K-6

    b. Teachers can show a schedule or lesson plan indicating that designated students receive **planned instruction** in primary language literacy.

    Comments: _____

    _____

    _____

3. Primary oral language and primary language literacy instruction are conducted in an organized manner.

    K-6

    a. Primary oral language and primary language literacy sessions are conducted only in the primary language.

    Comments: _____

    _____

    _____

4. The teaching staff is knowledgeable about the main features of the methodology used for primary language literacy instruction.

    K-6

    a. Participating classroom teachers can describe at least two main features of the methodology used for primary language literacy instruction.

    Comments: _____

    _____

    _____

5. Students in bilingual classrooms have access to a variety of reading materials in the minority language that are appropriate for their age and grade level.

    K-6

    a. In a sample of students who receive primary language literacy instruction, each student has a textbook or locally developed reader.

K-6
☑

b. Teachers can exhibit either 30 different books in the classroom or 50 different books in the library or media center.

Comments: _____

_____

_____

6. The primary language is used as a medium of instruction for at least two subject matter areas in the bilingual classrooms.

K-6
☑

a. Teachers can show a schedule or lesson plan indicating that each designated student receives **planned instruction** in social studies through the primary language.

and/or

K-6
☑

b. Teacher can show a schedule or lesson plan indicating that each designated student receives **planned instruction** in science through the primary language.

and/or

K-6
☑

c. Teachers can show a schedule or lesson plan indicating that each designated student receives **planned instruction** in mathematics through the primary language.

and/or

K-6
☑

d. Teachers can show a schedule or lesson plan indicating that each designated student receives **planned instruction** in an elective subject through the primary language.

[Indicate elective(s): _____]

K-6
☑

e. Lessons delivered through the primary language in the above subject matter areas are conducted only in the primary language.

Comments: _____

_____

_____

Component 2: Second-Language Acquisition

7. The teaching staff is knowledgeable about the distinction between second-language learning and second-language acquisition.

   K-6 ◩

   a. Teachers in participating classrooms are able to identify at least three differences between **communicative-based ESL** and **grammar-based ESL** instructional approaches.

   Comments: _____

   _____

   _____

8. Students of limited English proficiency are provided adequate exposure to **comprehensible second-language input** under optimal conditions.

   K-6 ◩

   a. Records in each classroom indicate that designated LEP students receive **planned instruction** in **communicative-based ESL.**

   K-6 ◩

   b. Records in each classroom indicate that designated LEP students receive **planned instruction** in English **immersion classes.**

   K-6 ◩

   c. During observations of planned instructional periods designed to provide L_2 acquirers with **comprehensible second-language input,** the teaching staff consistently demonstrates all of the following practices:
      (1) Maintains focus on communicative content rather than language forms,
      (2) Uses concrete contextual referents,
      (3) Does not restrict L_1 use by L_2 acquirers,
      (4) Groups students so that all participants receive substantial amounts of **comprehensible second language input,** and
      (5) Does not overtly correct language form errors of L_2 acquirers.

   Comments: _____

   _____

   _____

Component 3: Classroom Management

9. Students are placed in appropriate first- and second-language instruction based on information collected on the **individual student language profiles.**

   K-6
   ▨

   a. Teachers are able to show an **individual student language profile** for each student enrolled in the bilingual program.
   Comments: _____
   _____
   _____

10. The program has written **criteria for the introduction of formal English language reading instruction** to students of limited English proficiency.

    K-6
    ▨

    a. Teachers in the participating classrooms are able to describe the program **criteria for the introduction of formal English language reading instruction** to students of limited English proficiency.
    Comments: _____
    _____
    _____

11. Students of limited English proficiency are consistently placed in English reading instruction on the basis of the criteria established by the bilingual program.

    K-6
    ▨

    a. A sample of LEP student profiles and observations of English reading lessons indicate that only those LEP students who have met the **criteria for the introduction of formal English language reading instruction** are receiving such instruction.
    Comments: _____
    _____
    _____

12. Language minority students in the bilingual program receive L_1 instruction in ample amounts and on a consistent basis to adequately sustain academic achievement.

    K-6
    ▨

    a. A review of the student records indicates that at least 50 percent of the students who have been enrolled in the bilingual program for at least four full school years are at or above grade level expectancy on any appropriate measure of Cognitive/Academic Language Proficiency.

Comments: _____

_____

_____

Component 4: Staffing and Staff Development

13. Staff members are proficient in the minority language.

    a. Teachers have **bilingual credentials.**

    K-6 ☐

    b. Teacher aides meet the **criteria for minority language proficiency—teacher aides.**

    K-6 ☐

    Comments: _____

    _____

    _____

14. The training needs of each teacher and teacher aide have been assessed.

    a. Records indicate that the training needs of each teacher and teacher aide have been assessed during the current school year in at least the following topic areas:

    K-6 ☐

    (1) Cultural heritage of the minority students,
    (2) Primary language development,
    (3) Second-language acquisition,
    (4) Literacy instruction in the primary language,
    (5) Basic intent and content of a bilingual education program,
    (6) Language assessment procedures, and
    (7) Language development for teachers and aides (English or minority language).

    Comments: _____

    _____

    _____

15. The program provides training sessions that are based on the assessed needs of the staff.

    a. Teachers in the participating classrooms can give at least two examples of training sessions attended dur-

    K-6 ☐

ing the current school year that, in their opinion, enhanced their teaching skills in bilingual education.

K-6

b. Teacher aides in the participating classrooms can give at least two examples of training sessions attended during the current school year that, in their opinion, enhanced their skills in bilingual education.
Comments: _____

_____

_____

16. The minority language is sometimes utilized as the medium of communication at staff development sessions.

K-6

a. Staff members are able to identify at least two examples of training sessions conducted in the minority language.
Comments: _____

_____

_____

17. Periodic **formative evaluation reports** are distributed to and discussed with staff members.

K-6

a. During the current school year, each teacher and teacher aide has received at least one **formative evaluation report** that was discussed at a staff meeting.
Comments: _____

_____

_____

Component 5: Family Services

18. A **bilingual program orientation document,** written in both English and the minority language, is disseminated to the school community.

K-6

a. Each classroom teacher reports that at least three of the following approaches are used to disseminate the **bilingual program orientation document** to parents and community:
(1) Sent home with students or mailed

(2) Presented as a topic at parent meetings or work shops

(3) Explained during parent/teacher conferences

(4) Explained during home visits

(5) Other: _____
                     (specify)

Comments: _____

_____

_____

19. The school promotes home activities that are conducted in the minority language and that are designed to better prepare minority language students for the academic challenges of school.

K-6

a. Each classroom teacher reports that at least two of the following approaches have been used to promote L_1 activities in the homes of language minority students:

(1) Development and dissemination of parent/student activity guide,

(2) Parent training sessions, and

(3) Provision of L_1 reading materials for use at home.

Comments: _____

_____

_____

SUMMARY COMMENTS

SIGNATURES

_____   _____
School site administrator   Reviewer

_____   _____
District Title VII coordinator   Reviewer

GLOSSARY

1. **Additive Bilingualism:** a process by which individuals develop proficiency in a second language subsequent to or simultaneous with the development of proficiency in the primary language.

2. **Affective Filter:** a construct developed to refer to the effects of personality, motivation, and other affective variables on second language acquisition. These variables interact with each other and with other factors to raise or lower the affective filter. It is hypothesized that when the filter is "high," the L_2 acquirer is not able to adequately process "comprehensible input."

3. **Basic Interpersonal Communicative Skills:** a construct originally developed by James Cummins to refer to aspects of language proficiency strongly associated with the basic communicative fluency achieved by all normal native speakers of a language. Basic Interpersonal Communicative Skills are not highly correlated with literacy and academic achievement. Cummins has further refined this notion in terms of "cognitively undemanding contextualized" language.

4. **Bilingual Education Program:** an organized curriculum that includes: (1) L_1 development, (2) L_2 acquisition, and (3) subject matter development through L_1 and L_2. Bilingual programs are organized so that participating students may attain a level of proficient bilingualism.

5. **Cognitive/Academic Language Proficiency:** a construct originally proposed by James Cummins to refer to aspects of language proficiency strongly related to literacy and academic achievement. Cummins has further refined this notion in terms of "cognitively demanding decontextualized" language.

6. **Comprehensible Second-Language Input:** a construct developed to describe understandable and meaningful language directed at L_2 acquirers under optimal conditions. Comprehensible L_2 input is characterized as language which the L_2 acquirer already knows (i) plus a range of new language (i + 1), which is made comprehensible in formal schooling contexts by the use of certain planned strategies.

These strategies include but are not limited to: (a) focus on communicative content rather than language forms; (b) frequent use of concrete contextual referents; (c) lack of restrictions on L_1 use by L_2 acquirers, especially in the initial stages; (d) careful grouping practices; (e) minimal overt language form correction by teaching staff; and (f) provision of motivational acquisition situations.

7. **Communicative-Based ESL:** a second language instructional approach in which the goals, teaching methods and techniques, and assessments of student progress are all based on behavioral objectives defined in terms of abilities to communicate messages in the target language. In communicative-based ESL, the focus is on language function and use and not on language form and usage. Examples of communicative-based ESL instructional approaches include Suggestopedia, Natural Language, and Community Language Learning.

8. **Grammar-Based ESL:** a second language instructional approach in which the goals, teaching methods and techniques, and assessments of student progress are all based on behavioral objectives defined in terms of abilities to produce grammatically correct utterances in the target language. In grammar-based ESL, the focus is on language form and usage and not on language function and use. Examples of grammar-based ESL instructional approaches include Grammar-Translation, Audiolingualism, and Cognitive Code.

9. **Immersion Classes:** subject matter class periods delivered in L_2 in which teachers: (1) homogeneously group L_2 acquirers, (2) speak in a native speaker to non-native speaker register similar to "motherese" or "foreigner talk," and (3) provide L_2 acquirers with substantial amounts of "comprehensible second language input."

10. **Immersion Program:** an organized curriculum that includes: (1) L_1 development, (2) L_2 acquisition, and (3) subject matter development through L_2. Immersion programs are developed and managed so that participating students may develop proficient bilingualism.

11. **Limited Bilingualism:** a level of bilingualism at which individuals attain less than native-like proficiency in both L_1

and L_2. Such individuals invariably acquire Basic Interpersonal Communicative Skills in L_1 and often demonstrate Basic Interpersonal Communicative Skills in L_2 as well.

12. **Monitor:** a construct developed to refer to the mechanism by which L_2 learners process, store, and retrieve conscious language rules. Conscious rules are placed in the Monitor as a result of language learning. In order to effectively use the Monitor, L_2 users must: (1) have sufficient time to retrieve the desired rule, (2) be involved in a task focused on language forms and not on language functions, and (3) have previously learned correctly and stored the rule. These three conditions are rarely present in normal day-to-day conversational contexts.

13. **Partial Bilingualism:** a level of bilingualism at which individuals attain native-like proficiency in the full range of understanding, speaking, reading, and writing skills in one language but achieve less than native-like skills in some or all of these skills areas in the other language.

14. **Proficient Bilingualism:** a level of bilingualism at which individuals attain native-like proficiency in the full range of understanding, speaking, reading, and writing skills in both L_1 and L_2.

15. **Submersion Classes:** subject matter class periods delivered in L_2 in which teachers: (1) mix native speakers with second language acquirers, (2) speak in a native speaker-to-native speaker register, and (3) provide L_2 acquirers with only minimal amounts of "comprehensible second language input."

16. **Submersion Program:** an organized curriculum designed for native speakers of a language but often used with language minority students. No special instructional activities focus upon the needs of language minority students. Submersion programs are often referred to as "Sink or Swim" models. In such programs, language minority students commonly experience a form of subtractive bilingualism, usually limited bilingualism.

17. **Subtractive Bilingualism:** a process by which individuals develop less than native-like Cognitive/Academic Language Proficiency in L_1 as a result of improper exposure to L_1 and L_2 in school. In certain instances, some individuals addi-

tionally experience loss of Basic Interpersonal Communicative Skills in L_1. In such cases, L_1 Basic Interpersonal Communicative Skills are replaced by L_2 Basic Interpersonal Communicative Skills.

18. **Transitional Bilingual Education Program:** an organized curriculum that includes: (1) L_1 development, (2) L_2 acquisition, and (3) subject matter development through L_1 and L_2. In **Early Transitional** programs, students are exited to English submersion programs solely on the basis of the acquisition of L_2 Basic Interpersonal Communicative Skills. In **Late Transitional** programs, students are exited on the basis of attainment of native-like levels of both L_2 Basic Interpersonal Communicative Skills and L_2 Cognitive/Academic Language Proficiency sufficient to sustain academic achievement through successful completion of secondary school.